W9-ADJ-943

DETAINED

DETAINED

IMMIGRATION LAWS

AND THE EXPANDING

I.N.S. JAIL COMPLEX

Michael Welch

Temple University Press
PHILADELPHIA

Temple University Press, Philadelphia 19122
Copyright © 2002 by Temple University
All rights reserved
Published 2002
Printed in the United States of America

∞ The paper used in this publication meets the requirements of
the American National Standard for Information Sciences—Permanence
of Paper for Printed Library Materials, ANSI Z39.48-1984

Library of Congress Cataloging-in-Publication Data

Welch, Michael.
    Detained : immigration laws and the expanding I.N.S. jail complex / Michael Welch.
        p.   cm.
    Includes bibliographical references and index.
    ISBN 1-56639-977-7 (cloth : alk. paper) — ISBN 1-56639-978-5 (pbk. : alk. paper)
        1. United States—Emigration and immigration—Government policy. 2. Aliens,
    Illegal—Government Policy—United States. 3. Alien detention centers—United
    States. I. Title.
    JV6483 .W455 2002
    304.8'73—dc21

                                                                            2002018087

**To Lady Katie
& Francis Ford**

Contents

Acknowledgments

This work embodies the inspiration and assistance of many people. Over the years, I have learned a great deal about the plight of Immigration and Naturalization Service (INS) detainees from those committed to preservation of human rights, namely, Faye and Sandor Straus and the Project for the Indefinitely Detained, the Catholic Legal Immigration Network, American Civil Liberties Union Immigrants' Rights Project, Lawyers Committee for Human Rights, Amnesty International, Human Rights Watch, Women's Commission for Refugee Women and Children, Lutheran Immigration and Refugee Service, Detention Watch Network, Will Coley of the Jesuit Refugee Service, and Mark Dow.

At Rutgers University I am grateful to my colleagues who lend their support to my scholarship: Dean Mary Davidson, Dean Arnold Hyndman, Freda Adler, Gerhard O.W. Mueller, Lennox Hinds, Albert Roberts, and Carol Fine, as well as the staff at the University's libraries. Additionally, this project benefited tremendously from my research assistants Ania Dobrzanska, Brett Cortese, and Mike Zilberstein.

At Temple University Press I would like to acknowledge editors Doris Braendel, Peter Wissoker, and Jennifer French, along with Naren Gupte of P. M. Gordon Associates and Jean Anderson, who copyedited the manuscript. I also wish to thank Professor Mark Hamm, who offered valuable guidance for this work, and finally, I appreciate the wit and wisdom of Mike "Coffee Can" Beckerman, Dave "Bogart" Schreck, and Johnny "Sunshine" Stanton (a.k.a., The Retroliners).

DETAINED

Introduction

Immigrant bashing is a politically and psychologically cathartic practice for beguiling politicians and frustrated white people, regardless of its economic impacts.

Christian Parenti

I was sitting with other detained immigrants in the Hudson County Corrections Facility [New Jersey] on July 4, watching the special on NBC with Katie Couric. She talked about how this was the land of opportunity, freedom, and justice. We just howled with laughter. The motto of the Statue of Liberty in today's America is: "give me your poor, your tired and your hungry, because we still have empty jail cells."

Detainee Alejandro Bontia

It is like a hell here.

Sesay, a 54-year-old asylum-seeker from Sierra Leone detained in the Wackenhut Corrections Facility in Queens, New York

pon his return from a religious mission in the Dominican Republic in 1999, Reverend Frank Almonte, pastor and Hispanic television evangelist in Corona, Queens, New York, was arrested on drug charges at John F. Kennedy International Airport. Almonte was unaware that the 300 steroid tablets he had purchased legally in the Dominican Republic were a banned controlled substance in the United States. To no avail, Almonte explained to customs officials that he had obtained the steroids at the suggestion of a Dominican physician to help improve the appetite of his 12-year-old son, who, at 5-foot-four and 91 pounds, struggled to gain weight. Almonte was handcuffed and transported to a federal prison in Pennsylvania where he remained in detention for the next 10 days. Almonte, a legal immigrant, had no previous criminal record, had resided in the United States for 22 years, and had three children who are all American citizens. Despite being a well-respected member of his community, if convicted of drug charges Almonte could have been sentenced to seven years in prison and could have been deported as stipulated by the recently revised immigration statutes.

Under the Illegal Immigration Reform and Immigrant Responsibility Act and the Antiterrorism and Effective Death Penalty Act passed by Congress in 1996, the Immigration and Naturalization Service (INS) has enjoyed new and expansive powers that allow the agency to detain and deport any legal (and illegal) immigrant who has been charged with or convicted of a drug offense. Amid widespread community outcry denouncing his arrest, Almonte's drug charges were dismissed. One of Almonte's parishioners said that he and others "were shocked that they [the government] treated him like he was a common criminal" (Toy 1999: B10). The fairness and utility of the 1996 immigration and antiterrorism laws remain in serious question. Edward Juarez, president of International Immigrants Foundation, pointed to Almonte's ordeal as "a symbol of discrimination and anti-immigration feeling" (Toy 1999: B10), further insisting that the 1996 statutes be repealed since they stiffen penalties against immigrants charged with drug offense without distinguishing between illicit drugs such as cocaine and heroin and other substances like steroids, which are sold legally overseas (see Thompson 1999).

The case against Almonte is not an isolated one. Since 1996, when Congress bowed to growing nativism by passing new immigration legislation, the INS has ambitiously enforced laws that no longer permit judicial review, resulting in a record number of detentions and deportations. Proponents of tough law and order strategies praise the INS for its commitment to rid the nation of criminal aliens; however, immigration advocates argue that the laws unfairly target immigrants who have had minor brushes with the law. Under the 1996 immigration act, numerous crimes were reclassified as aggravated felonies requiring detention and possibly deportation, including minor misdemeanors such as shoplifting and low-level drug violations. Typically, persons convicted of those crimes rarely served jail terms and were placed on probation. To compound the harshness of the revised statutes, enforcement was retroactive, which means that persons who had been convicted before 1996 also were subject to detention and deportation; furthermore, judges have little or no discretion in determining under which conditions the law applies. In 2000, Garibaldy Mejia, a 54-year-old grandfather and livery cab driver, was stopped by immigration agents in the airport upon returning from the Dominican Republic, where he had attended his father's funeral. Mejia's green card and passport were confiscated and he was placed in detention because in 1985 he had been arrested with a small amount of cocaine, a misdemeanor. Given the minor nature of the offense, Mejia had pleaded guilty, paid a $100 fine, and agreed to serve two years' probation. Because Mejia was arrested while reentering the United States, he was not eligible for bail. Under the new laws, nearly all drug offenses, no matter what the magnitude, are grounds for deportation. Even though Mejia had established himself as a productive member of his community since his drug violation, he was transported to the Federal Correctional Institution in Oakdale, Louisiana, a prison specifically designed to hold criminal aliens, where he awaits his fate (Hedges 2000a).

Since 1996 thousands of immigrants—many whom are legal residents—have been treated cruelly by the INS, a bureaucracy still grappling to harness its newfound authority. In 1988, Mary Anne Gehris, a legal resident who was brought to the United States from Germany as an infant, was convicted of assault when she pulled the hair of another woman in a quarrel. A decade later, due to the retroactive clause in the revised immigration law, Gehris faced deportation. After much legal wrangling, however, Gehris avoided expulsion when she was granted a pardon for her offense. The Gehris case, and subsequent pardon, is testimony that repressive laws prompt legal maneuvering of the most unusual kind. While Gehris was spared the ultimate punishment contained in the revised immigration statute, others have not been as fortunate. In 2000, Claudia Young, the German wife of a U.S. citizen, was arrested in Portland, Oregon, as she nursed her year-old daughter. INS agents charged her with violating immigration law for not having the proper visa. Insisting that they had no other choice under the revised statute,

INS officials handcuffed and shackled Young, then strip-searched her twice. Young was then deported and barred from entering the United States for 10 years (Lewis 2000a).

Political Debate on Immigration

Although it is tempting to do, we should not frame the debate on immigration as a partisan stand-off between liberals and conservatives since many liberals support restrictions for immigration while many conservatives do not. As the arguments over immigration heated up in the early 1990s, political observers acknowledged that the issue had indeed created strange bedfellows. Among those opposing freer immigration were Patrick J. Buchanan, the conservative commentator and Republican Presidential candidate; Dianne Feinstein, the liberal California Democrat; and her fellow liberal counterpart Barbara Jordan of Texas. Proponents of freer immigration include conservatives William Bennett, Jack Kemp, Rudolph Giulliani, and Robert Dornan, a gay-bashing California Republican, along with Representative Barney Frank, the Massachusetts Democrat who is openly homosexual (Holmes 1996; Reimers 1998, 1992; Schuck 1998; Ungar 1995).

Rather than trying to force fit the dialogue on immigration into traditional categories of political party alliance, we should try to understand the topic in terms of the various immigration ideologies found among liberals and conservatives alike. For instance, *free marketeers* support immigration, arguing that the free flow of people across national borders, like that of goods and capital, contributes to prosperity, while on the other side of the issue, *nativists* oppose immigration policies that allow non-whites to enter the United States because they dilute the whiteness of American culture. Conversely, civil rights and ethnic advocates oppose immigration policies that discriminate against people of color, insisting that such an approach to immigration is racist and a violation of human rights. Some environmentalists and population control advocates recommend strict limits on immigration to the United States because they contend that overpopulation places undue strain on natural resources; similarly, job protectionists believe that immigration contributes to income stagnation and takes work from unskilled Americans. Rounding out the field, antigovernment libertarians oppose the call for a national identification card verifying citizenship status, while antitax advocates reject proposals requiring employers to pay a tax on every foreign worker they sponsor (Holmes 1996; Millman 1997; Stefancic and Delgado 1996).

It is important to realize that the political debate on immigration has been shaped by overt economic considerations. Whereas some commentators oppose immigration, arguing that U.S. citizens are adversely affected by job displacement as well as having their tax dollars spent on social services for illegal aliens (Auster 1990; Beck 1996; Borjas 1990; Briggs 1992; Brimelow 1995; Frey 1995a, 1995b, 1996), others argue that the economy benefits from immigration (Harris 1996; Millman 1996; Simon 1995). Recently, the National Academy of Sciences calculated the taxes a U.S. immigrant and his or her descendants are likely to pay over their lifetimes and then subtracted the cost of the government services they are likely to use. "The result: Each additional immigrant and his or her descendants will provide $80,000 in extra tax revenues over a lifetime" (Anderson and Cavanagh 1999: 27). Also, in the terms of overall employment, the National Academy of Sciences concluded that "immigration does not have a significant effect, since new entrants not only fill jobs, they also create jobs through their purchasing power and by starting new businesses" (Anderson and Cavanagh 1999: 27). In another recent report, the Bureau of Labor Statistics found that the number of immigrant workers jumped to 15.7 million in 1999, up 17 percent from three years earlier. Immigrants now represent 12 percent of the nation's workers, a shift in the labor force that is helping hold down wages in unskilled jobs (e.g., poultry plant workers, hotel housekeeping, building demolition workers, restaurant workers, seamstresses, and fruit and vegetable pickers) while providing many companies the employees needed to expand (Greenhouse 2000a; see Espenshade 1997; Reimers 1998; Reitz 1998; "Study Finds Immigrants Doing Well . . ." 1999).

In a democratic society, certainly debate over public policy ought to engage competing points of view along with systematic appraisals of legislation. Regrettably, however, revised immigration laws passed by Congress in 1996 were influenced less by sound policymaking and more by exaggerated political rhetoric that issued warnings that foreigners pose a threat to the American social and economic order. From a sociological standpoint, new legislation governing immigration was a culmination of demagoguery emblematic of moral panic, especially considering that popular perceptions of immigrants were channeled through the distorted lens of racial and ethnic stereotypes. Adverse societal reaction to immigrants is nothing new (see Glazer 1983; Glazer and Moynihan 1963; Portes and Rumbaut 1996). Throughout U.S. history, citizens have shunned immigrants, viewing them with contempt and suspicion, thus reinforcing social inequality, hostility, and discrimination. Still the degree of nativism evident in the 1990s is remarkable because it generated enormous public and political support, resulting in sweeping legislation that unfairly targeted immigrants, particularly people of color (Cose 1992; Hing 1997; Jonas and Dod Thomas 1999; Perea 1997; Welch 1997a; 1999a). As explored in the next chapter, controversy over immigration in the 1990s had all the elements of a moral panic.

Scope of This Book

One can only wonder how and why current immigration laws have become so rigidly conceived and ruthlessly enforced. With those concerns in mind, we explore recent legislation whose emergence has dramatically altered the way immigrants are treated by the U.S. government. Taking a sociological approach to the passage of these new laws, we turn our critical attention to the effects that they have on legal and illegal immigrants, their families, communities, and society at large. Together, those statutes demonstrate how government and the public view immigrants. In passing such sweeping legislation, Congress has funneled increasingly greater funds and resources to the INS, making it the largest federal law enforcement agency. With unprecedented power in dealing with immigrants, the INS stepped up its reliance on detention and deportation, policies that are fraught with contradictions and injustice.

As we shall see in this book, the 1996 immigration statutes have produced profound inconsistencies demonstrating the ironies of social control whereby immigrants are subject to self-defeating—and inhumane—government strategies (Chapter 4). Not only have recent changes in immigration law failed to accomplish their stated objectives, but because the laws emphasize confinement, those violating revised immigration laws are unnecessarily detained for protracted periods of time in facilities known for their harsh conditions. The punitive nature of INS detention policy and its tendency to simply warehouse detainees are examined in Chapters 5 and 6; similarly, Chapter 7 explores the controversial practice of detaining juvenile immigrants. It should be understood that key developments in INS strategies contributing to increased reliance on detention mirror policy shifts in the traditional criminal justice apparatus. Over the past two decades, crime control initiatives have increasingly adopted hard-line measures based on the three P's: penalties, police, and prisons. While neglecting crucial crime control strategies that attend to adverse societal conditions, including poverty and inequality, the new penology reinforces a commitment to coercive social control by relying more on prisons than alternatives to incarceration. Regrettably, the INS has taken cues from the prevailing criminal justice agenda by channeling more resources into enforcement and detention while neglecting its responsibility of providing services that help immigrants assimilate.

As the book nears its conclusion, critical attention is turned to the role of the INS in the expanding corrections–industrial complex, a controversial phenomenon in criminal justice whereby increased reliance on incarceration is driven by profit motives. The corrections–industrial complex portends tragic consequences for modern penology, given that prisoners are treated as raw materials that produce economic gain for local and private jails. A decade ago, the INS entered the corrections–industrial complex, creating the need for a larger number of detainees to fill an expanding number of expensive jail cells (Chapter 8). In light of the dehumanizing aspects of current immigration policies and practices, especially in the realm of detention, immigration lawyers and human rights activists have become increasingly concerned that the government and the INS have taken a wrong turn in their efforts to deal with illegal immigration. The concluding chapter surveys recent activities in the courts and Congress aimed at reducing the harshness of current immigration laws. Throughout the book, viable alternatives to detention are recommended; moreover, such enlightened policy changes are formulated according to compassionate logic rather than bigotry, racism, and classism.

This work concentrates on the 1996 legislation and its adverse effects on immigrants, but those controversies have moved to the forefront of the American conversation on immigration since September 11, 2001. Indeed, the terrorist hijackings and attacks on the World Trade Center and the Pentagon have given the debate over immigration control a new resonance. In the epilogue, we shall examine closely the government's campaign to fight terrorism at home, especially using racial profiling, mass detention, and secret evidence. As the country recovers from the tragedies of September 11, renewed discourse over immigration is imbued with anxieties over national security along with concerns for civil liberties.

Setting the stage for a critical and in-depth examination of INS detention, we consider in the following chapters the sociological underpinnings of the controversy over immigration as it took hold in the early and mid-1990s. At that point, the issue was grossly distorted by inflammatory rhetoric maligning immigrants depicted not only as different and foreign, but also as threats to the social and economic order. So that we may comprehend the sociological processes by which the 1996 laws governing immigration were conceived, we address the significance of *moral panic*, a turbulent and exaggerated response to a putative social problem.

2

Moral Panic over Immigrants

The [U.S. Supreme] Court routinely overrules the actions of local police boards, boards of education, and state laws under which they act. The beneficiaries of the Court's protections are members of various minorities, including criminals, atheists, homosexuals, flag burners, illegal aliens including terrorists, convicts, and pornographers.

Patrick J. Buchanan, 1996

It's based on an irrational fear of something different, something strange, that somehow they're going to take something away from us. . . . A lot of it is just undifferentiated fear of foreigners, of people who appear to have different values or different ways of doing things.

New York City Mayor Rudolph Giuliani, opposing immigration reform legislation

The Emergence of Moral Panic

Moral panic has armed sociologists with a useful concept to elucidate deviance, social problems, collective behavior, and social movements, especially in the context of pseudodisasters. Moral panic occurs when, "A condition, episode, person or group of persons emerges to become defined as a threat to societal values and interest; its nature is presented in a stylized and stereotypical fashion by the mass media and politicians" (Cohen 1972: 9). Sociologist Stanley Cohen learned that moral panic was a key component of a moral crusade, a social enterprise he discovered while studying societal reaction to youths in England. In his ground-breaking treatise, *Folk Devils and Moral Panics* (1972), Cohen explored the roles of the public, media, and politicians in constructing heightened concern over British youths in 1964 when the Mods and Rockers were depicted as threats to public peace as well as the social order. Together, the media and members of the political establishment publicized exaggerated claims of the dangers posed by the Mods and Rockers; in turn, such claims were used to justify enhanced police powers and greater investment in the traditional criminal justice apparatus. Since the 1970s, the study of moral panic has enjoyed growing popularity among scholars examining the social construction of deviance and crime. Among the more recent examples of moral panic are those involving crack cocaine use (Chiricos 1996; Reinarman and Levine 1997), crack mothers (Humphries 1999), youth gangs (McCorkle and Miethe 1998; Zatz 1987), satanic ritual abuse in day care centers (Best 1990), and flag burning (Welch 2000a; also see Best 1999; Glassner 1999).[1]

Moral panic helps us understand turbulent societal reactions to immigration, which lead to a disaster mentality in which there is a widespread perception that immigrants endanger American society. Indeed, such perceptions of threat perpetuate stereotypes of immigrants as intellectually inferior, morally corrupt, and prone to crime—and worse terrorism. As moral panic mounts, there is a sense of urgency to do something now or else society will suffer even graver consequences later, compelling social policy to undergo significant transformation in a rash attempt to diffuse the putative threat. Moral panic typically manifests in "strengthening the social control apparatus of the society—tougher or renewed rules, more intense public hostility and condemnation, more laws, longer sentences, more police, more arrests, and more prison cells" (Goode and Ben-Yehuda 1994: 31).

Looking at adverse reactions to immigrants through the prism of moral panic adds to a critical view of the harsh and contradictory aspects of the 1996 immigration laws. Previous research from that perspective has taught us important lessons about how moral panic reinforces demeaning stereotypes of immigrants. In his book, *The Abandoned Ones: The Imprisonment and Uprising of the Mariel Boat People* (1995), criminologist Mark Hamm investigated moral panic over Mariel Cubans who arrived in the United States in 1980. Because many Mariels appeared to be *different* from other Cubans (i.e., darker and poorer), they were met with suspicion and eventually labeled deviants, predators, and criminals; in turn, many Mariels were placed under unusually close supervision by the INS and other criminal justice agencies. As a classic self-fulfilling prophecy, many young Mariel Cuban men—with few economic opportunities in the United States—resorted to committing minor offenses such as drug peddling. As a result, many of them were labeled habitual criminals and returned to prison where they currently are detained indefinitely—a kind of "three strikes you're out" policy designed by the INS specifically for that ethnic population (Welch 1997b). As of 2001, more than a thousand Mariel Cubans who have been convicted of deportable crimes—including minor offenses—remain imprisoned because the United States and Cuba do not have a deportation agreement (Catholic Legal Immigration Network [CLINIC] 2001; see Chapter 5).

So that we may comprehend more precisely how moral panic specifically applies to the debate on immigration, we examine the concept's five criteria: concern, hostility, consensus, disproportionality, and volatility (Goode and Ben-Yehuda 1994). Drawing on evidence contained in the controversy over immigration in the early and mid-1990s, we discuss each of those social indicators as it pertains to moral panic.

Concern

The first component of moral panic is a heightened concern over the behavior of others and how their actions affect society. Sociologists insist that concern ought to be verifiable in the form of an observed and measurable manifestation, such as public opinion polls, public commentary in the form of media attention, proposed legislation, and social movement activity (Best 1989, 1990; Cohen 1972; Goode and Ben-Yehuda 1994; Welch 2000a; Welch, Fenwick, and Roberts 1997 and 1998). Although in many cases the level of concern does not have to reach that of fear, there must be a perception that a threat exists. Heightened concern over immigration in the early and mid-1990s, like other moral panics, created a tense atmosphere that American society was under siege, leading to a disaster mentality in which people felt an urgency to do something. In 1995, sociologist Nathan Glazer detected a latent anxiety over immigration: "We are a society less optimistic about our future, although there were comparable periods of angst before. We don't think we have any more wide open spaces to settle, however unpopulated we are compared to Asia" (Glazer 1995: E3). Sensing a political op-

portunity, elected leaders tapped into the communal anxiety over immigration, but rather than offering their constituency firm leadership
that would have produced sound and fair-minded policymaking, many
politicians fueled moral panic by pandering to popular fears. As a result,
concern over immigration escalated into public hysteria leading to numerous legislative campaigns, thus reinforcing hostility and discrimination against immigrants.

In the early 1990s, the perception that immigrants endangered American society gained considerable acceptance among political commentators and eventually the public. In 1992, conservative journalist, Peter
Brimelow published a controversial article in the *National Review*, "Time
to Rethink Immigration," in which he delivered a scathing attack on
current immigration policy, arguing that it was already destroying American society as we know it. The essay drew enormous attention, placing
the issue of immigration back on the political table; tragically though,
the debate over immigration degenerated into a crusade against immigrants. Brimelow and other nativists, including Patrick J. Buchanan, realized that they had hit a public nerve with the immigration issue (see
Auster 1990; Beck 1996; Borjas 1990). While Buchanan campaigned for
President, spewing his brand of nativist rhetoric, Brimelow expanded his
magazine article into a widely publicized book. In 1995, Brimelow, himself, an immigrant from Britain, unveiled *Alien Nation: Common Sense
about America's Immigration Disaster.* Casting apocalyptic images of a
doomed American society, *Alien Nation* epitomizes moral panic.[2] More
significantly, Brimelow's treatise was not viewed merely as nativist rant-
ing; rather, it inflamed fears of immigrants and heightened anxiety
among huge segments of the public. *Alien Nation*, along with growing
anti-immigrant sentiment, sounded the alarm that American was under
siege, galvanizing a nativist crusade that would succeed in revising federal immigration laws in 1996 (Reimers 1998).

Bolstering a disaster mentality, Brimelow engaged in claimsmaking
activities prevalent in the early stages of moral panic. Brimelow insisted
that "The United States has lost control of its borders—in every sense"
(1995: 4) and "The post-1980 approach to refugees has created a catas-
trophe—even by the generally disastrous standards of immigration policy" (p. 150; also see Auster 1990; Beck 1996). To prepare for writing
his book, Brimelow visited INS officials at the U.S. border. After wit-
nessing an illegal crossing, Brimelow writes, "I was momentarily dis-
tracted, brooding on this awesome spectacle of a great nation morally

incapable of defending itself against the most elemental invasion" (p. 238). What concerns Brimelow and other nativists most about current U.S. immigration policy is that it dilutes the whiteness of American society and culture (see Buchanan 1999). Given the high proportion of non-white immigrants permitted to enter the United States under current immigration policies, Brimelow believes that America will become "a freak among the world's nations because of the unprecedented demographic mutation it is inflicting on itself" (1995: xix). Exhibiting fear that the United States will lose its identity as a white nation, Brimelow introduces metaphors from natural disasters, saying that current immigration policy "may well prove a sociological San Andreas Fault" (1995: 69).

Brimelow's argument against immigration is driven further by previous legislation that he believes has created an immigration disaster, namely, the 1965 Immigration Act. That law serves as a basis from which Brimelow expresses his dissatisfaction for current immigration policy, and in doing so, he shows his disdain for the 1960s activism and the civil rights movement: "The 1965 Act can be seen to have invented one quite new type of immigration: a black inflow, both from Africa itself and from the Caribbean" (1995: 61). Brimelow continues, "Because of affirmative action quotas, it absolutely matters to me as the father of a white male how large the 'protected classes' are going to be. And that is basically determined by immigration. . . . To get a sense of perspective, we have to go back to the beginning. And in the beginning, the American nation was white" (p. 66). In his own defense for sounding racist, Brimelow longs nostalgically for white America before the civil rights movement desegregated the nation: "Suppose I had proposed more immigrants who look like me. So what? As of late 1950s, somewhere up to nine out of ten Americans looked like me. That is, they were of European stock. And in those days, they had another name for this thing dismissed so contemptuously as 'the racial hegemony of white Americans.' They called it, 'America'" (1995: 59).

Particularly in California, Texas, and Florida, as well as in the nation's capital, politicians took notice of growing public concern over immigration; however, instead of offering their constituents enlightened interpretations of the issue, many political leaders reinforced fears of immigrants. Politicizing immigration is significant because political rhetoric not only inflames public anxiety but also shapes the content of legislation. Just as fear of crime—rather than crime itself (Donziger

1996a; Glassner 1999; Reinarman and Levine 1997; Welch 1999b)—drives criminal justice policies, the undifferentiated fear of crime and immigrants consumed the 1996 immigration laws. As we shall see throughout the book, revised immigration legislation, much like crime and drug control strategies, is not only poorly formulated but also unjust and discriminatory against the poor and people of color.

In the early 1990s, California Governor Pete Wilson stirred public anxiety over immigration by introducing several proposals, including the abolition of birthright citizenship, a measure considered extreme even by nativist standards. During that period, California drew national attention for its Proposition 187, an initiative designed to clamp down on undocumented immigrants, prohibiting them from receiving publicly funded education, medical care, and social services. Critics observed that the "campaign was tuned to a range of Anglo anxieties and fears: a declining standard of living, and quality of life; a faltering and changing economy; a sense of being overwhelmed by a range of cultures and peoples of color, and concern for dilution of American values, institutions, and ways of life" (Mata 1998: 151; also see Calavita 1996; Gutierrez 1995; Quiroga 1995). Demonstrating widespread anxiety over immigrants, Californians overwhelmingly voted for Proposition 187 in 1994. However, California federal Judge Mariana Pfaelzer ruled that Proposition 187 was unconstitutional, a decision based on a 1982 Supreme Court case preventing Texas from denying illegal immigrant children an education (*Plyer* v. *Doe* 1982).

Similar legislative activity also gained momentum at the federal level. In 1994, a crime bill in Congress proposed that cities would be required to turn in the names of all illegal aliens discovered from all sources, including people who report crimes. Critics argued that such a measure would discourage some residents from reporting crimes in their community, thus compromising public safety (Firestone 1995). In 1995, the House passed a welfare bill that would deny food stamps, Medicaid, and welfare payments to legal residents of the country who are not citizens. Also that year, the Congressional Task Force on Immigration Reform, a Republican-dominated panel (46 Republicans and 8 Democrats) appointed by Speaker Newt Gingrich, issued dozens of recommendations for cracking down on illegal immigration. The proposals would require public hospitals to report illegal aliens who seek medical treatment and would force public schools to turn away students who are in this country illegally. Those recommendations, spearheaded by Gingrich, were strikingly similar to California's Proposition 187 (Firestone 1995).

Later in 1995, the Commission on Immigration Reform delivered their recommendations to Congress, including a proposal to cut immigration by one-third. The commission also suggested that immigration should become easier for minor children of U.S. citizens, but more difficult for adult children. Additionally, the commission called for the creation of a national identification card that documents their status as citizens or noncitizens. In his criticism of the commission, journalist Roger Hernandez (1995: 8) wrote, "If Congress follows the recommendations, it will legitimize xenophobia by making it appear that reasonable people believe there is an immigration crisis." In a similar vein, New York City Mayor Rudolph Giuliani condemned federal legislators for "pandering to an irrational fear of foreigners" ("Standing up for Immigrants" 1995: E14). Despite harsh criticism from advocates for immigrants, the nativist campaign reached critical mass in 1996 when Congress passed three profoundly significant laws: the Illegal Immigration Reform and Immigrant Responsibility Act, the Anti-Terrorism and Effective Death Penalty Act, and the Personal Responsibility and Work Opportunity Reconciliation Act. As we shall see throughout the book, those revised immigration laws continue to have adverse effects on immigrants throughout the nation.

Hostility

Sociologists remind us that moral panic arouses hostility toward an identifiable group or category of people who, in turn, are vilified as social outcasts. According to Goode and Ben-Yehuda, "Members of this category are collectively designated as the enemy, or an enemy, of respectable society; their behavior is seen as harmful, or threatening to the values, interests, possibly the very existence, of the society, or at least a sizeable segment of that society" (1994: 33). This component of moral panic is particularly relevant given that the debate over immigration often becomes so mean-spirited that elements of hostility are difficult to overlook. Still, unlike bona fide social problems that do not blame any one group of people, such as the aftermath of natural disasters, moral panic shifts blame to unpopular people who become scapegoats and folk devils. According to Goode and Ben-Yehuda (1994: 33–34), "not only must the condition, phenomenon, or behavior be seen as threatening, but a clearly identifiable group in or segment of the society must seen as responsible for the threat." Moreover, a distinction is made between us—good, decent, respectable people—and them—deviants, undesirables, outsiders, villains, criminals, and disreputable people (Cohen 1972; Humphries 1999). Unlike other moral panics such as the Red Scare of the late 1910s or McCarthyism of the 1950s, in which it was difficult to know exactly who was a "communist" since they did not look or speak differently than anyone else (Levin 1971), moral panic over immigrants is more apparent because they are easily identifiable, particularly those who are not white and of European descent. In the eyes of many nativists, non-Europeans or immigrants of color are viewed as threats to American society because they are seen as being different. In his work, Brimelow's persistent use of the word "they" in reference to non-white immigrants is laden with alarm: "They are still coming. Indeed, after a short hesitation, they seem to be coming about as strong as ever" (1995: 33; see Bustamante 1972).

Clinging to racial and ethnic stereotypes, nativists demonize immigrants, especially those who are non-white, claiming that they are a threat to public safety (i.e., dealing in drugs, crime, and terrorism), the economy, the welfare state, public education, and public health. Hostility contained in moral panic manifests in several ways; as we shall see in the next several sections, immigrants are vulnerable to being criminalized, pathologized, marginalized, and scapegoated.

Criminalizing Immigrants

Stoking anti-immigrant hostility, nativists and restrictionists commonly resort to criminalizing immigrants by casting them as predatory villains, drug dealers, and even terrorists (Beck 1996; Brimelow 1995; Buchanan 1996; also see Gordon 1994 and Marshall 1997). Compounding matters, stereotypes have a potent effect on America's psyche as the general public often is willing uncritically to accept inaccurate versions of tragic events. In 1995, the bombing of a federal building in Oklahoma City contributed to growing fears about terrorists and fueled suspicion of Arab immigrants. In the aftermath of the blast, the *New York Post* editorialized, "Knowing that the car bomb indicates Middle Eastern terrorists at work, it's safe to assume that their goal is to promote free-floating fear and a measure of anarchy, thereby disrupting American life" (Naureckas 1995: 6). Similarly, *New York Times* columnist A. M. Rosenthal wrote, "Whatever we are doing to destroy Mideast terrorism, the chief terrorist threat against Americans has not been working" (Glassner 1999: xiii). Eventually, investigators determined that the bombing was not the handiwork of Arab terrorists but that of Timothy McVey, a white U.S. citizen and former serviceman; nevertheless, Muslims had been stereotyped as terrorists and threats to American national security (Council on American-Muslim Research Center 1995; Glassner 1999; Glazer 1995; Shaheen 1984). In *Alien Nation*, Brimelow delivers a despicable blow to immigrants by associating them with a number of criminal events in the early 1990s:

> In January 1993, a Pakistani applicant for political asylum opens fire on employees entering CIA headquarters, killing two and wounding three! In February 1993, a gang of Middle Easterners (most illegally overstaying after entering on non-immigrant visas—one banned as terrorist but admitted on a tourist visa in error) blow up New York's World Trade Center, killing six and injuring more than 1,000!! In December 1993, a Jamaican immigrant (admitted as a student but stayed) opens fire on commuters on New York's Long Island Rail Road, killing six and wounding 19!!! WHAT'S GOING ON??!!? (1995: 6)[3]

Other opponents of immigration weighed in on the crime issue. Dan Stein, of the restrictionist group Federation for American Immigration Reform (FAIR), announced, "A series of jarring incidents in 1993 gave the public the unmistakable impression that immigrants are not all honest and hardworking. Some are here to commit crimes" (1994: 27; also see Tanton and Lutton 1993). In a another remark imbued with moral panic over illegal aliens, William Colby, former Central Intelligence Agency (CIA) Director, boldly stated, "The most obvious threat for the U.S. is the fact that . . . there are going to be 120 million Mexicans by the end of the century. . . . [The Border Patrol] will not have enough bullets to stop them" (quoted in Acuna 1996: 115; see Mata 1998). Whereas Roy Beck, in his book *The Case against Immigration* (1996), relies on rhetoric less inflammatory than that of Colby, Brimelow, and other nativist crusaders, there are numerous passages in which immigrants are blamed for lawlessness: "One of the most insidious costs of federal high-immigration policies is the increase in social tensions and crime," he states (1996: 215). Adding to his case against immigration, Beck writes, "Numerous organized crime syndicates headquartered in the new immigrants' home countries have gained solid beachheads of operations" (p. 17). Again, fears of crime and of immigrants are nearly indistinguishable, thus fueling greater public anxiety. Amid greater public outcry, legislators push for more of the three P's—police, penalties, and prisons. As I discuss at length in the next chapter, the federal Anti-Terrorism and Effective Death Penalty statute was passed by Congress in 1996 as a response to the bombing of the World Trade Center.

Pathologizing Immigrants

As another manifestation of hostility, immigrants tend to be patholo-gized, and hence perceived as a threat to public health. While aptly pointing out that immigration officials at Ellis Island routinely inspected immigrants for diseases such as cholera and smallpox (see Divine 1957), Brimelow remarkably claims that even in the 1990s, "the United States has never been so unprotected against immigrant's impact on its public health" (1995: 186). Arguing that the current immigration policy is cre-ating a public health crisis, Brimelow pathologizes immigrants, espe-cially those from Latin America and Southeast Asia, blaming them for spreading tuberculosis, measles, cholera, malaria, dengue fever, and even leprosy. Perpetuating a disaster mentality, Brimelow issues a catastrophic forecast for America's public health: "The U.S. Institute of Medicine has recently predicted *'with some confidence'* that if yellow fever, the in-curable mosquito-borne disease now resurgent in Africa and Amazonia, returns to New Orleans, public health defenses could be quickly over-whelmed: 100,000 people would become ill . . . and 10,000 would likely die within 90 days" (1995: 187).[4]

Brimelow's heightened fear of immigrants from a public health stand-point follows the classic formula of moral panic in which outsiders—foreigners—are pathologized. Throughout history, interpretations of plagues and epidemics have emerged in two forms. First, plagues are depicted in moral terms, sent by a higher power as a punishment for so-ciety's sins; second, plagues come from somewhere else. Sontag (1989) recalls that the syphilis epidemic in Europe during the fifteenth century, the bubonic plague during the eighteenth century, and the outbreaks of cholera during the nineteenth century were all characterized as dreaded foreigner diseases. Literally and figuratively, plagues are reified as pol-lution from alien and exotic lands. Remember, Sontag writes, "AIDS is thought to have started in the 'dark continent,' then spread to Haiti, then to the United States and to Europe. . . . It is understood as a trop-ical disease: another manifestation from the so-called Third World" (1989: 51–52). Popular beliefs on the origin of HIV/AIDS—commonly, although inaccurately, termed a plague—has fueled anti-African (black) prejudice in the Americas, Europe, and Asia: "The subliminal connection made to notions about a primitive past and the many hypotheses that have been fielded about possible transmission from animals (a disease of green monkeys? African swine fever?) cannot help but activate a familiar set of stereotypes about animality, sexual license, and blacks" (Sontag 1989: 52; also see Huber and Schneider 1992; Kraut 1994; Welch 2000b). Not surprisingly, fear of HIV/AIDS has affected immigration policy. In 1993, Congress passed overwhelmingly a measure that would continue to bar immigrants who tested positive for HIV or have AIDS from entering the United States, despite recommendations from the Centers for Disease Control that the illness be removed from the list banning potential immigrants (Reimers 1998; U.S. Congress, House 1990).

Certainly, lawmakers should continue to take seriously issues of public health; still, policies should be based on scientific research rather than on hysterical pronouncements that stigmatize immigrants and people of color. Paradoxically, moral panic over immigrants in the early and mid-1990s led to proposals that actually could have compromised public health. Because hospitals were instructed to notify the INS when undocumented immigrants sought medical attention, the ill would have been discouraged from seeking treatment, which, according to a *New York Times* article, "could well result in the spread of communicable diseases like tuberculosis, which has made a disturbing comeback" ("Standing up for Immigrants" 1995: E14).

Another common tactic in pathologizing immigrants is to depict them as intellectually inferior to those born in the United States, a stereotype that often is drawn along racial lines. "For the first time, virtually all immigrants are racially distinct 'visible minorities'" writes Brimelow (1995: 56), who then refers to the work of Richard J. Herrnstein and Charles Murray, whose *The Bell Curve: Intelligence and Class Structure in American Life* stirred enormous controversy in 1994. In their book, Herrnstein and Murray claimed that there is scientific evidence supporting the thesis that differences in intelligence can be traced to race. Brimelow goes on to note, "Herrnstein and Murray blamed the 1965 Immigration Act for a sharp deterioration in immigrant quality." According to Brimelow: "If they are right, of course, this suggests the consequences of current policy are far more disastrous than anything argued in this book" (1995: 56). Critics, however, argue that *The Bell Curve* distorts research findings on race and intelligence, becoming a classic example of pseudoscience and scientific racism (Fraser 1995; Gould 1995; Hacker 1995; Nisbett 1995).

Marginalizing Immigrants

Hostility, as a result of moral panic, also economically marginalizes immigrants, relegating them to the underclass. Nativists contribute to the stigma of immigrants by insinuating that they drain tax dollars in the form of public assistance, adding that immigrants are drawn to the United States because of "the magnet of the American welfare state" (Brimelow 1995: 33). Similarly, Robert Rector of the conservative Heritage Foundation opined, "The U.S. welfare system is rapidly becoming a deluxe retirement home for the elderly of other countries" (1996: 279). Depicting immigrants as people who do not want to work and expect to be supported by government assistance, nativists reinforce notions that immigrants are different from *us* hardworking tax-paying folks (see Gilens 1999; Mann and Zatz 1998). Also fueling hostility toward immigrants, Donald Huddle (1993), Rice University economics professor, reported that the net cost of immigration to government, including the welfare costs of native-born workers displaced by immigrants, exceeded $40 billion in 1992. Immigration and welfare specialists seriously questioned Huddle's figures. In 1993, *Business Week* reported that immigrants pay $90 billion in taxes and receive only $5 billion in services ("The Immigrants" 1993; see Chua 1995; Lemann 1995; Reimers 1998). Even when attempting to compliment certain ethnic groups, Brimelow reveals his suspicion of non-whites: "Like most New Yorkers . . . I am sentimental about Asian immigration. They seem law-abiding and hardworking (although I gather you aren't suppose to say this. And maybe it's just another immigration myth: there are growing reports of gangs and welfare dependency)" (1995:189).

Institutional biases reduce economic mobility for many of the nation's poor people, preventing them from rising above the poverty threshold and join those earning middle incomes (Wilson 1987, 1996). Inadequate education, a key barrier to achieving financial independence, commonly becomes apparent early in the education process. If it were not for some crucial rewriting of the revised 1996 immigration bill, that law would have had a huge impact on communities where schools would be required to turn away students who have immigrated illegally or who have been born of illegal immigrant parents. In New York City, for instance, that law would have thrown "60,000 children onto the streets and deprive them of the education they desperately need to become productive citizens. Inevitably, fear of being discovered would force parents to withdraw children from school" ("Standing up for Immigrants" 1995: E14). Undoubtedly, having tens of thousands of children on the streets of New York City would not only create opportunities for delinquency but also put both children and other residents at risk of being victims of crime (see Firestone 1995: A1).

Scapegoating Immigrants

By definition, scapegoating is "the placing of blame for one's troubles on an individual or group incapable of offering resistance" (Robertson 1981: 633). The public, angry over social and economic unrest, justifies scapegoating unpopular groups such as immigrants, who have already been criminalized, pathologized, and marginalized, because they are an easy target. Criminologist Michael Tonry sheds light on that phenomenon: "In an era of rapid social and economic change, many people feel threatened and insecure, and minority and immigrant groups may be blamed for much what seems wrong. Hate crimes are increasingly common, and violent attacks against minority groups are more evident in Europe" (1996: 1). Scapegoating creates unique paradoxes—or Catch-22's—for immigrants. On the one hand, immigrants are portrayed as lazy and unskilled, thus draining social and welfare services, and, on the other hand, they are blamed for stealing jobs from hardworking U.S. citizens (see Delgado 1992; DeSipio and de la Garza 1998; Harris 1996).

While revised immigration laws represent formal social control aimed at regulating and managing immigrants, community protest and physical attacks on immigrants represent informal social control. In Farmingville, New York, a small town on Eastern Long Island, undocumented immigrants from Central America gather each day with hope of being hired as day laborers by drive-by employers. Many townspeople, however, have expressed their disdain for those undocumented immigrants, calling them a public nuisance and blaming them for rising crime rates, even though police officials report that "there is no evidence linking an increase in crimes arrests in Farmingville to undocumented workers" (Rather 2000: B5). The immigrants say they take jobs that residents do not want and complain of harassment, abuse, and overcrowded living conditions. About 200 residents convened at the town hall to protest the immigrants. Some waved American flags and red, white, and blue balloons—popular symbols of nationalism exploited by nativists—and others carried signs with more direct messages, including, "Illegal aliens are criminals, not immigrants" and "Peaceful solutions through deportation" (McFadden 2000: 42). The local controversy drew regional attention when hostility over illegal immigrants spilled over into violence. Two Mexican immigrants were attacked with a shovel, a crowbar, and a knife by two men who had lured them to an abandoned building with the promise of work (LeDuff 2000a: B1; also see LeDuff 2000b). Two suspects were arrested and charged with two counts of attempted murder. Later they confessed to driving more than 50 miles with the motive "to go out and attack Mexicans" (Kelley 2000: B5; also see Baker 2000).[5]

At a higher level of abstraction, scapegoating is imbued with demonization, in which unpopular people are pronounced evil and morally corrupt and thus are vilified as folk devils (Cohen 1972; Katz 1988). Revealingly, Brimelow demonizes immigrants by quoting Alexander Hamilton in his 1802 Congressional speech: "The United States have already felt the evils of incorporating a large number of foreigners into their national mass. . . . it has served to divide the community and to distract our councils" (quoted in Brimelow 1995: 191). Brimelow similarly cites Enoch Powell, who warned fellow Britons of the dangers of immigration in 1968, proclaiming, "The supreme function of statesmanship is to provide against preventable evils" (quoted in Brimelow 1995: 92). In the eyes of Brimelow, the 1965 Immigration Act is not only a disaster but also a curse, adding, "The evils that this policy has inflicted upon the country will still be felt in a hundred years, quite probably even more intensely with the passage of time" (1995: 114). To argue in favor of restricting immigration is one view, but to rely on metaphors that demonize immigrants reminds us that the debate over immigration has been driven by moral panic. Likewise, hostility, a key criterion of moral panic, is clearly evident in attempts to criminalize, pathologize, marginalize, and scapegoat immigrants, especially racial and ethnic minorities.

Consensus

To become a recognizable phenomenon, moral panic requires a certain consensus among members of society. By no means does such agreement need to be universal or even representative of the majority. Still, there must be a widespread belief that the problem at hand is real, it poses a threat to society, and it should be rectified (Cohen 1972; Hall, Critcher, Jefferson, Clarke, and Roberts 1978; Zatz 1987). Moral panic comes in different sizes: Some grips the vast majority of the general public, while others affect smaller segments or regions of society (Goode and Ben-Yehuda 1994). With that distinction in mind, Californians, Floridians, and Texans exhibited more moral panic over immigration in the early and mid-1990s because a greater number of citizens perceived immigrants as threats to their communities and economies (see Holmes 1995). Indeed, Proposition 187 is a compelling example of consensus, especially considering that Californians passed the initiative by a two-to-one margin with more than five million votes. Public opinion polls offer additional evidence that many Americans view immigration as a social problem that ought to be remedied by revised legislation and enforced with measures borrowed from the criminal justice model, including more police, penalties, and prisons. In 1993, as moral panic over immigrants began reaching a critical mass, a *Newsweek* nationwide poll found that 60 percent of Americans believed that current immigration levels were harming the nation ("Why Our Borders" 1993). In regions where the issue is increasingly politicized, public concern over immigration was greater. A *Los Angeles Times* survey discovered that 86 percent of Californians thought illegal immigration into their state was a "major" or "moderate" problem and about 47 percent felt the same about legal immigration ("Illegal Immigrant Health" 1993). Although less reliable in accurately gauging public discontent, a call-in poll sponsored by the *Orlando Sentinel* reported that 95 percent of respondents supported a ban on all immigration for the next several years (*Orlando Sentinel* 1993). Interestingly, even among immigrants there is concern that immigration is out of control. An Empire State Survey published in the *New York Times* showed that 51 percent of immigrants believed that immigration was bad for New York City: Sixty-six percent of native-born New Yorkers agreed ("Immigration Hurts City" 1993; also see Beck 1996; Heller 1994; "Public Opinion and Demographic Report" 1994; Simon and Alexander 1993).

Public perceptions weigh heavily in the formation of moral panic over immigration, especially since the issue is commonly framed as a racial and ethnic threat to white America. Still, surveys reveal that Americans do not have an accurate perception of the racial and ethnic composition of their own nation, and perhaps such misperceptions contribute to fear of minorities. In the mid-1990s as the immigration issue reached noticeable levels of panic, white Americans believed that 49.9 percent of the population was white, but the figure was actually 74 percent. Similarly, white Americans thought the population was 23.8 percent black, while the actual percentage was 11.8 (Labovitz 1995).

Disproportionality

Another key component of moral panic is its *disproportionality*, meaning that the perceived danger is greater than the potential harm (Cohen 1972; Davis and Stasz 1990; Jones, Gallagher, and McFalls 1989). As mentioned previously, public perceptions that immigrants pose a threat to American society often are complicated by undifferentiated fear of minorities and fear of crime (see Covington 1995; Glassner 1999; Hacker 1992; Russell 1998). As a result, the actual harm that immigrants pose on American society is greatly exaggerated and in some instances completely unfounded. Whereas it might be difficult to determine whether a social issue, such as immigration, has been blown out of proportion, there are four indicators of disproportion, namely: exaggerated figures, fabricated figures, the existence of other harmful conditions, and changes over time (Goode and Ben-Yehuda 1994). The presence of these indicators of disproportion coupled with stylization and political hyperbole suggest that persons and groups involved in claimsmaking engage in disinformation campaigns, disseminating distorted messages to influence public and political opinion, which, in turn, alters legislation and its enforcement.

Exaggerated Figures

The criterion of disproportion is met when figures and statistics cited to measure the scope of the problem are grossly exaggerated. Huge discrepancies among figures usually point to the emergence of moral panic; suffice to say that bona fide social problems do not need to be exaggerated in order to convince the public that something should be done (e.g., the Great Depression, the polio epidemic). As the political debate over immigration heated up in the early and mid-1990s, Pat Buchanan proclaimed that the United States is undergoing an invasion of illegal aliens who enter from Mexico: "That is what's taking place when one, two, or three million people walk across our borders every year" (Buchanan quoted in Holmes 1996: B10). The figures on illegal entries commonly are exaggerated, thereby fueling public anxiety over immigrants and the perception that American society is under siege. According to Jessica Vaughan, assistant director for the Center for Immigration Studies, an organization that supports lower levels of immigration, commonly accepted estimates of illegal entries are considered somewhere between 300,000 and 400,000 per year. Contrary to the popular view that the vast majority of undocumented immigrants arrive in the United States illegally, more than half enter legally and merely stay when their student or temporary work visas expire (Holmes 1996: Reimers 1998).

As California's Proposition 187 gained momentum in 1994, Governor Wilson announced that Los Angeles County "had spent 946 million dollars in 1991–1992 on services to recent immigrants, adding that the county had only collected 139 [million dollars] of the $4.3 billion a year in federal, state and local taxes paid by immigrants" (Flanigan 1993: D1). Wilson's figures on social spending were immediately contradicted by reports published by governmental and nongovernmental groups, including the Urban Institute and the RAND Institute (Calavita 1996). Interestingly, the California Senate, in 1993, chided politicians "for their failure to heed admonitions that scapegoating immigrants won't begin to solve the state's economic woes" (Mata 1998: 152; see Stefancic and Delgado 1996).

Critics point out that Brimelow's work also lends itself to disproportion by disseminating exaggerated figures. According to Chua, "*Alien Nation* is presented physically [as] if it involved considerable research. . . . On inspection, [however,] Brimelow's reasoning is wildly convoluted and riddled with historical inaccuracies" (1995: 17; see also Reimers 1998). In his opposition to current immigration policy, Brimelow remains concerned about the putative problem of America's fading whiteness; furthermore, he introduces exaggerated statistics on the whiteness of the nation. Brimelow claims that as late as 1960, the United States was nearly 90 percent white, leaving critics wondering how that figure was calculated and questioning how Hispanic Americans were counted (Lemann 1995; see Chua 1995).

In his critique of *Alien Nation*, Nicholas Lemann writes, "When Mr. Brimelow tries to provide tangible details about the deteriorating fabric of life here caused by immigration, they often have exaggerated or unproved feeling" (1995: 3). Detecting elements of disproportion contained in *Alien Nation*, Lemann continues, "Mr. Brimelow is more an energetic pamphleteer than a reporter. He has done a good job of assembling printed material but, aside from one nocturnal visit to the Border

Patrol station south of San Diego, he has not gone out in search of first-hand, irrefutable evidence that immigration actually is eating away at the very core of the country in the way he says it is" (1995: 3). Rather than offering a sound and scholarly argument against immigration, *Alien Nation*, in the words of critic Richard Bernstein: "reads too much like one of those solicitations you get in the mail urging a contribution to a political cause" (1995: C17).

Fabricated Figures

As a more blatant form of disproportion, figures are not merely exaggerated but fabricated altogether, meaning that there is no factual basis for claiming that a particular threat exists. In a campaign to rid his Long Island, New York, community of undocumented immigrants whom he blames for rising crime rates, Joseph Caracappa, a Republican legislator, announced plans to bring court action to compel the INS to crack down on illegal immigration. Caracappa said that "enforcement of immigration laws would reduce the risk to public safety that undocumented people pose in areas like Farmingville, where Hispanic men congregate daily near street corners awaiting job offers as day laborers" (Rather 2000: B5). Contrary to Caracappa's claim, Suffolk Police Commissioner John C. Gallagher said, "there was no evidence linking an increase in crimes and arrests in Farmingville to undocumented workers" (p. B5). Caracappa's political opponents have challenged his public statements maligning undocumented workers as criminals. Maxine S. Postal, a Democratic lawmaker, expressed concern that additional anti-immigrant legislation could pass: "There is a lot of hysteria and fear out there" (p. B5). Nadia Marin-Molina, a lawyer and advocate for immigrant workers, detected a distinct racist undercurrent, adding, "This legislation seems to be an attempt to tell the INS to pick up people based on their skin color and the INS can't do that" (p. B5). INS spokesperson Mark Thorn concurs: "INS agents cannot simply approach a group of people and ask for their documentation without probable cause" (p. B5). Barbara J. Olshansky, an attorney with the Center for Constitutional Rights, believes that issuing fabricated statistics that claim that undocumented immigrants are responsible for an increase in crime, then passing legislation to combat the putative problem by clamping down on undocumented workers—many of whom are Latino—represent a clear "effort to intimidate people who are seeking a better life here" (p. B5).

Other Harmful Conditions

Consider, for instance, moral panic over crack (cocaine) babies in which claimsmakers deliberately failed to acknowledge that pregnant addicts also consumed alcohol, nicotine, and other drugs that adversely affected the health of the fetus; moreover, many pregnant addicts had poor nutrition and inadequate prenatal care. To place the blame solely on crack cocaine while ignoring those other harmful substances is politically manipulative, especially if such claims about the dangers of crack are used as a basis for public policy aimed at criminalizing drug use rather than developing medical and health care programs for addicted mothers and their children (Brewster 2000; Goode 1990; Humphries 1999; Welch 1997c, 1999a). Similarly, blaming immigrants for social ills such as crime, unemployment, and contagious diseases without conceding that those problems have multiple sources demonstrates the extent to which moral panic depends on disproportionate claims that ignore other harmful conditions. In *The Case against Immigration*, Beck does precisely that: "During the last decade of explosive immigration the rate of violent youth crime has soared. Youth arrests for major violent crimes rose from 83,400 arrests to 129,600 in 1992, a Justice Department study shows. And the rate is even higher in urban areas of high immigration" (1996: 225). As mentioned throughout this chapter, many advocates for restricting immigration have shifted blame to immigrants, scapegoating them for economic woes, lawlessness, and problems facing public health (Beck 1996; Brimelow 1995; Buchanan 1996, 1999).

Changes over Time

"If the attention paid to a given condition at one point in time is vastly greater than that paid to it during a previous or later time, without any corresponding increase in objective seriousness, then, once again, the criterion of disproportionality may be said to have been met," according to Goode and Ben-Yehuda (1994: 44). In the 1980s, for example, there were widespread claims that drug abuse was on the rise, thus contributing to a series of antidrug laws and enhanced enforcement. Conversely, studies had shown that drug abuse among Americans had actually declined (Goode 1990). Similarly, concern over immigration has ebbed and flowed throughout much of American history. In the early 1990s, politicians, sensing latent public anxiety over immigrants, exploited the issue for campaign purposes, especially in California, Florida, and Texas. Given the sheer size and population of those states, immigration, as a political issue, was greatly amplified, prompting lawmakers at the federal level to weigh in on the controversy. In 1996, Congress passed the most sweeping legislation governing immigration since the 1920s and 1930s (Holmes 1996). However, by 1999 moral panic over immigrants had already begun to wane. Even legislators who had supported revised immigration laws realized that they had gone too far and conceded that many immigrants, their families, and communities had suffered undue hardship (Lewis 2000a; see Chapter 9). As we will soon discuss, fluctuating public—and political—opinion on immigration is indicative of volatility, another key criterion of moral panic.

Stylization and Political Hyperbole

The immigration issue is not merely exaggerated, but, in the words of Cohen (1972), *stylized*. By sensationalizing the issue, immigration is hyped in a stylized manner that feeds public anxiety; as a result, immigrants are reduced to an array of stereotypes portraying them as predatory, criminal, lazy, stupid, and diseased (Fine and Christoforides 1991). Hyperbole also manifests in apocalyptic metaphors characteristic of a disaster mentality. Resorting to catastrophic rhetoric as his own brand of hyperbole, Brimelow writes,

- "The United States is not a pile of wealth but a fragile system—a lifeboat. And lifeboats can get overcrowded and sink" (1995: 245).
- "In effect, by allowing its borders to vanish under this vast whirlwind mass of illegal immigrants, the United States is running on the edge of a demographic buzz saw. One day, it could suddenly look down to find California or Texas cut off" (1995: 35).
- "Make no mistake: What we are looking at here is a demographic event of seismic proportions" (1995: 45; also see Beck 1996; Buchanan 1996; Chua 1995; Lemann 1995).

Likewise other nativists and immigration restrictionists issued books with catastrophic titles, such as *The Immigration Invasion* (Lutton and Tanton 1994), *The Immigration Time Bomb: The Fragmenting of America* (Lamm and Imhoff 1985), *Will America Drown? Immigration and the Third World Population Explosion* (Dalton 1993), *The Path to National Suicide: An Essay on Immigration and Multiculturalism* (Auster 1990). Hyperbole over the presumed harmfulness of immigration exemplifies moral panic; indeed, much of the political rhetoric represents tangible evidence indicating further that the issue was blown out of proportion. Public and political concern over immigration reemerged in the early 1990s, and mainline politicians scrambled to outdo one another over who could be tougher on illegal—and even legal—immigrants. Anti-immigration campaigns not only come from the right end of the political spectrum, including one of the more vocal opponents of immigration, Pat Buchanan, but also from political moderates and centrists. Most notably, President Clinton supported the Illegal Immigration Reform and Immigrant Responsibility Act, the Anti-Terrorism and Effective Death Penalty Act, the Personal Responsibility and Work Opportunity Reconciliation Act, producing the most restrictive immigration policies in more than 75 years (Holmes 1996). As mentioned previously, the more immigration is politicized, the more distorted and oversimplified it becomes; correspondingly, the issue strays from circumspection and reasonable solutions. According to Frank Sharry, executive director of the National Immigration Reform Forum, a pro-immigration group, "With the candidates, I think most of their ideas are silly sound bites rather than thoughtful policy pronouncements. . . . There is no relationship between the serious policy debate over immigration that is going on and what the candidates are saying" (Holmes 1996: B10).

Volatility

In the early 1990s, immigration emerged as a putative social problem, drawing the concern of a public that perceived immigrants as a growing threat to American society, its culture, and the economy. Illegal immigrants in particular were viewed as taking valuable jobs from struggling U.S. workers and consuming tax dollars for social services, health care, education, and welfare. In pandering to public anxiety over immigration, politicians in key states initiated legislation adversely affected immigrants. Sociologists remind us that moral panic often breaks out following a major crisis or event (Cohen 1972; Goode and Ben-Yehuda 1994). Even though moral panic over immigrants had surfaced in particular states, especially in California, Florida, and Texas, an alarming event fueled fear of immigrants at the national level. In 1993, a powerful bomb ripped through the World Trade Center in New York City, killing six people and injuring more than a thousand. Americans realized immediately that their nation was not immune from international terrorism, and after an expansive investigation, authorities arrested militant Muslim leader, Sheik Omar Abdel Rahman, a fundamentalist cleric from Egypt. Rahman was convicted in 1995 of seditious conspiracy and sentenced to life in prison (Fried 2000). The bombing inflamed fears not only of immigrants in general, but those of Middle Eastern descent in particular (Reimers 1998). The tragic explosion compelled legislators in the nation's capital to devise new immigration laws designed to combat terrorism (U.S. Congress, House 1993, 1994a, 1994b, 1994c; U.S. Congress, Senate 1995). Citing a threat to national security, Congress responded by passing sweeping legislation aimed at removing criminal aliens from the United States, a policy that has prompted a steady increase of deportations (Hedges 2000a).

As the term *volatility* suggests, moral panic erupts quickly (although the problem may lie dormant or latent for long periods of time), then fades or vanishes from the collective conscience or public psyche. Still, even though moral panic subsides, the changes made in policies and government institutions remain, eventually becoming obsolete and inappropriate for dealing with the problem. Because moral panic occurs suddenly, policies and legislation are often made in haste, driven more by emotion than rational decision-making; consequently, such laws are difficult to enforce fairly and without discrimination due to the sprawling nature of legislation. As noted, immigration laws passed in 1996 were questioned later by lawmakers who originally supported them (Lewis 2000a). Even INS officials concede that the 1996 legislation needs to be rewritten since it is unfair to treat all immigrants with equal harshness. According to INS spokesman, Bill Strassberger, "The law is sweeping, even overreaching. . . . We have told Congress that changes need to be made and some discretion needs to be returned to our immigration judges. But as the law stands now the ability of the immigration judges to look at all aspects of the individual's life, including the crime committed, whether they are members of the P.T.A., what their jobs are or if they have a family, is no longer possible" (Hedges 2000a: B3).

Volatility also implies that interest in the putative threat is subject to rapid decline, a feature of moral panic evident in the recent controversy over immigration. Whereas anti-immigration campaigns continue to linger among nativists, the issue did not consume the media or political institutions in the late 1990s as it did earlier in the decade. Simply put, moral panic over immigration waned along with its volatility. It is important to emphasize that moral panic fluctuates along with perceptions of economic threat (Cohen 1972; Hall et al. 1978). Moral panic over immigrants is no exception. By 2000, Americans were exhibiting less anxiety about immigration than in the mid-1990s, due in large part to an expanding economy and low unemployment, developments that served to reduce economic insecurity among U.S. citizens. "You have a very robust economy and full employment, and that always changes the terms of debate on immigration," said James P. Smith, an economist with the Rand Corporation who was chairman of a 1997 National Academy of Sciences study on the effects of immigration. "When there are plenty of jobs around, the finger pointing that goes on about immigration goes away," he stated (quoted in Greenhouse 2000b: A12). Congress also has adapted to the prevailing economic climate by viewing some immigrants as a resource rather than a burden or threat. In October 2000, Congress approved legislation that will increase significantly the number of work visas for educated skilled foreigners who are expected to fill specialized jobs in the high-technology industry. The vote in the Senate (96 favoring the proposal and one dissent) demonstrates how dramatically the debate over immigration and economics has changed since the early and mid-1990s. Senator Spencer Abraham, a Michigan Republican who cosponsored the bill, said, "The one thing on which I think almost everyone is in agreement is that we face a serious worker shortage with respect to high-tech employment and skilled labor in America today" (Alvarez 2000: A1). "The industry very much wants to make sure that we remain competitive globally. We either import workers or export jobs and industries," reasoned David Dreier, a California Republican who had sponsored a House bill similar to that of the Senate's (Alvarez 2000: A24).

Although a strong economy in 2000 had reshaped the debate over immigration, not all immigrants enjoyed renewed status. As the Senate deliberated over measures that would grant educated immigrants easier access to America's workforce, advocates for immigrants tried, unsuccessfully, to attach other immigration provisions. "I thought we would work together to restore some of America's lost luster on immigration issues and this did not happen," said Democratic Senator Patrick J. Leahy of Vermont, who has sought to legalize the immigration status of some Haitians, Central Americans, and others who have long lived illegally in the United States (Alvarez 2000: A24). Other inequities within immigration reform also are evident. Despite Congressional approval for increasing the number of visas for skilled foreigner to work in high-tech industries, from 115,000 per year to 195,000, other sectors of the economy did not necessarily benefit from low unemployment. That is particularly the case in agriculture, where there is enormous dependence on workers from Mexico—fully documented or not (DePalma 2000: C2). In Congress, Republicans generated support for the largest temporary worker legislation since the 1940s and 1950s, when the Bracero program brought more than five million Mexicans to the United States to work in agriculture (see Calavita 1992). The Clinton administration, however, rejected proposals to issue temporary work visas to Mexicans, a position that Vicente Fox, Mexico's president-elect, found hypocritical. Fox argued that it made no sense for the United States to spend nearly $1 billion a year to guard the border with Mexico if American businesses need Mexican workers. "I know many people in the United States want to see people as a burden, as a problem, but people are an asset. . . . The U.S. should allow Mexican workers to cross the Rio Grande as easily as the products that make up the $16 billion in two-way trade," Fox argued (quoted in DePalma 2000: C2). The General Accounting Office reports that approximately 52 percent of the nation's 1.6 million farm workers are in the United States illegally (DePalma 2000).

The increased value of labor in the United States continues to alter the view of immigrants who have the potential to fill significant voids in the workforce. Leaders of organized labor have taken notice of that economic shift. Labor unions, which once fought to keep illegal immigrants from entering the work force, are now eager to organize them (Greenhouse 2000b). Those economic and demographic changes also are having an impact on politics. Politicians who once led unforgiving attacks against immigrants—with measures to cut government benefits to the children of illegal immigrants—have realized that their nativist stance has backfired. In California, for instance, the fastest-growing Hispanic and Asian populations have moved to punish anti-immigrant politicians in the voting booth. In the Presidential race, Republican candidate George W. Bush, Governor of Texas, pushed pro-immigration rhetoric in an effort to avoid alienating Hispanic voters while also preserving his state's business ties to Mexico ("Blaming Immigrants" 2000; Greenhouse 2000b: A12; Schmitt 2000; also see Archibold 2000).

Conclusion

Summarizing the nature of pseudodisasters, Goode and Ben-Yehuda reiterate that moral panic "locates a 'folk devil,' is shared, is out of synch with the measurable seriousness of the condition that generates it, and varies in intensity over time" (1994: 41). In this chapter, evidence was introduced to demonstrate that public anxiety over immigrants in the early and mid-1990s satisfies each of the criteria of moral panic, namely, concern, hostility, consensus, disproportionality, and volatility. There was considerable concern then that immigrants posed a threat to the United States' social, cultural, ethnic, racial, and economic order; as a result, immigrants were demonized, stereotyped, and subjected to various forms of hostility. Although the danger of immigrants had been exaggerated greatly, public fears waned due in large part to favorable economic trends in the United States. Regrettably, however, moral panic over immigrants has left in its wake three acts of legislation, namely, the Illegal Immigration Reform and Immigrant Responsibility Act, the Anti-Terrorism and Effective Death Penalty Act, and the Personal Responsibility and Work Opportunity Reconciliation Act, all passed in 1996 at the peak of moral panic over immigrants. Experts characterize those statutes as being steeped in contradictions and inconsistencies (American Civil Liberties Union [ACLU] 2000a; Amnesty International 2000a; Lawyers Committee for Human Rights 2000a). As we shall see throughout this work, the revised immigration laws passed in 1996 have continued to affect adversely the lives of immigrants, their families, and communities.

It is crucial to keep in mind, however, that moral panic does not necessarily mean that there is no potential for a problem; rather, societal responses to the putative problem are fundamentally inappropriate (Chiricos 1996; Cohen 1972). Immigration, like all social policies, ought to be carefully formulated and mindful of ongoing worldwide demographic shifts (Heer 1998; Reimers 1998). Moreover, to achieve sound policy that does not discriminate against certain groups of people, legislators ought to resist hyperbole rooted in fear of immigrants (Andreas 1998; Dowty 1987; Jonas and Dod Thomas 1999). In his assessment of immigration policy, Bernstein agrees: "Those who think that system needs no fixing cannot responsibly hold to that position" (1995: C17). Correspondingly, Lemann adds that Brimelow, author of *Alien Nation*, "is right when he says that there is more risk from too much immigration than from too little, but he doesn't establish that the current situation justifies his level of alarm—and the reason is that he finds the simple fact of substantial nonwhite immigration to be sufficiently alarming" (1995: 3).

The overall purpose of this book is to examine critically the impact of the revised immigration laws enacted in 1996. In the chapters ahead, evidence is unveiled showing that those laws are fundamentally unfair and discriminatory, especially against the impoverished and members of racial and ethnic minorities—people who remain susceptible to being criminalized, pathologized, marginalized, and scapegoated. Those and other problems related to moral panic over immigration will be interpreted in the context of key developments in the controversy involving the 1996 legislation.

3

The Campaign against Immigrants

The combined forces of open immigration and multiculturalism constitute a mortal threat to American civilization.

Lawrence Auster

When the pressure built to "do something" about immigration, illegal aliens were a natural target. And that is precisely what Congress did.

David Reimers

uring the first year of the newly passed immigration laws, sweeps, raids, and roundups became increasingly common. Moreover, such tactics became so aggressive that they injected tremendous fear even among U.S. citizens who, according to law enforcement officers, *appeared* to be foreign. In 1997, 30 police and six Border Patrol agents descended on the barrio section of Chandler, Arizona, randomly stopping motorists and pedestrians and demanding that they produce verification of their U.S. citizenship. Those who resisted or attempted to flee were beaten. For five days, the warrantless dragnet, featuring house-to-house searches, terrorized the community. In the end, 432 illegal migrants—including two U.S. citizens—were swiftly deported, some wearing not much more than underwear. Upon investigation, the Arizona attorney general condemned the actions of the INS and local police as blatant violations of Fourth Amendment rights (Wood 1997). Also that year, a tactical team composed of 60 police and federal agents raided a low-income housing complex in the outskirts of Portland, Oregon. The roundup yielded more than a hundred undocumented immigrants who, along with a handful of alleged drug peddlers, were removed from the country (Bjorhus 1997). Similarly, sheriff deputies in Wyoming combined forces with Border Patrol officers, and together they stormed Jackson Hole, "snatching Latino workers from the kitchens of twenty-five restaurants, rousting them from their homes, and literally grabbing them as they rode on their bicycles" (Parenti 1999: 152). More than 150 people—including 50 legal residents and U.S. citizens—were corralled into a yard where authorities scrawled large identification numbers on their forearms; later, those who could not furnish documentation were hauled away in a manure-strewn cattle truck to be deported (Hacker 1996; Hubbard 1996).

As explored previously, moral panic over immigrants is a complex expression of public anxiety manifesting as undifferentiated fear of immigrants, people of color, and crime. Making matters worse, nativists and restrictionists fuel campaigns against immigrants by lobbying for regressive policies, including the use of aggressive law enforcement tactics. This chapter takes a closer look at the activities of anti-immigrant groups and the influence they have on legislators and the INS. To contextualize the phenomenon, we begin by discussing the process by which immigration emerged as a so-called social problem in the early 1990s. At that time, immigrants underwent a significant social transformation, becoming viewed as threats to American society, culture, and economy. As a formal response to that putative threat, political leaders embarked on tough legislative campaigns that produced greater measures of coercive control while allowing the INS to neglect its commitment to service.

Immigration as a Constructed Social Problem

According to the objectivist perspective, a major school of thought in the study of social problems, society's ills are detected easily since it is assumed they incur harm that can be verifiably assessed (Manis 1974, 1976). As a rival to the objectivist school, however, constructionism (or the subjectivist view) argues that social problems are driven by collective definitions that become so compelling that they influence the way the public perceives society. Constructionists Spector and Kitsuse contend that social problems are "activities of individuals or groups making assertions of grievances and claims with respect to some putative conditions" (1977: 75; see Best 1987, 1989; Schneider and Kitsuse 1985; Schneider and Ingram 1993). The subjectivist perspective adds tremendously to our understanding of the process by which the immigration issue was socially constructed in the early and mid-1990s. First, the so-called problem of immigration was created according to a collective definition along with several claims-making activities that warned about the putative threat from immigrants. Second, demands, particularly in the form of proposed legislation, were put forth to remedy the problem of immigration. Third, public opinion supported the perception that immigration was a social problem requiring revised laws and additional measures of social control. Fourth, the media offered heightened attention to those developments, thus amplifying moral panic over immigrants, contributing to its consensus, disproportionality, and volatility.

Although there is significant overlap between social problems and moral panic, there remain three distinct differences (Goode and Ben-Yehuda 1994). First, not all social problems involve a folk devil: consider, for example, an economic depression. Conversely, moral panic always is directed at a specific folk devil, a person or group whom moral entrepreneurs can blame and scapegoat for society's troubles. Disproportionality marks the second difference between social problems and moral panic. As noted in the previous chapter, a key criterion of moral panic is the discrepancy between the degree of concern over the issue and the magnitude of the putative threat; hence, panic stems from the process by which a danger is blown out of proportion. Bona fide social problems, by contrast, do not always provoke panic, and at times, policymakers caution against exaggeration so that the precise nature of the problem can be ascertained, such as the aftermath of a natural disaster. Again, moral panic implies volatility resulting in sharp fluctuations of concern: Simply put, moral panic *breaks out*. Such vacillation, however, is not a defining element of social problems. Based on those considerations, the immigration controversy of the early and mid-1990s did not constitute a bona fide social problem; rather, it manifested as moral panic containing folk devils along with a disproportionate degree of public concern that fluctuated over time.

The Nativist/Restrictionist Movement

Social movements harness the unbridled energy of collective conscience and funnel it into organized, coordinated actions aimed at social change rather than merely persecuting undesirable groups at random. Due to the defining impact of social movements, moral panic appears less erratic and more formalized. The anti-immigration movement of the early and mid-1990s, composed of nativists and restrictionists, expressed dissatisfaction with the status quo and offered proposals for social change. Whereas nativists and restrictionists share similar strategies to reduce immigration, they differ in some respects. Nativists proclaim that America should remain a nation of predominately white people of European stock; moreover, they rely on inflamed rhetoric intended to warn the public that non-white immigrants pose a danger to American culture (Brimelow 1995; Buchanan 1996). For restrictionists, however, the race or ethnicity of immigrants is not necessarily a prominent concern; rather, they issue claims that immigration should be restricted because more immigrants increasingly place an undue strain on the nation's economy and environment (Beck 1996; Briggs 1996). Of course, in the midst of moral panic over immigrants in the early and mid-1990s, it is difficult to distinguish between nativists and restrictionists given that each of their claims about the harmfulness of immigrants was excessive and exaggerated. Both nativists and restrictionists resorted to criminalizing, pathologizing, marginalizing, and scapegoating immigrants, pointing to well-publicized tragedies as evidence of the putative danger of immigrants, most notably the bombing of the World Trade Center. With those claims, nativists and restrictionists set out to alter the issue of immigration by lobbying lawmakers.

The leading restrictionist organization is the Federation for American Immigration Reform (FAIR). Formed in 1979, FAIR gained a reputation for strident views endorsing substantial cuts in immigration. FAIR's leadership, namely, Roger Connor, John Tanton, and Dan Stein, was successful in keeping its group in the political spotlight by appearing frequently in the media and at congressional committees. In 1985, FAIR helped open the Center for Immigration Studies (CIS), a research and policy group that would augment the campaign to revise immigration laws. By the early 1990s, as immigration weighed heavily on the public mind, FAIR had established itself as a formidable force in the debate over legislation, and by 1996, at the height of moral panic over immigrants, FAIR reported a membership of 70,000.

FAIR inspired other organizations gaining prominence in the restrictionist movement, including the American Immigration Control Foundation (AICF), founded in 1983. In the 1990s, several local and regional groups also joined the campaign against immigrants. In California, a grassroots organization captured the essence of moral panic over immigrants, calling itself Save Our State (SOS); its goals and activities mirrored another California group known as Voice of Citizens Together (VCT) as well as the Tri-Immigration Moratorium (TRIM) organized in New York City in 1995. Those groups disseminate anti-immigration literature, organize rallies, lobby lawmakers, and support candidates who endorse restrictions on immigration, such as Presidential candidate Pat Buchanan (Reimers 1998).

Despite the local impact of regional nativist and restrictionist groups, the national campaign to cut immigration was led by FAIR, headquartered in Washington, D.C., with an office in Los Angeles. John Tanton, an early leader of FAIR, was instrumental in turning immigration into a policy issue by frequent public appearances, fundraising, and writing. In promoting further its cause, Tanton currently publishes the restrictionist periodical *Social Contract* and manages Social Contract Press, which distributes anti-immigration literature, often featuring sensationalistic titles that suggest a disaster mentality, including *The Immigration Invasion* (Lutton and Tanton 1994). Whereas his supporters recognize Tanton for endorsing restrictionist policies based on concerns for the environment and overpopulation, his critics believe that his motives are driven by xenophobia, bigotry, and racism (Reimers 1998).

The campaign against immigrants, however, is not without its opposition. Among the most recognizable advocates for immigrants is the National Immigration Forum (NIF), an organization committed to promoting the positive aspects of immigration and dispelling the myths that feed nativism and prejudice. The pro-immigration coalition also consists of the Mexican American Legal Defense and Educational Fund (MALDEF) and the National Council of La Raza. Both groups are devoted to fighting restrictionist immigration proposals because they commonly are unfair to Latinos. Other organizations continue to lend their support to immigrants, such as the Asian-American Association, the National Council of Churches, the American Jewish Committee, the

Roman Catholic Church, CLINIC, the Jesuit Refugee Service, the Lutheran Immigration and Refugee Service (LIRS), the Immigrants' Rights Project of the ACLU, the Florence Immigrant and Refugee Rights Project, the Lawyers Committee for Human Rights, and the National Lawyers Guild.

Whereas critics felt that racism and bigotry were driving the campaign to reduce immigration, restrictionists publicly relied on the argument that more immigrants endangered the environment and its limited natural resources. In confronting FAIR's chief ecological claim, NIF issued a report debunking the theory that immigrants—particularly non-whites—harm the environment (NIF 1997). Interestingly, the environmental argument did not enter the policy debate at the national level. In fact, as the controversy over immigration peaked in the mid-1990s, Congress and government officials did not even address the environmental agenda; rather, political discourse on immigration centered on concerns for the economy, welfare, abuses within asylum procedures, and most prominently, curbing illegal immigration. Paradoxically, several of the provisions of the 1996 legislation compromised the environment by building new fences and barriers along the border. According to immigration historian David Reimers,

> The situation was ironic: the current movement to restrict immigration is heavily rooted in the population and environmental concerns growing out of the 1970s, but thus far the population and environmental issues surrounding immigration have rarely been debated in the political arena nor have the major environmental groups taken a stand on immigration. . . . Because of the difficulty in convincing Congress and the public of their case against immigration, the environmentalists in the restrictionist movement have turned to other issues in their call for cutting immigration. (1998: 63)

The campaign to curb immigration gained considerable momentum in the early 1990s as restrictionist groups took exception to the Immigration Act of 1990, which increased immigration by about 35 percent. In reaction to that legislation, restrictionists in Congress proposed the Immigration and Stabilization Act of 1993, designed to cap immigration at 300,000 per year while proposing additional funding for the INS, stricter asylum procedures, and swift deportation of criminal aliens. Similar measures followed suit. In a key proposal, Senator Alan Simpson, a leading Republican figure on immigration affairs, recommended that immigration be reduced by 100,000, while his GOP colleague Senator Bob Stump favored a reactionary position, calling for a moratorium on immigration in addition to expanding the INS and slashing benefits for legal residents. The Democrats, who controlled Congress at that time, successfully resisted legislative reform, thus stalemating the campaign against immigrants.

However, as the economy slowed in the early 1990s, anti-immigration sentiment among the citizens grew, and in several states immigration became a hot political issue. Legislatures in California, Florida, and Texas argued that the federal government should reimburse states for monies spent on social services for legal and illegal immigrants and subsidize the incarceration of criminal aliens housed in state prisons. In the aftermath of the World Trade Center bombing, along with well-publicized news stories of increasingly more Cuban and Haitian boat people trying to reach American soil in 1994, lawmakers could no longer ignore public anxiety over immigration. That year other significant events shaped further immigration as a policy issue; in particular, California passed Proposition 187 and Republicans took control over Senate and the House. Despite those developments, nativists and restrictionists struggled to achieve consensus among Republicans, especially given that the right wing of the party saw immigration as vital to expanding the labor force necessary to improve the U.S. economy. Similarly, many conservatives viewed immigration reform as an affront to family values since it would place restrictions on those seeking immigration to reunite families (Reimers 1998). Lawmakers from each major political party soon realized that the immigration issue was tremendously complicated, prompting them to sort out numerous facets of policy, including legal immigration (i.e., whether to institute reductions, and on what basis: job skills or family reunification), illegal immigration (i.e., resources for INS and law enforcement, including border patrol), criminal aliens (i.e., federal reimbursements for state prisons and funds for INS detention and deportation), social services for legal and illegal immigrants (i.e., education, health care, welfare benefits, and whether states or the federal government would bear the costs), and employment opportunities for legal residents and undocumented workers.

Faced with a complex and multifaceted issue of immigration policy, Congress formed a bipartisan Task Force on Immigration Reform in 1995. That panel, along with a report by the Commission on Immigration Reform (CIR 1994), sharply defined the parameters for policy considerations when it separated concerns over illegal immigration from those over legal immigration. By doing so, the task force made it easy for lawmakers to tackle the popular issue of illegal immigration while standing clear of the political fallout caused by cutting legal immigration (*Congressional Record* 1996). The final version of legislation was not ready for congressional vote until 1996, and by then the economy had improved to the extent that immigrants were no longer scapegoated for economic woes. Also during that time, the pro-immigration lobby had recruited powerful allies from corporations whose workforce could be maligned by reductions in immigration (i.e., IBM, Microsoft, Procter & Gamble). Due to those key developments, nativists and restrictionists had to settle for legislation that for the most part sidestepped the controversial issue of legal immigration,[1] thus concentrating on illegal immigration, asylum procedures, criminal aliens, and terrorists, none of which generated much opposition (Diamond 1996; Judis 1997; Reimers 1998). The campaign against immigration surged forward in the form of a well-financed attack on illegal immigrants and criminal aliens as Congress granted INS unprecedented authority and discretion.

As we look back at the events that produced a newly fortified INS, we ought not lose sight of the lasting impact of moral panic, particularly since the problem of immigration became socially constructed in the early 1990s, picking up momentum over the next six years. Amid the wars on crime and drugs and the crusade to "end welfare as we know it," a popular mantra of President Clinton that led to a major overhaul of the welfare system, the campaign against illegal immigrants had few opponents. Many politicians blatantly distorted the issue by repeating falsehoods about immigration and welfare policies, an example of a disinformation campaign typically found in moral panic. California Governor Pete Wilson, for instance, fueled hostility against illegal immigrants by proclaiming that hundreds of thousands of aliens come to the United States to take advantage of the welfare system. That rhetoric was particularly deceitful given that Wilson and his staff knew full well that welfare is not extended to immigrants who are undocumented; nevertheless, a dominant political myth was preserved, one that combined a derogatory view of welfare along with a condemnation of lawlessness in the form of illegal immigration. Compounding the issue of immigration was the popular tendency to racialize many of America's social ills, including crime, drugs, poverty; therefore, the problem of illegal immigration could easily be understood as another threat from people who are not white. Even immigration advocates realized that a sure way to reduce public and political animosity against legal immigrants was to divert that hostility to illegal immigrants, especially since the problem could be framed as a form of lawlessness that could be eradicated by strengthening the criminal justice apparatus.

Members of Congress rallied behind the campaign against illegal immigrants, proclaiming, "America's immigration system is in disarray and criminal aliens . . . constitute a particularly vexing part of the problem. Criminal aliens occupy the intersection of two areas of great concern to the American people; crime and the control over our borders" (U.S. Congress, Senate 1995: 1). Echoing popular complaints about the traditional criminal justice apparatus, lawmakers pronounced that the immigration system was broken; thus criminal aliens posed a growing threat to public safety. Moreover, even though "criminal aliens who commit serious crimes are subject to deportation under current law, the deportation system is in such disarray that no one, including the Commissioner of the Immigration and Naturalization Service can even say with certainty how many criminal aliens are currently subject to the jurisdiction of our criminal justice system" (U.S. Congress, Senate 1995: 1). Adding to moral panic and the perception that the immigration system had failed to protect the public, there were unsubstantiated reports that even when some criminal aliens were deported, they "often return to the U.S. in a matter of days or even hours" (U.S. Congress, Senate 1995: 3).

Given the scope of the 1996 immigration legislation, many elected leaders realized that they had encountered a win–win situation insofar as they could appeal to immigrant communities as a growing political constituency and at same time lend support to the always popular campaign for law and order. Equally important, politicians could enthusiastically voice their support for legislation targeting illegal immigrants in the same breath with anticrime, antidrug, and antiwelfare rhetoric, a simple task considering that immigrants, most notably illegal, are easily criminalized, pathologized, and economically marginalized. Whereas legal and illegal immigrants were often scapegoated before 1996, with the passage of new legislation, undocumented immigrants and criminal aliens became the primary folk devils.

Moral panic and social movements give rise to two mutually reinforcing classes of social managers, rule creators and rule enforcers (Becker 1963). Rule creators, most notably, lawmakers, politicians, and various inside players engaged in the legislation process, provide the legal justification for law enforcement campaigns. Through legislation, rule creators legitimize authority whereby the government increases its power to monitor and regulate the conduct of people. Rule creators purport that existing legal codes are insufficient to combat a persistent problem; therefore, they crusade for additional forms of social control. Operating on an absolute ethic, rule creators impose their fervent self-righteousness onto legislation. Throughout American history, legislative campaigns against immigrants resemble similar measures prohibiting alcohol and drugs insofar as rule creators depict their target population as inferior, immoral, and menacing (Bennett 1963; Gordon 1994; Gusfield 1963; Knobel 1996; Jones 1960; Reinarman and Levine 1997). Still, rule creators do not simply promote rules for their own sake; rather, they believe earnestly that their proposed laws are good for all citizens and society as a whole, thus projecting a greater sense of societal consensus based on shared values.

The INS as Agency of Social Control

While much of the discussion thus far has illuminated the role of rule creators in the campaign against immigrants, namely legislators and influential lobbyists, we turn attention to their counterparts charged with enforcing the rules. In his classic work, *Outsiders*, sociologist Howard S. Becker observed, "The most obvious consequence of a successful crusade is the creation of a new set of rules. With the creation of a new set of rules we often find that a new set of enforcement agencies and officials is established. Sometimes, of course, existing agencies take over the administration of the new rule, but more frequently a new set of rule enforcers is created" (1963: 155; see Bustamante 1972; Goode and Ben-Yehuda 1994). Rule creators realize that new laws are useless without sufficient enforcement; hence, rule enforcers are instrumental for social campaigns and their success. Unlike rule creators, enforcers tend to be less self-righteous and exhibit a more detached and pragmatic understanding of their tasks. Laws secure jobs for rule enforcers who know intuitively that they jeopardize the legitimacy of their agency should they not carry out their required duties (Becker 1963). Indeed, the involvement of rule enforcers as agents of social control becomes increasingly self-serving amid moral panic given that their agencies benefit from enhanced power, authority, and prestige along with greater funding and resources (Hall et al. 1978; Welch, Fenwick, and Roberts 1998). Consequently, rule enforcers are given credit—albeit falsely—for maintaining social order, an attribution that empowers further the criminal justice system and social control apparatus. According to Goode and Ben-Yehuda (1994: 27), "The thinking among agents of social control is that 'new situations need new remedies'; a national problem called for a drastic solution" (also see Cohen 1972). Scholars point out that social campaigns have figured prominently in the development of the INS. According to George Weissinger, "The Investigations Section [of the INS] and the Border Patrol seem to have their roots in moral crusades. The passage of the I&N Act of 1921 necessitated the creation of the Border Patrol to enforce the rules of the Act. The Investigations Branch evolved out of the desire to eradicate communism in the United States. Afterwards, the Investigations Unit expanded its mission to include all violators of the I&N Act inside the United States. Such a mission perpetuates the agency's existence. Survival is an underlying goal of all organizations" (1996: 48–49; also see Parenti 1999; Welch 2000c).

Nowadays, the impact of recent social campaigns is just as evident. In 1996, the Illegal Immigration Reform and Immigrant Responsibility Act passed overwhelmingly, prompting a renewed battle cry to stem the tide of illegal immigration. Moreover, there has been considerable bite to back up the bark, most notably in the realm of law enforcement. The INS continues to receive huge increases in funding, resources, and manpower; furthermore, law enforcement officials currently enjoy more stringent provisions in dealing with undocumented immigrants, including mandatory detention and expedited deportation of criminal aliens. Whereas legal immigration had been spared major reform, significant changes in the way the government confronts illegal immigration are left in the wake of legislative maneuvering, producing a larger, and arguably harsher, apparatus of social control.

As an agency of social control, the INS operates within the Department of Justice (DOJ), and its primary responsibility is enforcing the laws regulating the admission of foreign-born persons (i.e., aliens) to the United States and for administering various immigration benefits, including the naturalization of qualified applicants for U.S. citizenship. The INS also cooperates with the Department of State, the Department of Health and Human Services, and the United Nations in the admission and resettlement of refugees (INS 2000a; U.S. Congress, House 1981: 538).[2] As its mission suggests, the INS is a unique agency insofar as it has the duty to both enforce the law and provide services to immigrants, activities that create considerable strain for its personnel as well as its clients. Compounding the problems caused by a dual mandate is the fact that the INS remains one of the most criticized agencies in the federal government, frequently questioned about its controversial enforcement tactics and its lack of efficient service delivery (Calavita 1992; General Accounting Office [GAO] 1998; Reimers 1998).

Enforcement Mandate

The prevailing public image of the INS is that of a law enforcement agency responsible for preventing aliens from entering the country illegally and locating and removing persons who are living or working in the United States illegally. Still, the agency is vastly bureaucratic and even its enforcement mandate is dispersed into several major sectors within the INS. The Border Patrol division, operating as uniformed police, is charged with exterior enforcement against illegal entry. Guarding the interior United States, the investigations branch employs detectives in plain clothes who investigate violations of criminal and immigration law by undocumented immigrants and inspect places of employment for unauthorized workers. Monitoring 250 ports of entry, the inspections division screens all travelers arriving in the United States by air, land, or sea, while the antismuggling unit specifically investigates smuggling operations. Shoring up the enforcement mandate, the detention and deportation division is responsible for taking into custody criminals and undocumented aliens pending proceedings to determine whether they are to be removed from the United States (INS 1999).

In the early 1990s, popular perceptions driven by moral panic suggested that the immigration system was broken, allowing the nation to be invaded by illegal aliens. Fueling public anxiety, those views played a key role in strengthening the INS's enforcement mandate. In an attempt to fortify the nation's borders against illegal immigrants, Congress granted the INS resources to construct barriers along the Southwest border and the resources to hire additional personnel. Flexing its newfound muscle, the INS launched Operation Hold the Line in 1995, an initiative to strengthen a 20-mile barrier around El Paso, Texas. The following year, the INS embarked on Operation Gatekeeper in the San Diego, California, region, an aggressive strategy to halt illegal immigration by installing new fencing, high intensity lights, and more Border Patrol officers. Whereas INS officials insisted that those newly enacted operations served as effective blockades, critics argued that the barriers simply forced aliens to cross the border at other, less secured locations. Contributing to growing suspicion that fortified borders were not as effective as the government claimed was the accusation that INS supervisors falsified reports to make the plan look more successful (Reimers 1998). As ambitious as those operations have been, they paled by comparison to the proposals issued by nativists who argued that more extreme measures would be necessary to stop the influx of illegal aliens. Pat Buchanan proposed building a 200-mile-long "security fence" in areas along the United States–Mexican border. In Congress, some re-strictionists recommended authorizing the U.S. Army and the National Guard to patrol the southern border, while Lamar Alexander, a presi-dential candidate, proposed creating a new branch of the military to oversee the effort to stop the flow of illegal immigrants (Andreas 2000; Holmes 1996). Peter Brimelow, in *Alien Nation*, added, "Consideration should be given to jailing repeat offenders, perhaps in special prisons, for at least as long as is necessary to disrupt the economic patterns that have currently developed around lax border enforcement" (1995: 259).

In the 1990s and into the new millennium, even when Congress was cutting federal spending, the INS grew rapidly in large part because the agency persuaded lawmakers to remain fiscally committed to the fight against illegal immigration. Between 1993 and 2001, the INS budget increased by more than 230 percent—from $1.5 billion to $5.0 billion. During that period, spending for enforcement programs grew from $933 million to $3.1 billion, nearly five times as much as spending for citi-zenship and other immigrant services, which increased from $261 mil-lion to $679 million. The cost of shared support for the two missions increased from $525 million in 1993 to $1.1 billion in 2001. The INS also increased its full-time, permanent staff by 79 percent from 1993 (17,163) to 2001 (30,701). Most of this growth occurred in the enforce-ment programs, where the total number of employees, including offi-cers, grew from 11,418 to 23,364. Border Patrol led the way with an in-crease of 7,962 employees, or 159 percent. Additionally, the agency designated funds to expand its detention sector. Between 1995 and 2001, the INS more than doubled the number of detention bed spaces avail-able, with the current capacity at about 20,000 beds; furthermore, the Detention and Deportation staff nearly doubled, growing to 3,475 full-time permanent staff (INS 2002). Although the INS has allocated funds to improve services to immigrants, the lion's share of the budget is de-voted to "strengthening its successful multi-year strategy to manage the border, deter illegal immigration, combat the smuggling of people, and remove criminal and other illegal aliens from the United States" (INS 1999: 1).

To demonstrate the agency's accountability, the INS boasted substantial improvements in performance. In 1999, the INS successfully completed 45,131 criminal alien cases (they prosecuted, removed, or denied benefits as a result of investigation), an increase of 19 percent from 1998. Additionally, the agency removed 176,990 criminal and other illegal aliens in 1999; the number of criminal aliens removed (62,359) alone exceeded the total of all illegal aliens removed in 1995 (50,414).[3] In 1999, the Border Patrol apprehended 1,537,000 illegal aliens along the Southwest border. Finally, the INS reported collecting approximately $1.1 billion in fees for services in 1999, nearly twice the amount collected in 1993 (INS 2000a).

Whereas Congress lent its support to combating illegal immigration in the early 1990s, by the mid-1990s lawmakers were creating legislative changes that not only empowered the INS but also secured a steady stream of financial support. The Illegal Immigration Reform and Immigrant Responsibility Act of 1996 enhanced INS presence and enforcement at the border and increased criminal penalties for immigration-related offenses. The 1996 Act comprehensively reorganized the process of removal for inadmissible and deportable aliens, including an expedited removal process for inadmissible aliens arriving at ports of entry (INS 2000a). While groups backing renewed strategies to curb illegal immigration welcomed legislation changes, advocates for immigrants expressed concern that the government had adopted initiatives that compromised human rights. In particular, aggressive tactics designed to prevent illegal entries at the southern border have led to tragic incidents in which border agents have assaulted persons attempting illegal crossings. As mentioned previously, figures on illegal border crossings are greatly exaggerated by nativists and restrictionists who wish to inflame public anxiety that the nation is being besieged by illegal aliens. Regrettably, such disinformation also motivates some law enforcement officers to retaliate against undocumented immigrants during apprehension. Human Rights Watch (1993), a well-respected human rights organization, issued a report charging the Border Patrol with assaulting illegal aliens, prompting Congress to hold a hearing on the matter. In its defense, the INS disputed allegations that its agents had mistreated undocumented immigrants (U.S. Congress, House 1994b). Still, the issue lingered. In 1996, the public became increasingly aware of the problem of border violence when the media broadcasted a story in which sheriff's deputies in California searched a truck they suspected was transporting illegal aliens. During the apprehension, two aliens fled, and when they were caught, the officers beat them, an incident that was videotaped and shown on a national news program (Parenti 1999; Reimers 1998).

Since then, other incidents of abuse have caught the attention of human rights groups. In 1998, Amnesty International released a report documenting a pattern of officer misconduct, including unlawful lethal shootings, physical assaults, and ill treatment of detainees in custody. According to its investigation, steps taken in recent years to seal the border, coupled with the U.S. Army's role in assisting the INS in the "war on drugs," have increased the chances of human rights violations against people suspected of being illegal immigrants (Amnesty International 1998a). In 2000, a consortium of nongovernmental organizations announced that the INS, and in particular the Border Patrol, has elicited the most complaints about human and civil rights violations among law enforcement agencies over the prior two years. Fernando Garcia, coordinator of the Regional Abuse of Authority Campaign, accused INS agents and Border Patrol of racial profiling by stopping and questioning people who appear to be Hispanic (Valdez 2000). While human rights organizations do not take issue with the right of the United States to police its international borders, they insist it should be done in compliance with the country's international human rights obligations.[4]

Similarly, opponents of aggressive tactics point to the use of raids, swat teams, and sting operations that reach beyond the target population, thus intimidating legal residents and even U.S. citizens. In 1992 amid the riots in Los Angeles, the INS and Border Patrol swat teams, along with the officers of the Los Angeles Police Department, interrogated individuals to determine their citizenship, a clear violation of Los Angeles Special Order 40, which prohibits police from stopping and questioning an individual based on his or her ethnic appearance. As Hispanic residents became increasingly fearful of being detained by the government, community activists and local political leaders demanded that the INS discontinue its sweeps. In another controversial tactic, the INS issued sting letters intended to lure undocumented immigrants to government offices with the promise of legalizing their status; once they arrived, INS agents apprehended and deported them. While advocates of tough measures to curb illegal immigration often approve of such tactics, critics insist that they are ineffective and erode the public's trust in the government and especially the INS. Moreover, aggressive and deceptive enforcement tactics undermine the trust that the INS needs to effectively deliver services and benefits (Calavita 1992; Pastor 1992; Welch 1999a, 2000c). As we discuss later, enforcement strategies frequently interfere with the agency's service mandate.

Service Mandate

Although often overshadowed by its enforcement mandate, the INS is charged with assisting immigrants who are entitled to services and benefits. Specifically, the agency is responsible for administering status adjustments, work authorizations, applications for asylum and naturalization, as well as social services. Whereas the vast proportion of the INS budget is allocated to enforcement, between 1993 and 1999, spending for citizenship and other immigrant services grew from $261 million to $530 million. Budget increases for the service mandate were intended to keep up with demand. In 1999, the INS received 5.3 million applications for immigration benefits (including naturalization), nearly 25 percent more than received in 1993; the agency also received 6.4 million naturalization applications from 1993 through 1998, more than had been received in the previous 37 years combined. Since 1998, the INS opened 127 new Application Support Centers to fingerprint applicants for naturalization and other benefits. As a bureaucracy, the agency processes an immense volume of paperwork, currently holding more than 40 million files, including 19 million active files, which are created at a rate of nearly 60,000 per month. Since 1995, the agency added more than 6.5 million files to its computerized Central Index System, including 1.58 million in 1999 (INS 2000a).

The INS is not a static organization; rather, it is dynamic because it must respond to ongoing changes in legislation. The "get tough on immigrants" campaign manifested in the Illegal Immigration Reform and Immigrant Responsibility Act of 1996 placed restrictions on the eligibility of aliens for public benefits and imposed new requirements on sponsors of alien relatives for immigration (INS 2000a). Legislation governing welfare and social service instituted even more restrictions. The Personal Responsibility and Work Opportunity Reconciliation Act of 1996 denied Supplemental Security, food stamps, and Aid to Families with Dependent Children (AFDC) to legal immigrants during their first five years of U.S. residency; moreover, the new statute limited welfare to five years for all recipients (U.S. citizens and legal immigrants). Those laws not only altered the way INS operates, but as a service delivery system, the agency had the daunting task of deciphering the new provisions and clearly communicating the revised requirements to its clients. Confusion and anger soon followed as constituents complained that their elderly parents were adversely affected by recent legislation. Even sympathetic INS representatives were unable to offer remedies other than suggesting that voters take their complaints to federal lawmakers. In 1997, bowing to public pressure, Congress amended the 1996 legislation by reinstating social security benefits to elderly legal immigrants. In light of legislative reform that placed more restrictions on public benefits, along with mounting hostility toward immigrants, huge numbers of legal immigrants responded by filing applications for naturalization; as U.S. citizens they would remain eligible for social services and benefits. The surge in applications imposed an even greater burden on an already overwhelmed agency struggling to deliver services to immigrants. Moreover, those changes were occurring at a time when the INS was launching Citizenship U.S.A., a new program designed to expedite the naturalization process. INS representatives complain that funding for all of these services and programs was not keeping pace with their workload, adding to growing discontent among the rank and file staff (DeSipio and de la Garza 1998; Reimers 1998).

Certainly, undifferentiated fear of the impoverished, people of color, and immigrants played a key role in the emergence of legislation designed to curb illegal immigration, especially considering that the new laws rested on the stereotype that immigrants are drawn to the United States to take advantage of the welfare system. Indeed, the 1996 laws, combining such hot-button issues as welfare and immigration, reinforced the smug attitude that "they" (immigrants, particularly nonwhites) were different from "us" (white, hardworking U.S. citizens). Observers of the INS, including many of the agency's representatives, aptly pointed out that the service mandate takes a backseat to enforcement (Weissinger 1996; Welch 2000c). That realization is of little surprise considering that immigrants are tremendously marginalized by a society that has adopted the bigoted view that welfare breeds economic dependency on the part of racial and ethnic minorities (Gans 1995; Piven and Cloward 1971). As we see in the next section, the dual mandate contributes to the demotion of service providing since it has to compete with well-funded enforcement strategies, so-called police initiatives that enjoy public and political support because they personify the "get tough" sentiment contained in anti-immigration and criminal justice campaigns.

Strain of a Dual Mandate

The stress of competing directives contained in a dual mandate has been recognized by nearly everyone who has contact with the INS, including its representatives and clients and policymakers and scholars. In his research George Weissinger observed, "An apparent contradiction, the INS provides both a service and a control function. The contradiction involves an attempt by one organization to provide a service to the public while simultaneously attempting to enforce the law" (1996: 1; Morris 1985). Due to such conflict, there is a tendency for an organization to favor one activity over another. In the case of the INS, enforcement clearly retains its priority over service. INS agents, first and foremost, regard the agency as a law enforcement operation, and only secondarily as a service provider, a view widely shared by politicians, lawmakers, and the public.

Especially in light of the campaign against illegal immigration, the INS earns public and political support by demonstrating its effectiveness in the realm of apprehensions, detentions, and deportations, performance measures that mirror "law and order" initiatives in the traditional criminal justice apparatus. That feature of the agency is unmistakable, prompting Weissinger and other scholars to concur, "the processing of aliens by the INS parallels the American criminal justice system" (1996: 124; Parenti 1999; Welch 2000c). Although INS officials remind Congress that its agency values its commitment to service, funding disproportionately favors enforcement, setting the tone for its main mission, halting the tide of illegal immigration. Indeed, the INS currently is the largest federal law enforcement agency authorized to bear arms and make arrests.

Imbalance in the dual mandate perpetuates major contradictions at the INS. As more funds are designated to enforcement, fewer resources are available for service, contributing to the backlog of applications for naturalization and other services. Moreover, as the INS increasingly promotes itself as a law enforcement agency, it tends to alienate and at times intimidate its clients, a problem that compromises the agency's ability to offer services to legal immigrants. Simply put, the dual mandate creates a unique form of strain by which the agency is at odds with itself (GAO 1991).

Whereas the agency itself often is blamed for not improving its commitment to service, it is important to consider its key personnel who prefer tasks related to law enforcement. As their title suggests, INS Special Agents (also known as investigators) see themselves as law enforcement officers; they "view *paperwork* and service activities as *dirty work* and will avoid places where one completes such work. This accounts for the normally empty offices of most police and investigative units. Law enforcement officers believe that their work is *on the street*" (Weissinger 1996: 46). Scholar Peter Manning agrees: "When the reality of police work is on the street, then all other forms of reality assume a lesser significance" (1980: 220). Understandably, INS Special Agents find the delivery of services to be repetitive, routine, and bureaucratized, making the nonroutine nature of enforcement and investigation much more interesting by comparison. In his research, Weissinger unveiled a distinct police orientation prevalent among INS Special Agents:

> As law enforcement officers, Special Agents [of the INS] view their status and morale in terms of how closely their tasks mirror the expected role previously alluded to *real police work*. Among these agents there is a hierarchy of tasks upon which they measure their status. Investigators consider criminal investigation to be the most important task. The length of sentence often determines the severity of the crime and worthiness of the investigation. Control agents consider only tasks directly related to law enforcement as worthy. (1996: 2)

There is little surprise that INS Special Agents internalize their police role, given that the agency grants its personnel the power to arrest criminal law violators without a warrant and carry firearms and are considered to be working under hazardous conditions. Moreover, the status of police work has a polarizing effect on INS agents who feel they must continuously prove that they too are part of the larger police fraternity. "Law enforcement personnel are sensitive to peer review, and seek the approval of their peers. Police share solidarity and view their position in society as *we* against *them*" (Weissinger 1996: 46; Skolnick 1966). Weissinger concludes, "If [INS] investigators view their professional goals law enforcement, then service related activities are inappropriate. Even if the organization has a preference for the service activities, the enforcers view service providers negatively. The goals of the investigator often compete with the goals of the agency" (1996: 46).

Intraorganizational competition over which particular division is considered the "real" police unit contributes to polarization toward law enforcement and away from service. Weissinger found that INS Special Agents believe that their agency caters to the Border Patrol, a realization that demoralizes "the investigator who believes that interior enforcement is just as important as border enforcement" (1996: 119). Emulating a traditional police department, Special Agents operate as plainclothes detectives, while Border Patrol officers serve as uniformed patrol officers. Special Agents see themselves as truly professional law enforcement officers similar to other agents in the U.S. DOJ. Moreover, Special Agents view Border Patrol officers as mere "cops on the beat," a condescending perspective shared by other members of the Justice Department. According to Stephen G. Nelson, a U.S. District Attorney in San Diego, "The Border Patrol is 50 percent mediocrity, 40 percent stupidity, and 10 percent corruption. It is absolutely the worst federal law enforcement agency. No service does more to stifle bright young guys than the INS" (Neff 1981: 1). Special Agents view the Border Patrol as one dimensional, given that their main duty is to patrol the U.S. borders to prevent illegal entry. Unlike Special Agents, Border Patrol officers do not conduct investigations, nor do they have the same 1811 personnel classification that Special Agents have in common with agents in the Federal Bureau of Investigation (FBI) and Drug Enforcement Administration (DEA). Still, Special Agents feel slighted by the INS because the agency devotes more funds and resources, along with greater status and prestige, to Border Patrol than to the investigations branch.

For INS agents, perceptions of their professional worth also are complicated by the status structure within the DOJ, where a rigid sense of elitism places the FBI at the top of the hierarchy and the INS at the bottom. Drawing on his research, Weissinger found that Special Agents "believe that federal law enforcement agencies such as the FBI, DEA, U.S. Customs, Secret Service, and ATF [Bureau of Alcohol, Tobacco and Firearms], consider the INS to be low in law enforcement hierarchy" (1996: 114). In sum, competition over which division in the INS is regarded as truly the law enforcement sector and self-perceptions that their agency is consigned to the lowest rung of the Justice Department prompt INS agents to gravitate increasingly toward its enforcement mandate, thus neglecting service.

Making matters worse, recent investigations suggest that the strain of the dual mandate has contributed to an abusive and racist culture within some INS departments. In 2000, published reports revealed that in the INS Portland, Oregon, office, "some supervisors and officers call foreigners 'wets'—for 'wetbacks'—and 'tonks,' U.S. Border Patrol slang for the sound of a flashlight hitting an illegal immigrant's head. Employees complain that an officer, later promoted to supervisor, tells an African American colleague and others he can't stand 'niggers and white trash'" (Read 2000a: EV1). Members of Congress say that the INS often refuses to discipline its staff for abuse and mismanagement. Representative Janice Schakowsky (D–Illinois) said that complaints about the agency constitute 80 percent of her calls from constituents: "The enforcement side of the INS dominates the culture of the agency so that all too often everybody is viewed as a potential criminal . . . and all they're asking for is to get their passport stamped" (quoted in Read 2000a: EV2). Michael Bromwich, the inspector general who investigated the INS and other Justice Department agencies from 1994 to 1999, added that the INS consistently accounts for far more misconduct and corruption than the FBI, the DEA, the Bureau of Prisons, and the Marshals Service (Read 2000a). In 1999, the INS and the inspector general's office launched a record 4,551 internal investigations: one per seven workers in an agency that employs 32,000; that compares with one per 31 ATF employees and one per 89 Secret Service employees (Walth, Christensen, and Read 2000).[5] According to Bromwich, "The INS is notorious for having the most serious and pervasive management and misconduct problems of any part of the Justice Department. This has been the case for many, many years. Part of the problem is the culture of the agency which has resisted the management controls necessary to impose accountability" (Read 2000a: EV3).

With those concerns, members of Congress issued a proposal to split the INS into two independent agencies so that service would not compete with enforcement. In 1998, Congressman Harold Rogers (R–Kentucky) sponsored legislation that he insisted would improve the INS by reducing problems perpetuated by a dual mandate, including mismanagement, waste, and abuse. Rogers recommended that the Bureau of Immigration Enforcement be created within the Justice Department, constituting a new agency responsible for preventing illegal entry, conducting investigations, and detaining and deporting undocumented immigrants and criminal aliens. INS Commissioner Doris Meissner and her executive staff resisted that proposal and urged the Clinton administration to allow the agency to remain intact while separating enforcement and service functions. Still, such restructuring requires approval from Congress and as of 2001 plans to reorganize the INS remain in progress (see Chapter 9). In the meantime, the INS still must contend with problems that derive systemically from a dual mandate. As we see in the next several chapters, INS efforts to enforce immigration laws and provide services to immigrants contribute to ongoing conflicts, contradictions, and multiple ironies of social control.

Conclusion

Fueled by moral panic, the campaign against immigrants beginning in the early 1990s set out to reduce both legal and illegal immigration; however, by the mid-1990s, the economy improved and pro-immigrant groups garnered sufficient support to protect the interests of legal immigrants while redirecting public hostility to illegal immigrants. In 1996, legislation embodied renewed fervor to crack down on illegal aliens, endowing the INS with unprecedented powers and resources that would motivate the agency to pursue its enforcement mandate, leaving service at the margin. The police function of the INS continues to overshadow service in large part because its personnel view the organization as an agency of social control not unlike other sectors of the criminal justice apparatus. Weissinger adds to our understanding of that phenomenon, noting, "INS investigators share the philosophy of the law enforcer and experience great difficulty in coping with the service priority of the INS" (1996: 119).

As we explore with greater detail in the following chapter, the INS's tendency to emulate the traditional criminal justice paradigm produces unique problems for an agency that is also charged with serving immigrants. The campaign to "get tough" on illegal aliens has led to recent laws whose content and enforcement are rife with contradiction, often regressing into measures that either fail to solve the problem or make matters worse. Reimers reminds us that, "Even if the border were secure, however, by the mid-1990s more than half of all undocumented aliens were estimated to enter with some type of temporary visa and then stay in the United States illegally" (1998: 72; Holmes 1996). Consequently, enforcement methods, particularly those installed at the border, would have no effect on illegal immigration by those entering with some type of temporary visa, then overstaying (GAO 1995). Similarly, evaluations of enforcement strategies show that illegal immigration is not significantly deterred by policies administered by the INS, including fortified border patrol, penalizing employers who hire undocumented workers, or imposing greater restrictions on welfare and social services (Andreas 1998; Bean 1990; GAO 1990).

4

Ironies of Immigration Control

Most illegals view themselves as victims of circumstance rather than as criminals. For the most part, their behavior involves a survival strategy and appropriate response to poverty.

George Weissinger

While the INS agreed with Congress' attempt to more efficiently remove people who came illegally or visitors who committed crimes, the laws "can generate results that are too harsh and go too far."

Bo Cooper, INS general counsel

Scientific and humanistic understanding, as well as better professional practice, require attention to paradox, deception, incongruity, trade-offs, and irony as central themes in modern life.

Gary T. Marx

n 1997, a year after Congress passed sweeping legislation designed to bolster its fight against illegal immigration and criminal aliens, Jesus M. Collado, a 43-year-old restaurant manager and legal resident of the United States, found himself at the center of the debate over the fairness of revised INS policies. Upon returning from a two-week trip to the Dominican Republic with this wife and children, an inspector at Kennedy International Airport checked the INS records and found that Collado had been convicted of a criminal offense 23 years prior. Collado was arrested then sent to a county jail in rural Pennsylvania where he would be detained while the INS prepared a deportation order. Under the Illegal Immigration Reform and Immigration Responsibility Act of 1996, the INS was granted uncontestable authority to detain and deport criminal aliens; still, even supporters of that legislation were astonished by how harshly the new law would be enforced. At the age of 19, Collado was convicted of statutory rape for having consensual sex with his 15-year-old girlfriend; in accordance with sentencing guidelines for that misdemeanor, the judge placed Collado on probation for one year in 1974. Since then, Collado had lived a law-abiding life. Nevertheless, the INS viewed Collado as a criminal alien who should be deported to the Dominican Republic where he was born, even though he had not resided there since he was 17 years old. For more than six months Collado languished in custody, fearing that he would be transported out of the country, leaving behind a wife and three children, all of whom are U.S. citizens (Ojito 1997a).

Fortunately for Collado and his family, the INS bowed to pressure from sustained media and political attention. Collado was released after the INS reversed its interpretation of the 1996 statute, conceding that the new provisions were not intended for law-abiding long-term residents. Curiously though, less than a year after the new law was passed, more than 200 legal permanent residents who had minor brushes with the law were apprehended and detained by the INS. Congressional leadership pointed to the contradictions of immigration control, particularly the use of scarce resources to crack down on immigrants convicted of minor offenses. Senator Spencer Abraham, a supporter of the new immigration laws, criticized the INS: "Either because of an ability to set priorities, difficulty in interrelating the many different sections of the immigration bill or a combination if both, they seem to be pursuing some admittedly minor cases aggressively" (Lewis 1999; Ojito 1997b: B3). Despite concern by lawmakers and even INS officials who believe that the Illegal Immigration Reform and Immigrant Responsibility Act and other immigration statutes enacted in 1996 have gone awry, little has been done to change it. Critics argue that the new immigration statutes are fundamentally unfair, including a host of provisions that have raised serious constitutional questions (ACLU 1997, 2000a; Human Rights Watch 1998a; Lawyers Committee for Human Rights 2000a; Tebo 2000).

Whereas previous legislation affecting immigrants has been shaped by such considerations as the economy (i.e., a demand for cheap labor) and family reunification, the Illegal Immigration Reform and Immigrant Responsibility Act of 1996 was driven primarily by a criminal justice agenda. After all, when Congress was forced to act, they focused on illegal rather than legal immigration. Due to the prevailing criminal justice perspective, however, the nature of the problem became increasingly criminalized. Much like the wars on crime and drugs, the clampdown on illegal immigrants is riddled with contradictions; most notably, valuable resources are wasted on apprehending persons who have committed minor offenses. "Despite the law's name, the *Illegal Immigration Reform and Immigrant Responsibility Act,* its impact has been not primarily on illegal immigrants, but on lawful permanent residents of the United States who at some time in the past ran afoul of the criminal law" (Greenhouse 2001a: A10; see ACLU 2000a).

In this chapter, the contradictions and ironies of immigration control are examined critically, including the most controversial aspects of immigration legislation passed in 1996: court-stripping provisions, use of secret evidence, and a growing register of deportable crimes. It is important to remain mindful of the social context from which the problem of illegal immigration emerged, namely, moral panic over immigrants, a phenomenon compounded by the bombings of the World Trade Center in 1993 and the federal building in Oklahoma City in 1995. Those tragic events fueled public fear of crime, terrorism, and minorities, reinforcing a distorted view that immigrants threaten American society. Even though public anxiety over immigrants had waned along with economic worries, drastic changes in legislation continue to disrupt the lives of many immigrants and their families. As we look back on 1996 and the formulation of revised immigration policies, it is not difficult to see that today's problems are the result of yesterday's solutions. We begin the discussion with a succinct overview of the history of U.S. immigration policies.

A Brief History of U.S. Immigration Policies

Whereas contemporary U.S. immigration policies have been concerned with imposing limits on immigration, in 1864, when the first immigration office was established, the federal government encouraged immigration as way to populate America's vast frontier and to provide labor for an expanding industrialized society. By the 1890s, immigration was in full swing as 24 inspection stations, most famously Ellis Island, processed a huge influx of European immigrants. During that era, the Bureau of Immigration had moved from the U.S. Treasury Department to the newly established Department of Commerce and Labor, where it would administer the Naturalization Act of 1906. Following several immigration waves, the modern immigration apparatus took shape, and by 1933 an executive order had formally instituted a dual mandate—service and enforcement—for the INS (Auerbach 1955; Gordon and Gordon 1979).

Despite the seemingly progressive and benevolent side of U.S. immigration policies, restrictionists have persisted in using legislation to discriminate against unpopular racial and ethnic groups. In 1789, Congress passed the Alien and Sedition Act, a law that reinforced suspicion of foreigners. During the 1840s, manifest destiny inspired White Anglo-Saxon Protestants (WASPs) to uphold a racist ideology, professing that they were an elite people chosen by God to cultivate and civilize the country. That pernicious version of nativism condemned immigrants as cultural, political, and economic threats to a WASP-dominated society. Such militant nativism reached flashpoint in Philadelphia, where in 1844 members of the Native American Party unleashed their fury on Irish Catholics, sparking three days of violence known as the Kensington Riots, in which the homes, schools, and churches of Irish immigrants were burned and razed (Guenter 1990). During the 1880s, discrimination against Asians peaked when Congress passed the Chinese Exclusion Act of 1882, a law halting immigration from China and even stripping Chinese Americans of their U.S. citizenship. Eventually, similar hostility was directed at Southern and Eastern Europeans during the immigration wave of the 1910s (Bennett 1963, 1989; Jones 1960). In years leading up to World War I, mistrust of foreigners, especially those suspected of being political dissidents, influenced the passage of the Immigration Act of 1917. During the Red Scare of that period, thousands of foreign-born people suspected of political radicalism were arrested and brutalized by federal law enforcement officers; hundreds also were deported without a hearing (Jaffe 1972; Murphy 1972). The 1917 law also established various classes of undesirable immigrants who would be denied admission to the United States, including illiterates, vagrants, alcoholics, the mentally ill, and those perceived as being immoral. Additionally, the statute along with the Immigration Act of 1924 (also known as the National Origins Act) contained restrictions against Asians and Africans (Higham 1988; INS 2000a).

Given the scarcity of jobs during the Great Depression, immigrants again were scapegoated and accused of taking jobs away from so-called "real" Americans. Lawmakers responded to growing anti-immigrant sentiment; for example, California passed legislation in 1931 forbidding the hiring of illegal immigrants. At that time, more than 500,000 Mexican nationals and Mexican Americans were repatriated (Ruiz 1998; Sanchez 1993). In 1940, at the onset of World War II, as international tensions loomed, the INS was transferred to the DOJ, where the agency would become increasingly vigilant over new arrivals, reflecting concerns over national security. During that time, under immigration regulations passed in the 1920s, many Jews fleeing Nazi Germany were denied refuge in the United States. Although not formally an immigration policy, the internment of Japanese Americans during World War II embodied racism and xenophobia, reinforcing wartime hysteria. Following the bombing of Pearl Harbor in 1941, 120,000 Japanese Americans (including children) were officially labeled enemies of the state and quickly rounded up to be detained in what amounted to concentration camps located predominately in western states. Compounding their misery of being locked up for three years, Japanese Americans also lost their homes, property, and businesses (Daniels 1993; Hansen 1995; Nishimoto 1995; Smith 1995; Yoo 1996; Yoshino 1996).[1] Congress eventually offered the internees a formal apology in 1988, and under the Civil Liberties Act the federal government pledged restitution to 60,000 Americans of Japanese descent who were incarcerated during the war. Curiously, in the 1980s, the federal government reactivated one of its internment camps in Arizona so that the INS could detain hundreds of Central American refugees who crossed the border to escape a war financed by the U.S. government (Kahn 1996).

With U.S. involvement in World War II, the labor force became increasingly depleted as young men entered the armed services. In an ambitious effort to furnish labor for American industry and agriculture, the State Department, in cooperation with the Department of Labor, the DOJ, and the INS instituted the Bracero Program in 1942, which became the largest foreign worker program in U.S. history. For the next 22 years, the so-called farmhand program would import more than five million Mexicans to work as growers and ranchers in 24 states. However, as American workers replenished the labor force, many Mexicans were discarded. Many Bracero workers, along with hundreds of thousands of undocumented immigrants, were deported in the 1950s under Operation Wetback. As a vast enforcement campaign charged with cracking down on illegal immigrants, Operation Wetback mirrored the repatriation of Mexicans during the Depression. Between 1954 and 1959 nearly four million Mexicans were forced south of the border while at the same time allowing one million others to stay due to a demand for cheap labor during the Korean War. For the Mexican workers who remained under the Bracero Program, life in the U.S. meant low wages and abysmal working and living conditions (Calavita 1992; Gutierrez 1995; Samora 1971).[2] With a booming economy, postwar America became a preferred destination for immigrants and refugees, and in 1965 Congress passed the Immigration and Naturalization Act, a law that replaced nationality and ethnic considerations with a system concerned with the reunification of families, skilled immigrants, and the needs of refugees.

Beginning in the mid-1960s, the prevailing trend in immigration had shifted from Europeans to Latin Americans and Asians (Hutchison 1981). Due to an economic recession in the early 1980s, immigration had once again become politically charged. To discourage employers from hiring workers from outside the United States, Congress enacted the Immigration Reform and Control Act of 1986, which imposed sanctions and penalties on employers for knowingly hiring undocumented workers. Still, lawmakers were aware that there were many long-term undocumented immigrants residing in the United States, and in the spirit of humane legislation, Congress granted amnesty and allowed the approximately three million people who had been in the country since 1982 to become legal residents. In 1990, the Immigration Act raised the overall immigration ceiling and more than doubled the annual employment-based immigration to meet the demand for a skilled labor force. Additionally, the 1990 law featured criminal justice initiatives that would become more pronounced in forthcoming legislation, including allocating greater resources to enforcement and border patrol as well as enhanced efforts to deport criminal aliens (INS 2000a; Reimers 1998; also see Reimers 1992). Upon signing the 1990 Immigration Act, President George Bush touched on key social forces shaping immigration policy, proclaiming that the new law "is good for families, good for business, good for crime fighting, and good for America" (Ostrow 1990: 39). As we shall see in the next section, the national mood over immigration in the early and mid-1990s, prompted by uncertainties in the economy and workforce, took a turn for the worse, casting a dark shadow on newcomers, especially racial minorities.

Moral Panic over Immigrants and the 1996 Legislation

As discussed in the previous chapter, moral panic over immigrants emerged in the early and mid-1990s, pressuring the public and political institutions to reevaluate immigration policies. Whereas recent immigration laws were formulated according to such concerns as skilled labor and family reunification, legislation passed in 1996 was shaped by a tendency to criminalize immigrants. Indeed, revised immigration policies issued a forceful criminal justice mandate driven by moral panic and an undifferentiated fear of crime, terrorism, foreigners, and people of color. The Illegal Immigration Reform and Immigrant Responsibility Act of 1996 included increased criminal penalties for immigration-related offenses and measures designed to enhance INS presence and enforcement at the border. Under the new statute the INS instituted an expedited removal process that allows agents to deport immediately persons arriving in the United States without proper documents; moreover, the INS has the authority to bar illegal immigrants from reentering the United States for as long as 10 years. Coinciding with President Clinton's campaign to *eliminate welfare as we know it*, the Personal Responsibility and Work Opportunity Reconciliation Act of 1996 reinforced the derogatory view that immigrants are motivated by welfare rather than work. The law took away a wide range of federal benefits and services from both undocumented and legal immigrants (e.g., food stamps and Supplemental Security Income [SSI]) and instituted new requirements for sponsors of alien relatives for immigration (ACLU 1997; INS 2000a).[3] Lumping together a host of social problems, former Congressman Jim Bunn, a Republican from Oregon, remembers how lawmakers clamped down on immigrants: "We were saying, 'Let's do something; let's get tough on crime, on welfare and on illegal immigrants'" (Sullivan and Walth 2000: EV1).

While anti-immigrant attitudes were gaining public prominence, manifested in regional social movements such as California's Proposition 187, a law intended to deny most basic services to anyone suspected of not being a citizen or legal resident, including education, health, and social services, the problem of illegal immigration became a national obsession when organized terrorism came to U.S. soil. "The 1993 bombing of the World Trade Center in New York City caused many Americans to shudder with the sudden recognition that they could be targets even on their home soil" (Tebo 2000: EV1). Two years later, when the Alfred P. Murrah Federal Building in Oklahoma City was bombed, "the immediate reaction of law enforcement officials and many citizens was to assume that it, too, was the act of foreign terrorists" (Cole 1999; Tebo 2000: EV1). Although investigations led authorities to U.S.-born Timothy McVeigh, and not to foreign terrorists, public hostility against immigrants persisted. As is typically the case with moral panic, politicians weighed in on the controversy and in 1996 Congress passed the Anti-Terrorism and Effective Death Penalty Act, which complements the Illegal Immigration Reform and Immigrant Responsibility Act of 1996. Increased funding for the fight against illegal immigration made the INS the largest federal law enforcement agency; more significantly, both Acts granted the agency unprecedented authority to seek out and deport immigrants deemed a threat to national security.

Scholars of moral panic remind us that pseudodisasters commonly precipitate new laws that place additional restrictions on existing freedoms, liberties, and due process (Cohen 1972; Goode and Ben-Yehuda 1994; Welch 2000a). The 1996 immigration and antiterrorism laws did just that, especially considering that for many years the immigration review process was becoming progressively fairer. In fact, INS hearing judges had been attending to individual circumstances while the courts reviewed the officers' decisions, acting as final arbiters of whether particular cases met constitutional muster. The new statutes, however, gutted due process, issuing the INS unparalleled powers and limiting judicial review of deportation and detention decisions made by immigration judges. The laws authorized the INS to use secret evidence to detain and deport suspected terrorists and expanded the scope of crimes considered aggravated felonies, which are grounds for deportation. Underscoring its coercive and punitive nature, Congress made the new law retroactive, meaning any person convicted of a crime now reclassified as an aggravated felony could be deported, regardless of how old the conviction. The INS also had the newly created power to denaturalize nonnative-born U.S. citizens convicted of certain crimes and indefinitely detain deportable aliens even when there was virtually no chance their former countries would allow their return. Because the United

States has no official diplomatic ties with Cambodia, Cuba, Iran, Iraq, Laos, and Vietnam, former satellites of the Soviet Union, and Gaza, the Palestinian homeland, much of which is technically not a part of any country, there are no means for repatriation. As a result, detainees from those countries along with those persons who are not citizens of any country, having given up or been stripped of their birth citizenship when they immigrated to this country, remain in detention indefinitely (ACLU 2000a; CLINIC 2001; Tebo, 2000; see Chapter 5).

To reiterate, legislation on immigration in 1996 was imbued with an undifferentiated fear of crime, outsiders, and minorities. Legal expert Margaret Graham Tebo agrees: "some speculate it's because the INS knows that despite rhetoric to the contrary, Congress wants the agency to tighten the nation's borders, particularly to minority immigrants" (2000: EV9). On a similar plane, Gregory T. Nojeim, an ACLU Legislative Counsel, opined, "Everyone in Congress knew that the '96 anti-terrorism law was in large part an immigration law" (Tebo 2000: EV9; also see Christensen, Read, Sullivan, and Walth 2000). As we shall see, recent litigation has questioned the constitutionality of the new law and many of its more controversial components, most notably its court-stripping provisions, the use of secret evidence, and the new criteria for deportable crimes and as their retroactive power.

Court-Stripping Provisions

Although foreigners do not have the legal right to enter the United States, once here, the Constitution protects them from discrimination based on race and national origin and from arbitrary treatment by the government. Still, the INS retains the authority to determine who can stay in the country and who shall be deported. That power, however, is checked and balanced by the courts, which require the government to adhere to basic due process; for instance, before a noncitizen can be deported, the government must participate in a hearing that meets constitutional standards (*Yamataya* v. *Fisher* 1903). Over the past century, immigration law has evolved tremendously, particularly along lines of constitutional rights and civil liberties. Nowadays, persons facing deportation are entitled to several procedural safeguards governing the removal process, including: a hearing before an immigration judge and review, in most cases, by a federal court; representation by a lawyer (but not at government expense); reasonable notice of charges and of a hearing's time and place; a reasonable opportunity to examine the evidence and the government's witnesses; competent interpretation for non-English speaking immigrants; and clear and convincing proof that the government's grounds for deportation are validated (ACLU 1997: 2; also see Benson 1997; Cooper 1997; Medina 1997; Scaperlanda 1997).

As noted, the government periodically draws on popular fear and anxiety over crime (and terrorism) in its attempt to restrict people's rights; indeed, claims that public safety or national security are at risk—producing a disaster mentality—often accompany moral panic. Still, new laws restricting individual rights rarely affect the lives of people in the mainstream. Rather, enforcement campaigns tend to target those at the margins of society, namely, the poor, minorities, and immigrants. Such discriminatory enforcement practices persist because members of the mainstream are either unaware of such injustices or are indifferent to them, especially since they are aimed at unpopular groups who are easily scapegoated for social and economic unrest. Not only have the 1996 immigration and antiterrorism laws adversely affected the lives of many immigrants and their families, many of whom are low-income people of color, but Congress also took extraordinary measures to strip the courts of their authority to review and monitor key aspects of immigration policies, most notably deportation procedures. From a civil rights perspective, that legislative component remains particularly distressing considering, "No other law enforcement agency has as many armed officers with arrest powers as does the INS, and no other law enforcement agency arrests as many people. To strip the courts of jurisdiction to hear claims that the INS has acted illegally is to invite abuse" (ACLU 2000a: EV5).

American jurisprudence regards judicial review essential to the administration of justice; this is a safeguard that ensures fairness for people subjected to a deprivation of their liberty and promotes professionalism in law enforcement because officers must justify their activities to a neutral decision-maker. The Illegal Immigration Reform and Immigrant Responsibility Act of 1996 is remarkable because, by eliminating judicial review, it disrupts the separation of power between the courts and the executive branch of government. Without judicial review, immigrants are prevented from challenging abusive practices and policies of the INS in court (ACLU 1997, 1999a, 2000a). Concerned with that provision, Aryeh Neier, president of the Open Society Institute, remarked, "We had tended to regard legal immigrants as entitled to equal protection of the law. When you put them in a separate class, with less rights, that fundamentally takes away from their civil liberties" (Lewin 2000: EV1; see Sullivan and Walth 2000).

Lucas Guttentag, director of the ACLU Immigrants' Rights Project, also characterizes the 1996 immigration law as grossly unfair and, particularly in light of its court-stripping provisions, blatantly unconstitutional:

> First and fundamentally, that an alien subject to deportation from the United States has a right to have the legality of that order reviewed by a federal court. The Constitution requires review in these circumstances and we believe that the existing federal habeas corpus statute authorizes it. Congress has the power to change the jurisdiction of the federal courts and to decide which court will hear which types of claims. But there are constitutional limits to how far Congress can go, and it cannot bar judicial review altogether when the liberty of an individual is at stake. Deportation orders necessarily involve the rights and liberties of individuals. Therefore, judicial review of those orders is constitutionally required. (Guttentag quoted in ACLU 1999a: 3)

Despite criticisms by legal scholars, the INS has continued processing deportation cases without the court's oversight, prompting immigrants' rights organizations to file suit against the government. To reinstate judicial review, attorneys representing immigrants have requested that the courts consider fundamental issues of due process in their assessment of new immigration policies (see Guttentag in ACLU 1999a; and landmark judicial review case *Marbury* v. *Madison*).[4]

For human and civil rights advocates, 1996 is remembered as a benchmark year for regressive legislation. That year, Congress, to crack down on illegal immigration, terrorism, and welfare, significantly curtailed individual rights while also stripping the courts of their ability to review the actions of government officials.[5] Similarly, Congress took aim at people behind bars, including detained immigrants, because of a popular perception that prisoners were abusing their right to sue correctional systems for violating the Eighth Amendment's ban on cruel and unusual punishment. For more than 30 years, federal courts have been monitoring prisons and jails where inmates have shown evidence of assaults by staff, inadequate medical services, and inhumane conditions of confinement, problems that have worsened with increased crowding. Curiously, the Prison Litigation Reform Act of 1996 imposed new restrictions on federal courts that previously had the authority to ensure that correctional conditions and practices met constitutional standards. As a result of that statute, prisoners currently have fewer opportunities to have their complaints reviewed by the judiciary (Lewin 2000; Robertson 2000, 2001). As we shall see in upcoming chapters, court-stripping provisions contained in the Prison Litigation Reform Act continue to compound problems facing detained immigrants confined in facilities notorious for their harsh conditions and abusive staff.

Secret Evidence

Moral panic over immigrants, embodied in an undifferentiated fear of crime, terrorism, and foreigners, not only contributed to legislation that took the extraordinary measure of stripping the courts of judicial oversight, but citing the bombing of the World Trade Center, it also instituted the use of secret evidence. With the threat of terrorism on American soil, Congress created provisions for the Illegal Immigration Reform and Immigrant Responsibility Act and the Anti-Terrorism and Effective Death Penalty Act, allowing the INS to deport noncitizens and to deny them bond and asylum and other benefits based on secret evidence. As of 2001, the government has continued its reliance on secret evidence in two dozen cases; moreover, charges of bigotry persist because almost all such prosecutions target Arabs and Muslims. Gregory T. Nojeim of the ACLU noted, "the use of secret evidence is a feature of totalitarian governments that goes against everything our country stands for. People in this country whose liberty is at stake have the right to know the evidence against them and to be given an opportunity to rebut it" (ACLU 2000a: 5; Cole 1999).

Joining other human and civil rights groups, the ACLU has adopted the cause, arguing that detaining and deporting people on the basis of secret evidence is fundamentally unconstitutional. In a recent case, the INS relied on secret evidence to detain Dr. Mazen Al-Najjar, a former University of South Florida engineering professor (*Al-Najjar* v. *Reno*). Al-Najjar had never been charged with any crime or terrorist activity; however, by introducing secret evidence that even his attorney cannot review, the INS accused him of being politically affiliated with the Palestine Islamic Jihad, a group the U.S. government has designated as "terrorist" (ACLU 2000d). Al-Najjar, a native of the United Arab Emirates, entered the country on a student visa in 1981 and stayed after the visa expired. Since then he married a fellow Muslim from Saudi Arabia and together they have three young daughters, all American citizens. Al-Najjar's father and two siblings are naturalized U.S. citizens, and his mother is a legal permanent resident. In 1985, the INS opened deportation proceedings against Al-Najjar for having overstayed his visa, but a hearing official dropped the matter in 1986, allowing him to remain in the United States. Ten years later, he requested that that his case be reopened so he could apply for political asylum and permanent residency, but his petition was rejected in 1997 on the grounds that he did not demonstrate a credible fear of persecution in the United Arab Emirates. Then, in a strange turn of events, the INS detained Al-Najjar as a deportable alien, citing secret evidence that he was "suspected of affiliation with a known terrorist organization" (Tebo 2000: EV2). At the request of the government, an immigration judge denied bond, keeping Al-Najjar detained for next three years.

On behalf of Al-Najjar, civil liberties advocates challenged the INS in court. Andy Kayton, Legal Director of the ACLU of Florida, argued, "Jailing someone on the basis of secret evidence is inconsistent with justice and the basic principles of our legal system" (ACLU 2000d: 3). And, pointing to the insurmountable task of fighting the government's use of secret evidence, Kayton added, "If you do not know what you are accused of, how can you defend yourself?" (ACLU 2000d). Al-Najjar's attorney, Martin Schwartz, called on the Justice Department to disclose evidence showing that his client is a threat to national security: "If Al-Najjar is suspected of conspiracy with the Islamic Jihad, he should be charged and tried. The fact that no charges have been filed while Al-Najjar remains in jail is a violation of his due process rights" (Tebo 2000: EV3). Schwartz furthered his reasoning: "If they have evidence that my client did something wrong, charge him, have a trial, let us see and defend the charges. Otherwise, let him go. That's the way our system is supposed to work" (Tebo 2000: EV3).

In 2000, a federal district court in Florida ruled in the Al-Najjar case that the use of secret evidence violated due process, ordering a new detention hearing. The court stated that the INS must either share the nature of the allegations with Al-Najjar's lawyers or not introduce that evidence in the new hearing (Tebo 2000). After being held for three years, Immigration Judge R. Kevin McHugh ordered Al-Najjar's release, stating that the government failed to give him enough information to defend himself; upon review of the classified information, McHugh said that the evidence was insufficient to keep Al-Najjar detained. David Cole, Al-Najjar's other attorney and a Georgetown University law professor, stressed that his client's release proves that he should never have been imprisoned: "If he was truly a threat to national security, why would she [Attorney General Janet Reno] allow him to go free?" (Asseo 2001a: EV1). Cole said he would seek damages for wrongful imprisonment. Al-Najjar's detention indeed weighed heavily on him and his family. During the first three years of his imprisonment, Al-Najjar had been allowed only once-a-year visits from his daughters, and in only in the last six months of his detention was he allowed to see them weekly along with the rest of his immediate family.

David Cole, who has represented 13 men detained through use of secret evidence (all of whom have since been released), said that in those cases where the evidence has come to light, none of the cases would have been provable in court under criminal law standards. That, say Cole and other lawyers representing targets of secret evidence, is exactly the reason why the government wants to keep it secret in the first place. "There has been no coherent explanation for why secret evidence is OK in immigration but not in the criminal context," replied Gregory Nojeim of the ACLU (Tebo 2000: EV6). Referring to the use of secret evidence as a "modern-day version of McCarthyism," Cole observed, "There's a pattern here. People are investigated by the FBI, which is unable to find enough evidence to charge them. So the FBI turns to the INS and asks them to deport the guy instead, using secret evidence" (Tebo 2000: EV6).

Several lawmakers have realized that the secret evidence provision of the 1996 immigration and antiterrorism statutes grossly undermines due process. To correct the problem, in 1999, Congressmen David Bonior (D–Michigan) and Tom Campbell (R–California), along with more than 100 cosponsors, unveiled the Secret Evidence Repeal Act (H.R. 2121), a bill that would drastically restrict, although not eliminate, the use of secret evidence (Cole 2000). In a series of public hearings, legislators were appalled at some of the Kafkaesque testimony by former detainees and their family members who likened the practice to "tactics of totalitarian regimes, including, ironically, some of the very regimes secret evidence detainees have fled" (Tebo 2000: EV6). In one such case, Nasser Ahmed, a 37-year-old Egyptian immigrant and father of three, was detained in solitary confinement for more than three years on the basis of secret evidence. Ahmed quickly came to the attention of federal authorities because he worked as a legal assistant for the defense of Sheik

Omar Abdel Rahmen, who stood trial for plotting to blow up the World Trade Center and other New York landmarks. Ahmed, who had never been accused of any terrorist activity, was arrested after the INS determined that secret evidence suggested an "association with a known terrorist organization" (Weiser 1997: B2; see Cole 1997). Following a lengthy legal battle, an immigration judge ordered the release of Ahmed in 1999, contending that he was not a threat to national security and should, in fact, be granted political asylum in the United States (Rhode 1999). In a strikingly similar case, Hany Kiareldeen, a 31-year-old Palestinian, was detained after authorities said secret evidence linked him to one of the men convicted in the World Trade Center bombing case. After 19 months in detention, Kiareldeen was released when a federal district judge ruled that the use of secret evidence violated due process (Amon 2000a; "Palestinian Jailed on Secret Evidence Released" 2000; Smothers 1999). The INS decided not to appeal Kiareldeen's release, conceding that he does not pose a threat to national security; in other words, critics charge, the government was simply "crying wolf" ("Smashing Secrecy" 1999: 5; see Cockburn 2000; Cole 1999; Viorst 2000).

Despite arguments that use of secret evidence is unconstitutional and that it is used as a form of "racial profiling" aimed at Arabs and Muslims, the policy does have its supporters. David Ray, Associate Director of FAIR, strongly believes disclosure of secret evidence risks endangering antiterrorism efforts at home and abroad: "The information should not be disclosed because it could endanger the lives of innocent U.S. and foreign citizens" (Tebo 2000: EV6). Currently, at least five federal district courts have banned the use of secret evidence on the grounds that it violates due process; nevertheless, the INS continues to employ the practice in other jurisdictions. In his effort to ban the government's use of secret evidence, Gregory Nojeim argues, "Just as our country's leaders rightly condemn Iran for using secret evidence to protect 'national security' in trials there, we have to practice here what we preach abroad. It is time to end this ugly chapter of American history" (ACLU 2000b: 5; see Ufford 2000).

New Deportable Crimes

As of 2001, Olufolake Olaleye, mother of two small children, faces deportation to Nigeria because eight years previously she was convicted of shoplifting baby outfits worth $14.99. Her troubles began when she attempted to return some baby items without a receipt. The store manager accused her of shoplifting, and Olaleye, thinking that the matter could be easily resolved, appeared in court without a lawyer. After insisting that she had purchased the merchandise, Olaleye pleaded guilty as a means to end the ordeal. Olaleye was fined $360 and given a 12-month suspended sentence and 12 months probation, which was terminated two months later when she paid the fine in full. The INS did not consider her a felon when the agency approved her application for citizenship in 1996, after classifying her shoplifting conviction as a petty offense. However, under the newly passed Illegal Immigration Reform and Immigrant Responsibility Act, a shoplifting offense with a one-year sentence is treated as an aggravated felony, for which there is no possibility of relief (ACLU 2000e).

Adding even greater controversy to the recent immigration law, Congress expanded the list of deportable crimes to include such minor offenses as shoplifting, petty theft, drunk driving, and even low-level drug violations, all of which have been reclassified as aggravated felonies, a category that includes murder, rape, terrorism, and kidnapping (see Rodriguez 2000). The statute applies retroactively to all immigrants (and lawful permanent residents) who have ever committed a crime, even those that occurred in the distant past, and to those crimes for which no sentence was served.[6] In many cases, "people who pled guilty to minor offenses years ago in exchange for probation are now finding the rules have been switched on them and they are facing a new sentence: detention and deportation" (Amnesty International 2000a: 2). Although many members of Congress earned political support from their constituents for forging together such popular campaign issues as crime, terrorism, illegal immigration, and welfare, several high-ranking officials in the INS were appalled by the new register of deportable offenses. INS Commissioner Doris Meissner, who frequently ran afoul of advocates on both sides of the immigration debate, battled unsuccessfully to keep from the list of deportable crimes from expanding. For taking a stand against overzealous lawmaking, Meissner once again became a prime target for law-and-order conservatives who demanded her resignation, accusing her of being soft on crime and illegal immigration (Eggen 2000). Similar to the government's use of secret evidence, the new roster of deportable crimes continues to devastate the lives of immigrants and their families. Amnesty International agrees: "This is discrimination against immigrants. It also affects people of color disproportionately, since they are more likely to pass through the criminal justice system, thanks to racial profiling by law enforcement and discrimination in our courts" (Amnesty International 2000a: 2).

In 2000, 22-year-old Joao Herbert was deported to Brazil, where he had not been since an Ohio couple adopted him from a Sao Paulo orphanage when he was 8. Having been convicted of selling fewer than eight ounces of marijuana, his first and only drug charge, Herbert was subjected to the full force of the 1996 immigration law as the INS treated his offense as a deportable crime. Interestingly, Herbert took on a public persona in the Brazilian media that portrayed him as a victim of America's "zero tolerance" of immigrants who commit minor crimes, including drug violations. For his transgression, Herbert was sentenced to two years' probation and six months in drug rehabilitation beginning in 1997. At that time, he was informed that because his parents had never had him naturalized after his adoption, the INS could begin deportation proceedings against him. Fearing deportation, Herbert fled but was apprehended a year later when he visited his mother. The INS then placed him in detention for the next 20 months as deportation proceedings gained momentum. Herbert's case generated enormous support from immigrant rights groups and, to keep him from being deported, the Ohio state parole board unanimously recommended clemency, but Governor Bob Taft rejected the petition. His parents, Nancy Saunders and Jim Herbert, wracked with guilt over the failure to have their son naturalized, struggled to overturn the deportation order (Buckley and Levine 2000).

To no avail. Joao Herbert, after a 20-minute goodbye visit with his parents, was returned to a land he barely remembers and where he does not speak the language. Herbert does not hide his anger at the U.S. government for enacting harsh new laws that have stripped him of his family. Herbert feels betrayed further because of recent changes in legislation—in part a response to cases such as his—that now grant automatic citizenship to virtually every foreign-born child adopted by an American. However, that provision, enacted in 2001, applies only to adoptees under 18. "I made a mistake, and I'm remorseful for what I did, but I don't think I was treated fairly," he said. "If the Brazilians did to an American what America did to me, Americans would be up in arms. . . . What am I supposed to do if my father—my father is a paraplegic—if something happens to him? What if my mother got sick? I couldn't go back to see her without going to prison. I barely had time to give them a hug before I left" (Buckley and Levine 2000: EV5). His parents fear they may never see their son again because of the cost and difficulty of traveling to Brazil (also see Darling 2000).

Despite their devastating effects on immigrants and their families, the tough new provisions contained in the 1996 immigration law do have their defenders. Representative Dana Rohrabacher (R–California) fought aggressively to stem the tide of illegal immigration to the United States, saying that criminal aliens put "our country at a security risk" (Christensen, Sullivan, and Walth 2000: EV9). As a key political figure who championed the 1996 law, Rohrabacher says that its tragic consequences do not weaken his conviction that anyone found in the United States illegally should be removed: "Look, a lot of these stories might tear at your heart, but we can't let our hearts tear apart helping someone who is not an American citizen if it has a bad impact on the lives of the American people" (Christensen, Sullivan, and Walth 2000: EV9). According to Rohrabacher: "Their families need not be split. They can take their families with them when they go" (2000: EV9).

In its criticism of the new deportable crimes, the ACLU and other immigrant rights advocates remind us of the fundamental unfairness of the statute:

> Normally, if a person commits a crime in the United States, they pay their debt to society and they go on with their lives. The 1996 laws changed this normal state of affairs for many immigrants. The 1996 laws require the INS to detain even lawful permanent residents who committed minor criminal offenses for which they had long ago paid their debt to society. In some cases, an immigrant may have pleaded guilty to a crime for which he was advised there would be no adverse immigration consequences. But Congress changed the law retroactively. Now when the immigrant applies for nationalization, he can receive a one-way ticket to an INS lock up or a local jail. (ACLU 2000a: EV4)

Because of other provisions in the tough "one-strike-you're-out" immigration law, immigrants convicted of aggravated felonies currently face greater difficulty in maintaining their U.S. residency, because recent provisions have stripped the courts of judicial review. Even if those immigrants can demonstrate that they would not flee and are not a danger to the community, Congress took from immigration judges the discretion to release them while their cases are pending; therefore, they must remain in detention until further determination of their case is made (see Rodriguez 2000). Worse still, mandatory detention can become permanent for certain types of immigrants: "The 1996 laws have resulted in an explosion in the number of immigrants facing indefinite detention—approximately 3,500—because they were ordered removed and no country, including their own, will accept them" (ACLU 2000a: EV4; CLINIC 2001). In the next chapter, we examine in greater detail how the 1996 laws have perpetuated rather than resolved the problem of indefinite detention.

Ironies of Social Control

Whereas traditional sociologists have long argued that crime and rule-breaking stem from the absence of social control (Hirschi 1969; Reiss 1951), other scholars insist the presence of social control also contributes to such infractions—albeit inadvertently (Becker 1963; Hawkins and Tiedeman 1975; Lemert 1972). Adding to a critical understanding of that phenomenon, sociologist Gary T. Marx discovered that social control has the potential to be ironic, thus escalating the very behavior it sets out to deter (1981; also see Schneider 1975; Welch 1999b). Such ironies, or contradictions, are deeply imbedded in social structures that rely heavily on authorities charged with ridding society of its lawlessness. Accordingly, many law enforcement tactics—especially the aggressive ones—tend to make matters worse and in doing so perpetuate rather than resolve the problem: Consider, for example, the war on drugs (Brownstein 1996; Reinarman and Levine 1997; Welch, Bryan, and Wolff 1999; Welch, Wolff, and Bryan 1998). Looking at the crackdown on illegal immigrants and criminal aliens from the perspective of irony sharpens our view of how strict new laws have compounded the problem as well as created others (e.g., a massive increase in detained immigrants, racial discrimination, denials of due process, and various human and civil rights violations). In his conceptual framework delineating the key aspects of ironic thought, Marx introduces three basic components, namely, escalation, nonenforcement, and covert facilitation. Undoubtedly, those ironies of social control figure prominently in the campaign against illegal immigrants.

Escalation

Under certain circumstances, authorities can play a crucial role in the creation of law-breaking by redefining the problem and then intervening in a manner that produces an ironic, or escalating, effect (Marx

1981). In 1996, Congress passed laws that fundamentally transformed the social control apparatus aimed at illegal immigrants and criminal aliens. More specifically, those statutes issued revised definitions of what constitutes a violation of immigration law. By lowering the threshold of deportable crimes to include nonviolent offenses and misdemeanors, legislators constructed new categories of rule breakers who would be subject to arrest. Because the new law is retroactive, overnight there were thousands more violators of immigration law. Making matters worse, legislators devised new and controversial ways to intervene. Most significantly, Congress granted the INS unprecedented powers to employ secret evidence, expedite removal, and enforce mandatory and indefinite detention. Additionally, Congress augmented those tactics with court-stripping provisions that eliminated judicial review, thus centralizing power in the government's executive branch, namely, the office of the U.S. Attorney General. Due in large part to new definitions of rule-breaking, both lawmakers and rule enforcers have engaged in a form of escalation that has generated a growing population of violators.

To the dismay of critics, however, the new tactics of social control have worsened matters given the pattern of racial discrimination and human and civil rights violations (ACLU 1999, 2000a; Welch 1996a). Still, the clampdown on illegal immigrants continues, incorporating some unusual measures. In 2000, the INS in Atlanta began using drunk driving charges against illegal immigrants, mostly Mexicans and Central Americans, as a means of deporting them. INS authorities insist that the tough new policy will allow them to enforce the law without the disruption spot checks put on businesses and neighborhoods. "People who are illegally here in the U.S., have no right to be here," said INS official Fred Alexander. "We're not deporting these people because they got a DUI [driving under the influence]. We're deporting these people because they are illegally in this country. A DUI arrest is a method that we use to locate them" (Osborn 2001: EV1). INS officials locate illegal immigrants by checking arrest records of DUI detainees in county jails. If the INS determines that they are illegal immigrants, deportation proceedings begin immediately. During the last six months of 2000, drunken-driving arrests in Atlanta have led to the deportations of nearly 200 illegal immigrants. Proponents of the new tactic believe that it is a way to improve public safety while upholding immigration laws. Conversely, critics say it unfairly targets undocumented workers who enter the country to build a better life. Pointing to the demand for labor in the U.S. economy, Mexico's consul general in Atlanta, Teodoro Maus, argues, "What the INS says is they are going after criminals, but they are lumping together the real criminals with people who are just working and just happen to have a DUI" (Osborn 2001: EV1). To reiterate, escalation involves new definitions of what constitutes rule-breaking, thus expanding the pool of potential violators. The problem is then worsened by the use of heavy-handed tactics.

Nonenforcement

Another irony of social control is nonenforcement, whereby authorities intentionally permit rule-breaking by strategically taking no enforcement action (Marx 1981). As noted previously, economic forces, specifically the demand for labor, commonly dictate enforcement patterns in immigration control. During periods when jobs are scarce, undocumented workers are blamed for taking jobs from citizens; however, in prosperous times, undocumented workers are barely noticed by the general public, let alone scapegoated. INS enforcement patterns generally reflect such economic determinants. When the demand for labor is low, the INS steps up its monitoring of worksites suspected of hiring undocumented workers and issues employer sanctions as a means of deterrence. However, the INS eases its enforcement of worksite violations when jobs are plentiful and there is a high demand for labor, especially cheap labor, the kind provided by undocumented workers (Uchitelle 2000).

In the late 1990s, amid better economic times, Congress backed away from getting tough with employers who hire illegal immigrants—even though a few years earlier a bipartisan committee had concluded that "reducing the employment magnet is the linchpin of any strategy to curb illegal immigration" (Reimers 1998; Sullivan and Walth 2000: EV2). In 2000, a compromise plan emerged in Congress that allowed as many as one million illegal farm employees to stay in the country permanently and added perhaps one million more foreigners temporarily through an expanded visa program (Jansen 2000). As an irony of social control, when immigration laws are not enforced, undocumented workers and their employers are encouraged to break the rules. It should also be noted that businesses themselves have also resorted to notifying the INS as a means of deterring union activities among their undocumented workers who set out to improve working conditions and wages. The INS Operation Vanguard "attempts to purge undocumented immigrants from the work force en masse by terrorizing them into leaving their jobs. Behind the rhetoric of law enforcement, the program makes it easier for companies to exploit workers" (Bacon 1999a: 18; 1999b; Sack 2001; also see Hegstrom 2000). Again, patterns of nonenforcement, as an irony of social control, are greatly influenced by economic forces, especially as a means of regulating labor.

Covert Facilitation

In covert facilitation, authorities resort to deceptive enforcement actions intended to lure rule breakers and apprehend them as part of sting operations. In the realm of controlling illegal immigration, covert facilitation is particularly problematic because the INS operates with a dual mandate and therefore must both enforce the law as well as administer services to immigrants eligible for services. To the dismay of immigrants rights advocates, covert facilitation through the use of deceptive sting operations aimed at arresting illegal immigrants undermines the trust the INS needs to deliver services to legal immigrants and permanent residents. It is precisely in this sense that covert facilitation remains a form of ironic immigration control.

In Monticello, Kentucky, in 2000, 14 Hispanic men went to the Wayne County Courthouse expecting to pay fines on traffic tickets. To their surprise, they were arrested by INS agents who had hid in a backroom while waiting to ambush these undocumented immigrants. The Hispanic men sat all morning among the residents of Wayne County. Just before lunch, District Judge Robert Wilson announced that the INS wanted to talk to them; then undercover INS officers, wearing blue jeans and pistols in their jackets, arrested them. Two years prior, a chicken-processing plant opened in neighboring Clinton County, attracting many Latino immigrants in search of jobs. For the most part, residents and criminal justice officials had left them alone. In fact, many of the undocumented workers lived together in an apartment located next to the courthouse and local jail. Recently, however, police have cracked down on illegal immigration by arresting those who drive without valid licenses, charging some of them with felony possession of a fake driver's license. As a result, the INS has grounds to begin deportation proceedings against those violators (Tagami 2000a, 2000b).

Some residents of Monticello were clearly angered by the INS sting operations. Given the surplus of jobs in the community where the local unemployment rate had fallen from 9.3 percent in 1994 to 2.7 percent in 2000, some people believed that the campaign against illegal immigrants was fueled by racism (Tagami 2000b). As the Hispanic men were led away in handcuffs, Shannon James, a manager at the plant and one who had befriended many of the undocumented workers, broke into tears: "They weren't doing anything wrong," she said. "They just came here to work" (Tagami 2000a: EV2). Sister Barbara Walsh, of St. Peter's Catholic Church, who has been tutoring Hispanics to read English, agreed: "The Hispanics are not criminals, they are hard workers. Why punish the people who are trying to do something with their lives?" (Tagami 2000b: EV6). Local police, however, defended their involvement in the INS sting operation. Monticello Police Chief Ralph Miniard denied that he was deliberately targeting Hispanics. Rather, Miniard said, "he was targeting workers who were driving to Cagle's [the chicken-processing plant] without valid licenses" (Tagami 2000a: EV2). Interestingly, the INS agents who made the arrests told residents that they would be investigating the chicken-processing plant for hiring unauthorized workers. However, when asked later whether the agency had initiated an investigation of the plant, Roy Schremp, INS chief for Kentucky, replied, "To the best of my knowledge no, not at this point. And I can't answer whether there will be or not" (Tagami 2000a: EV3, 2000b).

The sting operation in Monticello sheds additional light on the paradox of immigration control: Curiously, individual violators, undocumented workers, are arrested, detained, and subject to deportation, while an organizational violator, the employer company, continues its practice of rule-breaking by hiring unauthorized workers. In essence, covert facilitation along with the other ironies of social control demonstrate that contradictory initiatives in immigration control have a disproportionate impact on poor immigrants, especially non-whites. Due to that imbalance in social control, businesses and economic institutions are left virtually unscathed by enforcement campaigns (see Parenti 1999).

In summary, Gary Marx (1981: 241) offers a critical look at the ironies of social control as an effort to develop a "sensitizing theoretical perspective." As we continue our examination of social control aimed at illegal immigrants and criminal aliens we shall remain mindful of its various contradictions. Often we see how self-defeating laws and policies perpetuate injustices against unpopular people who have few resources to defend themselves against ambitious enforcement campaigns, particularly those fueled by moral panic, bigotry, and racism.

Conclusion

When we take into consideration the ironies of social control, various contradictions of immigration policy are placed into a conceptual and theoretical perspective, including the use of secret evidence, court-stripping provisions, and the expanding roster of deportable crimes. Even legislators and rule enforcers concede that changes in immigration laws in 1996 are fraught with ironies that—especially in a democratic society—are fundamentally unfair, unnecessary, and self-defeating. Representative Barney Frank (D–Massachusetts), a member of the subcommittee on immigration for 16 years, remains critical of his congressional colleagues: "It was outrageous. They couldn't crack down on legal immigration; so they decided to make it as tough as possible for those already here" (Sullivan and Walth 2000: EV2). Many conservative lawmakers agree. "Since the House and Senate failed to do anything with legal immigration, they got very restrictive, almost draconian with the illegal immigration," said Alan Simpson, former Republican senator from Wyoming (Sullivan and Walth 2000: EV2).

Rule enforcers also agree that many of the 1996 provisions are too harsh, and high-ranking INS officials have made efforts to ease their enforcement (Martinez 2001). In one of her final acts in office, INS Commissioner Doris Meissner approved orders giving immigration authorities more discretion in how they enforce the statutes, particularly regulations on deportable crimes and their retroactive clause. "The majority of criminal removals are entirely appropriate, but I don't think anyone ever intended the law to split up families because of a 15-year-old minor conviction," said INS spokesman Bill Strassberger. "That is what led us to examine how we use our discretion" (Benjamin 2000a: EV1). Still, critics argue that granting immigration officials more discretion does not completely eliminate problems stemming from the 1996 laws. The INS concurs. For instance, even though the INS may decide not to deport certain immigrants convicted of a deportable offense, the felony, no matter how old, drastically limits the benefits they can receive under immigration law. Among the most significant restrictions imposed for those convicted of a deportable offense are disqualification for citizenship and not being allowed to travel outside the United States. In the words of Strassberger, "They will still be in limbo" (Benjamin 2000a: EV2). Whereas the INS has the authority to modify the enforcement of immigration rules, only Congress can actually change the law. Many lawmakers see the need to restore fairness in immigration policy by passing new legislation; however, Congress has yet to make any corrections in the statutes (ACLU 1999a, 2000a, 2000c; Cheng 2000; see Chapter 9).

Recent posturing over how immigration statutes ought to be enforced has caught the ire of restrictionists who suspect the INS of deliberately using draconian tactics to undermine the 1996 laws spearheaded by Republicans. Dan Stein, of FAIR, has launched the most direct accusations at the INS: "Clearly there was some kind of collusion between the political managers of INS and the immigration bar to bring forward these cases with bizarre fact patterns. The goal should be for INS to enforce the law the way that Congress intended. Instead they are chipping away at the law and trying to wear the system down through attrition" (Benjamin 2000a: EV2). In defense of the INS, Strassberger explained that Meissner did not do this in 1997 immediately following the passage of the 1996 statutes because the INS had not foreseen the types of cases that would run afoul of immigration reform. He denied that the agency acted to undercut Congress: "Three years ago, I don't think anyone realized exactly what the harsh effects of this law were going to be" (Benjamin 2000a: EV2; Cheng 2000; see Chapter 9).

As we discuss at length in the next chapter, the ironies of social control compounded by the government's criminal justice approach to immigration has produced tragic consequences for other segments of the immigrant population. In particular, the 1996 immigration laws adversely affect asylum seekers and refugees who face insurmountable obstacles upon entering the United States in large part because new legislation fails to distinguish them from criminal aliens. Consequently, many asylum seekers and refugees are unjustly forced into detention where they are subject to various forms of abuse and human rights violations.

5

Criminalizing Asylum Seekers and the Indefinitely Detained

In 1993, people who had entered the country by asking for asylum were linked to the World Trade Center bombing in New York and the shooting of CIA workers outside the agency's headquarters in Virginia.

Fredric Tulsky

People yearning to be free should not languish behind bars.

INS Commissioner Doris N. Meissner testifying before a 1998 Senate subcommittee examining the nation's asylum policy

Stop treating refugees like criminals.

Sigourney Weaver, actor, member of the Board of Directors of the Lawyers Committee for Human Rights

Upon graduating from medical school in Afghanistan in 1992, Dr. X looked forward to a career of helping and healing people; however, his modern view of medicine soon clashed with the traditional Taliban edicts of his homeland. After assisting a patient and her infant through a life-threatening labor, government officials arrested him for defying Taliban law prohibiting male doctors from touching women. For that infraction, Dr. X was tortured and thrown into solitary confinement. Later, when Dr. X refused Taliban orders to amputate a thief's hand, he was arrested again and told he would be executed for twice disobeying the Taliban.[1] During civil unrest in Afghanistan, Dr. X escaped from prison and eventually made his way to the United States, where he was arrested by the INS for not having a valid travel visa. Compounding his ordeal, Dr. X was stunned to find himself treated like a criminal—shackled, just as he had been by the Taliban, and transported to jail. Dr. X informed the INS that he was seeking asylum and that it was unrealistic to secure a passport from a government seeking his death. INS inspectors determined that his fear was credible but then denied his request for release even though he had an American relative eager to take him in. Fortunately, the plight of Dr. X came to the attention of the Lawyers Committee for Human Rights and several attorneys who worked diligently to secure his freedom (Weaver 2000: EV1–3).

As discussed throughout this work, moral panic over immigrants marginalizes and scapegoats those perceived as being outsiders, a societal reaction that is more pronounced during harsh economic times. Moreover, immigrants also are subject to being criminalized, due in large part to the prevailing criminal justice agenda dictating immigration policy. In the previous chapter, we explored how the growing inventory of deportable crimes has snared increasingly more violators into an expanding net of immigration control, including those convicted of nonviolent and petty offenses. Compounding criticism of the 1996 Illegal Immigration Reform and Immigrant Responsibility Act, the long arm of the INS has reached another segment of the immigrant population, namely, asylum seekers and refugees. Without having even a minor brush with the law, asylum seekers and refugees are criminalized and forced into detention because the sweeping scope of the 1996 law fails to distinguish between people fleeing persecution and those convicted of deportable crimes. In this chapter, we explore the harsh treatment of asylum seekers and refugees trapped in a control apparatus that has adopted criminal justice rather than other—more humane—models of immigrant processing. As we continue our examination of the ironies of social control, in this chapter we also delve into another ongoing controversy, indefinite detention. Because the U.S. government does not have official diplomatic ties with Cambodia, Cuba, Iran, Iraq, Laos, and Vietnam, former satellites of the Soviet Union, and Gaza, persons born in those nations who have been convicted of deportable offenses in this country are detained indefinitely. As of 2001, more than 4,400 so-called lifers remain behind bars, many of whom having already served prison sentences for their crimes (Indefinite Detention Project 2001; see Clendenning 2000a).

Bureaucratic Gauntlets and Their Effects on Asylum Seekers and Refugees

In the aftermath of World War II, the United States, along with many of its European allies, ratified international and domestic laws requiring them to provide a safe haven for people who demonstrate a credible fear of persecution because of their race, religion, national origin, social group, or politics. Fifty years later, human rights advocates are infuriated to find that the government has reneged on its commitment to refugees and those seeking political asylum. According to the ACLU, "Although hundreds of thousands of political refugees have been admitted into the U.S. since World War II, our government has too often been guided by political, rather than humanitarian, considerations and countless numbers of people have been returned to their countries of origin only to be jailed, tortured and even killed" (1998b: 1). Key events in recent history have contributed to the politicization of the asylum process. During the 1980s when Central America was ravaged by civil wars, the Reagan administration, which played an important role in fueling that violence, denied 97 percent of Salvadoran and 99 percent of Guatemalan asylum applications. Conversely, the United States routinely had granted applications from people fleeing countries whose governments the Reagan administration opposed, such as Nicaragua and Cuba. The United States eventually agreed to give new asylum hearings to 240,000 Salvadorans and Guatemalans after civil and human rights groups filed a class-action suit charging the INS with discrimination (ACLU 1998; Kahn 1996; also see ACLU 1998a). Similar criticisms of discrimination were leveled against the Bush administration for its policy of returning 20,000 Haitian refugees whom the Coast Guard had intercepted in international waters. To no avail, the Haitian refugees petitioned the United States for political asylum on the grounds that they feared persecution if returned to their homeland. Concerned for the plight of the Haitians, a federal judge accused the U.S. government of returning refugees "to the jaws of political persecution, terror, death and uncertainty when it has contracted not to do so" (ACLU 1998b: 2; Human Rights Watch 1998b).

Amid moral panic over immigrants in the early and mid-1990s, Congress forced the INS to impose greater restrictions on political asylum. As mentioned, the bombing of the World Trade Center prompted many legislators to view political asylum as one more way terrorists and criminal aliens were able to enter the United States. Along with an undifferentiated fear of crime, terrorism, and non-white immigrants, there was growing suspicion that under existing asylum proceedings, "People would show up, ask for asylum and then disappear, and of course stay in this country indefinitely" (Congressman Lamar Smith [R–Texas] quoted in Tulsky 2000a: EV3). However, experts insist that using asylum-seeking as a means of gaining entry to the United States is a high risk for terrorists because all asylum applicants are fingerprinted, thoroughly interrogated, and face the prospects of months or years in detention (Amnesty International 2000b).

Expedited Removal

As is the case with other provisions contained in the Illegal Immigration Reform and Immigrant Responsibility Act, new policies restricting political asylum are extreme. Even over the objections of the INS, Congress imposed *expedited removal*, a new tactic designed to seal the border against illegal entry. Under the revised asylum procedures, immigrants arriving at U.S. airports and other ports of entry without proper documents would be escorted to a secure area, handcuffed, and screened by armed INS inspectors. Being interrogated by government agents about one's fear of persecution is particularly traumatic, especially for asylum seekers who have been victims of torture or rape. For many asylum seekers and refugees who do not speak English, the summary interview is complicated by language and cultural barriers along with fears that their disclosures will be shared with government officials in their homeland. According to Kathryn Jastram, an official of the United Nations High Commissioner for Refugees (UNHCR) in Geneva, the screening process is "akin to filling out a tax form in another language. And if you do it wrong, you get sent back" (Tulsky 2000a: EV3). The ACLU's Immigrants' Rights Project also has issued forceful criticism of the INS and its policy for expedited removal:

> The system of expedited removal, in a misguided attempt to increase efficiency and decrease bureaucratic backlog, was implemented by the 1996 legislation supposedly to streamline the procedure in which aliens are refused entry into the United States. In practice, the expedited removal system operates in secrecy and erects an unprecedented barrier to the asylum process. Fleeing refugees are denied entry as they arrive in the United States and are not even allowed to apply for asylum unless they first persuade a low-level immigration officer in an on-the-spot proceeding of the validity of their claim for refugee protection. Problems of interpretation, legal understand-

ing, fear, humility and confusion all conspire to render this process discriminatory at best and meaningless at worst. (ACLU 1999b: 1)

Under the 1996 law, INS inspectors have the power to deport immediately anyone whose testimony they do not believe constitutes a credible
fear of persecution. Moreover, new court-stripping provisions also extend to asylum screening; thus judges no longer have the power to review such decisions. Even Commissioner Meissner objected to authorizing INS inspectors and thereby eliminating due process, a crucial
mechanism needed to reduce mistakes that result in sending back persons who are likely to be persecuted in their homeland. Although the
INS has instituted training for its 4,900 inspectors, critics charge that it
is unrealistic to assume that they have the background and skills needed
to assess accurately cases of persecution, a duty previously entrusted to
immigration judges. Meissner agrees: "You don't recruit inspectors for
international relations, or for counseling asylum seekers" (Tulsky 2000a:
EV4). Human rights groups continue to document cases in which the
INS has mistakenly removed persons needing protection (ACLU 1999b;
Amnesty International 2000b; Lawyers Committee for Human Rights
1998a, 1999a; Read 2000b).

In 1997, a 29-year-old woman from Albania came to the United States
fleeing political persecution. At the time, Albania was politically unsta-
ble and rife with violence. The woman's husband aggressively had been
recruited to join one of the political factions and, fearing for his safety,
he remained in hiding. Eventually, masked gunmen searched the woman's home in search of her husband and when they could not find him,
they retaliated by gang-raping her. Being a rape victim in a conservative
community stigmatized her, even though it happened through no fault
of her own. So that she could escape the relentless fear of being attacked
again, her brother-in-law gave her a fake passport and a plane ticket to
the United States. However, when she arrived in the United States, INS
inspectors discovered that her documents were fraudulent and immediately she was issued a document explaining the expedited removal procedures, printed in English, a language she could not understand. During the interview with the INS, her humiliation and fear of reprisals
from Albanian political leaders kept her from revealing all the details
about being gang-raped; as a result, she did not pass the credible fear test.
Because the 1996 law eliminated the appeals process, she was deported
back to Albania. Later, refugee rights' lawyers petitioned the U.S. government, arguing that the woman had been denied a fair opportunity to

apply for asylum. In a rare victory for refugees since the passage of the harsh immigration laws, the INS allowed the Albanian woman to reenter and reapply for asylum. Ultimately she was granted asylum (ACLU 1999b).

Alluding to the ironies of social control, the Lawyers Committee for Human Rights argues, "Expedited removal was unnecessary in the first place, because it was meant to address a problem that did not exist. And we fundamentally doubt that it can ever operate without making tragic mistakes" (1998a: EV2). Nevertheless, because expedited removal already has been instituted, asylum experts insist that monitoring is necessary to reduce errors in screening; for instance, orders of expedited removals should be reviewed by nongovernmental organizations and by the UNHCR. Additionally, the INS should inform individuals before the inspection that the interview will be their only opportunity to inform U.S. authorities that they need protection, and permit arrivees to contact outside agencies, family, attorneys, and translators before the screening begins (Lawyers Committee for Human Rights 1998a, 1999a; see GAO 2000; Musalo, Gibson, Knight, and Taylor 2000).

Detaining Asylum Seekers and Refugees

Another controversial feature of the 1996 law requires those who pass the credible fear of persecution test to be placed in detention while their application for asylum moves to the next stage of review.[2] Although some asylum seekers are detained briefly—ranging from a few days to several weeks—others remain incarcerated for months and sometimes years. Without notice, Patrick Mkhizi was awakened at 2 A.M. in his jail cell in York, Pennsylvania, then handcuffed and escorted to a van, which transported him to the perimeter of the INS processing center in Elizabeth, New Jersey. After three and one-half years in detention, Mkhizi, an asylum seeker from the Congo, was declared a free man. INS officials informed him that the Immigration Board of Appeals reversed its previous decision, granting him asylum. Upon careful review of his case, the U.S. government finally believed his claim of being tortured by soldiers. Dr. Allen S. Keller, director of the Bellevue–New York University Program for Survivors of Torture, who examined Mkhizi, reported, "Patrick had physical and psychological evidence corroborating his reports of torture and mistreatment in the Congo" (Hedges 2000b: EV2). Mkhizi luckily had escaped from his captors in the Congo, making his way to South Africa where he boarded a Greek freighter, which brought him to the United States. The crew turned him over to the INS. Inspectors determined that Mkhizi, who spoke little English and did not have an interpreter or lawyer present, failed to demonstrate a credible fear of persecution. When he resisted his deportation while being forced onto an airplane to Africa, the INS returned him to detention, where he was reinterviewed; at that point, another INS official found reason to believe that he, in fact, had been tortured (Chambers 2000).

Despite making considerable progress with his case, Mkhizi remained in detention. After two hunger strikes, protesting conditions of confinement, INS staff labeled him a "behavioral problem" and transferred him to a county jail that housed convicted felons. There, he was placed in solitary confinement for possessing "contraband items," which they described as "a several-day-old bagel, and a two-inch paper clip, wallet-size photos and a roll of tape" (Hedges 2000b: EV3). Upon his release, Mkhizi called Charles Mulligan, a 60-year-old former Catholic priest who with his wife, Geri, had visited him in detention as part of a program run by the Jesuit Refugee Service. Referring to the bureaucratic gauntlet that consumed Mkhizi, Will Coley of the Jesuit Refugee Service said, "Just about everything that could go wrong in the system in his case did go wrong" (Chambers 2000; Hedges 2000b: EV2).

Whereas experts agree that there are limited circumstances in which detaining asylum seekers is appropriate, generally the practice violates human rights.[3] Citing the Universal Declaration of Human Rights, advocates clearly state, "the right to seek and enjoy asylum is a basic human right; individuals must never be punished for seeking asylum" (Human Rights Watch 1998a: 7; see UNHCR 1995). It is widely understood that some members of Congress intended to use the 1996 law to target asylum seekers so as to deter those fleeing to the United States, an immigration control tactic that violates the Refugee Convention. As international refugee law scholar Arthur Helton explains,

> Detention for purposes of deterrence is a form of punishment, in that it deprives a person of their liberty for no other reasons than their having been forced into exile. It is a practice that is legally questionable under *Articles 31* and *33* of the *United Nations Convention* and protocols *Relating to the Status of Refugees*, which prohibit the imposition of penalties and restrictions on movement as well as refoulment. (Helton 1989: 5)

Detaining asylum seekers and refugees also contributes to criminalization whereby they are stereotyped as being threats to public safety and national security (Amnesty International 1998b). That is particularly the case when asylum seekers and refugees are transferred to county jails where they are confined along with criminal offenders. In many instances, the INS does not even bother to inform jail administrators that its detainees are asylum seekers rather than criminal aliens; therefore, from the standpoint of the correctional staff, asylum seekers are not viewed any differently from prisoners who have committed crimes. Because correctional facilities are unaware of the unusual circumstances that have prompted asylum seekers to flee their homeland, jail staff fail to recognize the source of perceived misconduct. In one incident, an asylum seeker who had been raped previously by guards in his homeland refused to undergo a strip search in a county jail; as punishment, he was locked up in solitary confinement (Rizza 1996). Human rights groups also oppose the detention of asylum seekers, especially in county jails, because it greatly limits their ability to consult with attorneys (and translators) and prepare their claim for asylum.[4] Additionally, the debilitating and demoralizing effects of incarceration may also cause some to abandon their claims for asylum and request deportation, even if it means risking persecution and imprisonment in their homeland (Amnesty International 2000b; Lawyers Committee for Human Rights 1998b, 1999b; Weaver 2000).

As we discuss in Chapter 6, the 1996 law has forced the INS to rely on a detention policy that is best characterized as massive warehousing. As of 2001, the INS held more than 20,000 detainees (including criminal aliens awaiting deportation, the indefinitely detained, asylum seekers, and refugees) in a vast a network of about 18 detention centers, and due to limited capacity at INS facilities, the agency also sends its detainees to more than 900 county jails with which it contracts. The INS estimates that there are approximately 1,000 asylum seekers in detention; oddly, the agency does not have precise data on the number of asylum seekers in its system even though Congress has required it to do so (INS 2001).[5] Due to the enormous impact that the 1996 legislation has had on immigration control, the INS has grown faster than its ability to handle its booming detainee population. As a result, the agency has lost track of detainees on numerous occasions. In one particular case, an asylum seeker was denied his appeal in federal court when he did not appear; later the INS realized that he was still in its custody but had failed to locate him in time for his hearing. Available jail capacity has become a significant factor determining whether an asylum seeker or refugee is detained, and the rate of detention is higher in districts, such as New York, that have ample detention space (Tulsky 2000a). In a rather bizarre case of detention management, a Central American asylum seeker was released by INS district authorities in El Paso—where there were no available beds at the time—under the condition that he check in each month. The next month when he reported to the INS, he was detained because the district had located a bed for him (Rizza 1996; see Chapter 8).

To understand fully the controversy over detaining asylum seekers and refugees, it is important to take into consideration the governing body of international law. Under UNHCR (1995) guidelines, all people in INS detention have the right to be held nonarbitrarily, humanely, and in conditions that are not punitive. Those guidelines explicitly state that refugees and asylum seekers should "not be accommodated with persons detained as common criminals, and shall not be located in areas where their physical safety is endangered" (Human Rights Watch 1998a: 28). However, refugees and asylum seekers detained by the INS are routinely subjected to conditions and correctional practices that violate international law. According to Amnesty International (1999a: 1), "asylum-seekers are not criminals and they should not be treated like criminals." Still, many asylum seekers are "confined with criminal prisoners, but unlike them, they are frequently denied any opportunity of parole. They are held in conditions that are sometimes inhuman and degrading, and are stripped and searched, shackled and chained, verbally or physically abused" (Amnesty International 1998b, 1999b: 1).[6] Amnesty International related,

> Yudaya Nanyonga, an asylum-seeker from Uganda, began crying uncontrollably on learning that she had been assigned to the maximum security section of York County Prison. Prison officials responded by stripping her naked, injecting her with sedatives and placing her in a four-point restraint.
> She says she regained consciousness two days later with no memory of how she had been removed from the restraints, or how and when her underwear had been put back on. During her interview with Amnesty International, Yudaya seemed deeply troubled over her loss of memory. She has told her attorney that she experiences frequent nightmares about the incident. (1999a: 2)

Dahir Nur, a refugee who fled Somalia after his sister was murdered and he received death threats from opposing religious fundamentalists, spent nine months in a county jail outside Chicago where he and other asylum seekers were incarcerated with convicted criminals. Adding to his ordeal, Nur was handcuffed during two days of testifying at his immigration hearing. Eventually, the judge determined that Nur's claim had substantial merit, and he was granted political asylum in the United States; still, he had been treated like a criminal for nearly a year ("Law Students Needed" 2001). Amnesty International and other human rights groups remain critical of the INS for detaining refugees and asylum seekers: "Once asylum-seekers are caught in the labyrinth of the INS detention system, its complexity and almost complete disregard of the needs of refugees create a trial by ordeal. Only the most persistent, courageous or lucky emerge unscathed" (1999a: 3; see Casimir 2001; Walth 2000; Zucker and Flink 1987).

While asylum emerged as a state-sponsored mechanism to protect people who face persecution based on their race, religion, national origin, social group, or politics, now other forms of victimization have begun to transform asylum policies, namely, domestic violence and attacks on gays. In 2000, the U.S. DOJ proposed a new rule for gender-based asylum claims intended to shield victims of domestic abuse: "The proposed rule recognizes the longstanding principle that gender can be the basis for membership in a particular social group. It can, on this basis, include victims of domestic violence who cannot obtain protection from their own government" (2000: 1). The proposed rule brings the United States in line with other nations that extend asylum to victims of domestic violence, including the United Kingdom, Australia, New Zealand, and Canada.

Human rights advocates welcome the new guidelines that expand the category "social groups" to encompass victims of domestic violence because they recognize that women sometimes face persecution because of their gender. In 1996, the INS began its policy of extending asylum to women facing genital mutilation, a ritual still practiced in some in parts of Africa. With the proposed change, "women applying for asylum would still have to show that they are victims of domestic violence, that they would likely continue to be victims or that their country is unable or unwilling to protect them" (Jelinek 2000: EV2). As progressive as the new policy is, its critics denounce the change as the latest example of expanding the definition of asylum beyond a traditional reading based strictly on government repression. Ira Mehlman of the Federation for American Immigration Reform contends that expanding the rules for asylum attracts fraudulent claims and "the intent of the political asylum law was to protect people from political persecution, now it's protecting people from a whole variety of misfortunes that might befall them" (McDonnell 2000: EV1). The INS dismisses such criticism and believes that the new rule will not open the floodgates for asylum; in fact, the agency does not expect to receive more than a few hundred asylum seekers annually (U.S. Department of Justice 2000).

Historically, homosexuals have faced immense persecution. In the 1930s and 1940s, under Hitler's Third Reich, gays were rounded up and confined to concentration camps where many of them were executed (Plant 1986). In 1994, the United States finally recognized asylum claims by homosexuals. Since then, formal efforts to help gays facing persecution have emerged. For instance, the South Florida chapter of the New York–based Lesbian and Gay Immigration Rights Task Force, composed of lawyers and civil rights advocates, has reached out to those who have been victimized for their sexual orientation, a small but growing segment of asylum seekers. In 1999, two gay men fled to the United States from Bogota, Columbia, after receiving a series of death threats from persons who identified themselves as members of La Mano Negra, or the Black Hand, one of several vigilante groups engaged in "social cleansing." With the assistance of human rights and asylum experts, the men eventually were granted political asylum (Benjamin 2000b).

Asylum is still a new and uncertain territory for would-be immigrants who claim to be persecuted because they are lesbian or gay. "People making cases like this were not being recognized as legitimate until recently," said Cheryl Little, executive director of the Florida Immigrant Advocacy Center (Benjamin 2000b: EV2). "As an asylum seeker you face all kinds of obstacles regardless of what claim you're making. But with these cases, it has been particularly uphill. There is a sense of shame that [the applicants] bring to this issue. They have been programmed not to disclose that part of their lives. Gaining their trust is often the most difficult part" (Little, quoted in Benjamin 2000b: EV2). Much like those who oppose asylum protection for victims of domestic violence, immigration restrictionists oppose expanding the social group category of asylum law to include lesbians and gays. "When you take asylum out of the political realm and persecution sponsored by the government and move it into people's personal lives, you invite fraud," said David Ray, of FAIR: "It's moving us toward a slippery slope" (Benjamin 2000b: EV3). It is not known publicly how many people have won political asylum because of persecution based on sexual orientation. The INS says it does not record the information, partly to protect applicants' privacy, and because it does not want the information to be used as a pretext for seeking asylum (see Diaz 2001).

The Ultimate Containment: Indefinite Detention

As discussed in the previous chapter, under the 1996 Illegal Immigration Reform and Immigrant Responsibility Act and the Anti-Terrorism and Effective Death Penalty Act, the INS has the authority to impose mandatory detention on noncitizens who are waiting to hear if they will be deported. If the government decides that those convicted of deportable offenses should be removed from the United States, the noncitizens are placed in detention until deported. Still, there are 4,400 other INS detainees convicted of deportable offenses who are detained indefinitely because the U.S. government does not have official diplomatic ties with their nation of origin, including Cambodia, Cuba, Gaza, Iran, Iraq, Laos, Vietnam, and former satellites of the Soviet Union (Clendenning 2000b). Like those in mandatory detention, "these people have served criminal sentences," said Judy Rabinovitz, senior lawyer for the ACLU's Immigrants' Rights Project. "It's only because they are not citizens that the government takes the position it can detain them for the rest of their lives if need be" (Clendenning 2000b: EV2).

Legal experts argue that the government's use of indefinite detention is unconstitutional and violates international laws (ACLU 2000f; Human Rights Watch 1998a; Indefinite Detention Project 1999). Prior to 1990, there was a six-month detention limit for a noncitizen with a final order of deportation. After the six-month period expired, the noncitizen had to be released under supervision unless he or she was obstructing deportation. The law was changed in 1990 when Congress created an exception to the six-month release rule for aggravated felons; then in 1996 the new immigration laws expanded the definition of aggravated felony to include a host of nonviolent and petty crimes. Civil liberties and human rights organizations insist that the indefinite detention policy is tragically flawed:

Indefinite detention is a feature we expect of repressive regimes, not of our own. The INS's authority to detain a non-citizen ordered removed derives from one purpose: effectuating removal. Once it becomes clear that removal is not possible, the rationale for continued detention evaporates and the non-citizen's liberty rights demand that he or she be released under supervision. It is grossly unfair to detain a person forever, after they have served their time in prison, just because the INS has been unable to remove them. (ACLU 2000f: EV2).

According to the INS, it is required by law to hold these detainees until an opportunity to deport them somewhere arises, "even though there is virtually no prospect on the horizon for that" (Tebo 2000: EV2).

Plight of the Mariel Cubans

In exploring the ongoing controversy over indefinite detention, it is important that we take into account how the practice emerged, particularly in light of the arrival of the Mariel Cubans. In 1980, more than 120,000 Cubans evacuated from the Port of Mariel with dreams of American citizenship. This became known as the Freedom Flotilla, and it marked the largest exodus in Cuban history. Initially, the Mariels were hailed by American political leaders as courageous people who risked their lives on the open sea to escape the Communist satellite of the USSR, what President Reagan called the "Evil Empire." Soon the United States was processing many more Mariels than government officials had anticipated. While the INS struggled to keep up with the enormous volume of Mariels, it also began to detect that many of the Cuban men were more hardened and rougher in appearance. That perception prompted the growing suspicion that Fidel Castro had used the immigration accord to reduce its rabble population of hard-core prisoners and chronic psychiatric patients. That belief took on a life of its own as the media uncritically broadcasted disinformation, feeding moral panic over Mariel Cubans. By falsely claiming that many of the Mariels posed a threat to the American communities, the INS justified its indefinite detention of several thousand newly arrived Cuban men. After more than seven years of detention in federal prisons, thousands of Mariels held at the Atlanta penitentiary and the Oakdale (Louisiana) correctional facility rioted against horrific conditions of confinement and the lack of progress in their immigration hearings (Hamm 1995; Welch 1997b).

It is crucial to acknowledge the predisposing forces underlying the Freedom Flotilla from Cuba, most notably the "push factors" (e.g., economic woes in Cuba) and "pull factors" (e.g., the glamour of American consumerism and myths of quick prosperity) that inspired hundreds of thousands of Cubans to immigrate to America. The sheer volume of Mariels reaching U.S. shores in 1980 caught the INS officials unprepared. To deal with that immigration emergency, the INS set up two large relocation facilities in south Florida, and later transported Mariels to other camps around the country (e.g., Fort McCoy, Wisconsin; Fort Indiantown Gap, Pennsylvania; Fort Chaffee, Arkansas). As the INS packed the relocation camps, the disinformation campaign concerning the Mariels gained momentum. Soon politicians and the INS publicized their suspicion that Castro had exported Cuba's social outcasts to the United States; as a result, Mariels were stereotyped as predatory and dangerous. Resettlement figures, however, contradicted that wave of disinformation; in fact, less than one-half of one percent of the Mariels were found to have a serious criminal history. By comparison, criminality within the general U.S. population was approximately 17 times greater than that among the Mariels. Eventually, even the U.S. Deputy Attorney General Arnold I. Burns conceded (in 1987) that nearly 97 percent of the Mariels had become "productive, law-abiding members of their communities" (Hamm 1995: 65). Nevertheless, the Mariels faced tremendous stigma and marginalization. An INS official boldly (and falsely) told *People* magazine that as many as "85 percent of the refugees are convicts, robbers, murderers, homosexuals, and prostitutes" ("Freedom Flotilla" 1980: 29). Unfortunately, a confrontation with the Arkansas State Police at the overcrowded camp at Fort Chaffee reinforced the disparaging view that Mariels posed a threat to society: That two-hour riot left one Cuban dead, 40 Cubans seriously wounded, and 15 state troopers injured (Hamm 1995).

The process of stigmatizing and criminalizing the Mariels proved to be an easy task for U.S. government officials; after all, the Cubans who joined the boatlift in 1980 were quite different from the Cubans who immigrated to America in the 1950s. In contrast to the middle-income professionals (of European ancestry) who fled Cuba a generation before, the Mariel boatlift included many more impoverished and people of color. Compounding matters, many of the Mariels observed the customs of Santeria, an Afro-Caribbean religion that blends African ancestor worship with Roman Catholicism. Due to the Santeria ritual of sometimes plentiful body tattooing, the physical appearance of those Mariels clashed with American cultural sensibilities. For many Mariels, fitting into American society was difficult, compounded further by racism and classism. Even Cuban Americans often rejected the Mariels; consequently, many of the newly arrived Cubans were denied membership to a community support system vital to their assimilation. It seemed that from the beginning the Mariels were destined to become another form of human rabble eligible for state-sponsored warehousing (see Irwin 1985; Welch 1999b). The harsh campaign against the Mariels also was fueled by financial gain for the INS. Treated as raw materials, Mariels were commodified in ways that generated much-needed revenue for the INS, a relatively obscure agency until the so-called flotilla boatlift. Congress generously compensated the INS for detaining thousands of Mariels; by 1988, the INS budget soared to $2.2 billion, a 100 percent increase over six years (Hamm 1995; see Chapter 8).

Eventually, some members of Congress recognized the plight of the Mariels. In 1986, a congressional subcommittee led by Representative Robert W. Kastenmeier investigated the Atlanta penitentiary and its mistreatment of the Mariels. A congressional report documented that none of the 1,869 Mariels detained there was serving a criminal sentence. Overcrowded conditions at the Atlanta penitentiary, contributing to violence and suicide, placed an enormous strain on health care and psychological services for detainees (U.S. Congress, House 1986). In 1988, Congressmen Kastenmeier and Pat Swidall introduced to the Committee on the Judiciary legislation extending due process to the Mariel Cubans. The bill was defeated in the House on a 144–271 vote (see Kastenmeier 1988). Consequently, the Mariels would be pushed so deeply into the incarceration machinery that even concerned members of Congress, the judiciary (e.g., Judge Marvin Shoob), and activists including the Coalition to Support Cuban Detainees (a group armed with resourceful and dedicated attorneys and advocates) struggled to have the detainees released.

The Campaign to Abolish Indefinite Detention

Responding to political and legal pressure, the INS, through its Cuban Review Plan, paroled hundreds of Mariels to halfway houses where they remained under INS supervision. Still, by 1997 more than a thousand Mariels languished behind bars, prompting many human rights advocates to question the INS's commitment to resolving the plight of the indefinitely detained. That year, a conference entitled How Long Is "Temporary" Detention: The Status of the Mariel Detainees, underwritten by the Straus Family Fund, convened at the University of California at Berkeley (Boalt) Law School. At the meeting, more than 25 attorneys, law professors, and immigration experts examined the lingering forces keeping the Mariels in detention. As a result, the Coalition to Support Cuban Detainees reorganized its mandate to facilitate the release of the Mariels in INS detention. In 1998, the Coalition to Support Cuban Detainees placed itself under the direction of the CLINIC, where strategies to assist the Mariels were expanded to include other immigrants in indefinite detention. The Indefinite Detention Project continues its mission to secure the release of those placed in indefinite detention by offering them legal representation and establishing contacts with agencies capable of offering support and aftercare supervision in the community:

> In light of the anti-immigration sentiment as expressed in the Anti Terrorism Act and other recent immigration legislation, the plight of the indefinitely incarcerated Cuban is sure to be a difficult endeavor. However, law and policy makers of the United States should understand that when the U.S. invited Cuban parolees or refugees into this country, we surely did not intend for them to suffer extraordinary human rights violations, such as the kind they experienced when they left Cuba. (Indefinite Detention Project 1999: 2)

On behalf of the so-called lifers, attorneys and human rights groups have turned to the courts to abolish the INS practice of indefinite detention. In 1991, the Ninth Circuit in *Alvarez-Mendez* v. *Stock* ruled in favor of the INS and its use of indefinite detention, stating that its practice is not an excessive means for protecting society from potentially dangerous aliens. Three years later, in *Barrera-Echavarria* v. *Rison* (1994), the Ninth Circuit showed signs of judicial compassion, ruling that the INS cannot indefinitely hold the Mariel Cubans; still, the court allowed continued use of indefinite detention, viewing it as a temporary solution to the problem. Also that year, the status of the Mariel Cubans was placed within the discretionary powers of the Associate Commissioner of the INS, who would have the unilateral authority to dictate the practice of indefinite detention.

In 1993, as moral panic over immigrants began shaping federal legislation, the Fifth Circuit ruled in *Gisbert* v. *U.S. Attorney General* that the Mariel Cubans are not entitled to due process because immigration proceedings are not criminal proceedings. Legal scholars, however, insist that due process remains at the heart of the dispute about what to do with the detainees being held indefinitely. Advocates for the "lifers" argue that indefinite detention is a form of punishment and therefore "due process considerations apply to their continued incarceration" (Tebo 2000: EV5). Moreover, attorneys maintain that it is irrelevant whether charges are civil or criminal. According to David Cole, a professor at Georgetown University Law Center, "There are differences between civil and criminal law, but there's no other proceeding where you're allowed to lock people up indefinitely" (Tebo 2000: EV5). Unfortunately for the "lifers," *Gisbert* became the prevailing court view, establishing a climate for similar judicial opinions. In *Cuban American Bar Association* v. *Christopher* (1995), the Eleventh Circuit declared that the Mariel Cuban (and Haitian) detainees are not entitled to legal representation and that the government is under no obligation to provide access to organizations like Due Process, Inc., and Legal Alliance, Inc., who might want to represent them.

Despite years of wrangling over the constitutionality of indefinite detention, the immigrants' rights movement persists. A growing coalition of concerned groups have joined the campaign to dismantle the practice of indefinite detention, including the ACLU, American Immigration Law Foundation (AILF), the Asian Law Caucus, CLINIC, Detention Watch Network, Federal Defenders, the Florence Project, the Florida Immigrant Advocacy Center (FIAC), the Indefinite Detention Project, the LIRS, and the National Association of Criminal Defense Lawyers. Still, the legal battles continued. In 1999, the Fifth Circuit Court of Appeals, in *Zadvydas* v. *Underdown* (1999), ruled that it was not a violation of due process to detain indefinitely a person with a final order of removal. In that case, Kestutis Zadvydas was released from a Texas prison where he had served a sentence for a drug conviction. Upon his release, the INS took Zadvydas into custody and since then he has been in indefinite detention (for more than four years) because the government has been unable to deport him. Zadvydas was born in a refugee camp in Germany after World War II to parents believed to be Lithuanian. But German and Lithuanian officials refused to accept Zadvydas, making him a stateless person. A federal judge ordered his release, but the Fifth U.S. Circuit Court of Appeals in New Orleans overturned the decision.

In 2000, the ruling in *Ma* v. *Reno* (2000) offered detainees a ray of optimism when the Ninth Circuit Court of Appeals decided that it was unlawful to detain persons with final removal orders for more than a reasonable period of time. The case involves Kim Jo Ma, a Cambodian immigrant who served several years on a manslaughter charge in Washington state before being detained by the INS pending deportation. Ma has been indefinitely detained because the United States has no deportation agreement with Cambodia. According to Judy Rabinovitz of the ACLU, the "ruling marks a victory for fundamental fairness in America. This is the first circuit to grapple with the issue of whether congress actually authorized the INS's policy of indefinite detention. . . . We are hopeful that other courts, as well as the INS, will rethink their position" (ACLU 2000g: EV1). Setting the stage for a final showdown, in 2000 the U.S. Supreme Court granted a petition for certiorari in *Ma* v. *Reno* and *Zadvydas* v. *Underdown*. The High Court agreed to hear the case in part to settle that split among the lower courts (in *Zadvydas* v. *Underdown* and *Ma* v. *Ashcroft*; see Clendenning 2000b; Indefinite Detention Project 2000). During oral arguments, it became clear that there remains a tendency to criminalize and demonize immigrants, even among members of the Supreme Court. Conservative Justice Antonin Scalia gave an indirect and colorful explanation of why the INS might be justified in detaining the men. Scalia pressed Ma's lawyer, Seattle Assistant Federal Public Defender Jay Stansell, to suggest what the INS should do with a "'really evil person,' who had served his time yet had no country to go to. What if you're talking about a real Hannibal What's-his-name?" Scalia asked, referring to the fictional flesh-eating character Hannibal Lecter (Gearan 2001: EV2). Conversely, Justice Stephen Breyer seemed troubled by the lack of outside oversight when the INS makes detention decisions: "To my mind, putting a person in jail or confinement for the rest of his life, no matter how bad deportation is, this is much worse" (Gearan 2001: EV2; see Chapter 9). At year end 2001, the INS still held approximately 1,000 indefinite detainees (Indefinite Detention Project 2001).

Conclusion

By detaining asylum seekers and those who cannot be deported because their nation of origin will not accept them, the INS perpetuates the ironies of immigration control. Not only are such detention policies unnecessary, costly, and self-defeating, but legal scholars contend that they also violate the U.S. Constitution and international law (ACLU 1999a; Tebo 2000). According to Amnesty International, "Detention policies and practices in the USA clearly fail to follow the United Nations High Commissioner for Refugees (UNHCR) guidelines and violate fundamental standards of international human rights law" (1999a: EV1). Amnesty International and other human rights groups recommend that the U.S. government revise its detention law and policy in the light of international law that requires that the detention of asylum seekers normally should be avoided. Moreover, those organizations call on the UNHCR to monitor U.S. compliance with international guidelines and report its finding publicly (Amnesty International 1999a; Lawyers Committee for Human Rights 1999a).

For the United States to comply with international standards for the treatment of asylum seekers, significant alterations to the 1996 immigration laws are necessary. Despite ongoing human rights violations stemming from the Illegal Immigration Reform and Immigrant Responsibility Act and other laws affecting immigrants, such legislation is difficult to amend because the statute is more than a mere immigration law; it is also viewed as a criminal justice initiative aimed at "getting tough" on illegal immigrants and criminal aliens. Although asylum seekers who have not been charged with a criminal offense do not officially fit into either of those categories, the sweeping nature of the 1996 law has criminalized them nonetheless. Because the 1996 statute fails to distinguish between criminal immigrants and asylum seekers, those who have fled their homelands fearing persecution are forced into INS detention and required to be handcuffed and shackled when they appear at their immigration hearings. American Bar Association President Martha Barnett, who has exerted pressure on lawmakers to amend the 1996 laws, notes that some politicians—including those who initially supported the legislation—say the consequences are not what they intended. Still, Marisa Demeo, regional counsel for the Mexican American Legal Defense and Education Fund, has found that many politicians "are hesitant to change the policies out of fear they'll be accused in elections of allowing criminal immigrants to remain in the country" (Gamboa 2000: EV3). With those obstacles in mind, small group of senators ventured out to correct the injustices caused by the 1996 immigration laws. In 2000, the Refugee Protection Act was introduced by Senators Patrick Leahy (D–Vermont), Sam Brownback (R–Kansas), Russell Feingold (D–Wisconsin), Jim Jeffords (R–Vermont), Edward Kennedy (D–Massachusetts), John Kerry (D–Massachusetts), and Frank Lautenberg (D–New Jersey). Human rights groups believe that measure would help restore fair treatment to refugees seeking asylum (ACLU 2000a; Amnesty International 1999a; Lawyers Committee for Human Rights 1999a; see Chapter 9).

In the realm of indefinite detention, similar legislation also has been proposed. The Restoration of Fairness in Immigration Law Act [H.R. 4966], introduced in 2000, was designed to reign in the power of the INS to detain noncitizens ordered removed after it becomes clear that they are clearly not removable. That law limits indefinite detention to a maximum of one year. If after that time the INS sees no reasonable possibility for deporting the detainee soon, the detainee is to be released on parole and remain subject to deportation at any time should the opportunity arise, such as an improvement in diplomatic relations between the United States and his or her home country. The statute included built-in exceptions for those deemed a flight or crime risk; still, such cases required open review of the evidence of risk, not secret hearsay. The Restoration of Fairness in Immigration Law Act also was designed to end mandatory detention of noncitizens whose immigration cases are pending as well as correct a number of other problems in the immigration laws (ACLU 2000f). "We fully support that," says Melanie Nezer, immigration policy director for Immigration and Refugee Services of America in Washington, D.C. "The INS role is to deport. If they're not deportable, we can't just lock them up forever" (Nezer, quoted in Tebo 2000: EV3). Joe Cook, executive director of the Louisiana ACLU, concurs, adding that indefinite detention "ranks right below death as one of the worst things that could happen to a person. You lose all sense of your freedom and you cannot carry on in any way with any type of meaningful life behind bars" (Clendenning 2000b: EV3).

Much like other proposals to amend the 1996 laws, releasing indefinite detainees into the community faces strong political and public resistance, especially given the weight of moral panic over criminal aliens. Recently, 50 Vietnamese convicted of felonies and who served prison time in Massachusetts were released by the INS rather than being placed in indefinite detention. That particular experiment with parole has been met with harsh criticism from local law enforcement and members of the community who view Vietnamese former convicts as threats to public safety, referring to them as the "walking deported." Thomas P. Todd, a probation officer at Dorchester (Massachusetts) District Court who works extensively in the Vietnamese community, wondered, "If they know they can't be deported, what's to stop them?" Even though Todd has yet to find evidence of new criminal activity by paroled felons, giving in to moral panic, he remains wary that "some former inmates could have a corrupting influence on the current generation of Vietnamese teenagers" (MacQuarrie 2000: EV2).

6

Warehousing Illegal Immigrants

The INS is shipping immigrants off to local jails where they don't belong. This practice violates international standards, and it must stop.

Kenneth Roth, executive director of Human Rights Watch

We're warehousing people running from unspeakable horrors. This is the welcome that we give to today's refugees.

Frank Lipiner, chief immigration attorney at the Hebrew Immigrant Aid Society

I've never been in prison before, but this place is a prison. I'm watching and hearing people getting sexually assaulted. I just can't take another six months in this hell hole.

Detainee Peterson Polidor

n 1995, detainees at the INS detention facility located—interestingly enough—in the warehouse district of Elizabeth, New Jersey, rioted in reaction to the harsh conditions of confinement compounded by abuse and harassment by the jail's guards. The INS surveyed the disturbance at the jail that had been operated by ESMOR, a private corrections corporation, and found many incidents of serious abuse. According to the assessment team's report, ESMOR guards were involved in numerous acts of physical abuse and theft of detainee property. Female detainees complained that they had been issued male underwear on which large question marks had been made in the area of the crotch. Other accounts of harassment included the unjustified waking of detainees in the middle of the night under the guise of security checks (INS 1995). The assessment team also reported that ESMOR did not have sufficient personnel and resorted to inappropriate uses of overtime. Moreover, low salaries for guards not only contributed to turnover but also exacerbated the ongoing problem of poorly qualified staff being placed on duty without the mandatory training required by the INS. As is the case with most INS detention centers, detainees at the ESMOR facility were subjected to protracted periods of detention due to lengthy processing and inefficient administrative hearing procedures; there, the estimated average length of detention was 100 to 115 days. The INS discovered that detainees were denied proper access to natural light, privacy in some toilet and shower areas, and an outdoor recreation area (INS 1995). Additionally, immigration lawyers complained about detainees' lack of access to counsel and the inappropriate use of shackles by ESMOR staff (Peet and Schwab 1995).[1]

When the ESMOR facility was closed, detainees were transferred to either other INS detention centers or county jails in New Jersey and Pennsylvania. Unfortunately for many of those detainees, the harshness of treatment not only continued, in some cases it also worsened. For instance, 25 detainees (who had not participated in the riot) were sent to the Union County Jail (N.J.), where they were met by a unit of guards who formed a gauntlet, punching and kicking the detainees, an ordeal that lasted more than four hours. "The guards broke one detainee's collarbone, shoved other detainees' heads in toilets, used pliers to pull out one man's pubic hair and forced a line of men to kneel naked on the jail floor and chant, 'America is No. 1'" (Sullivan 1995a: A1). Six guards eventually were arrested and charged with the beatings of INS detainees; still, prosecutors contend that at least two dozen officers participated in the assaults. In 1998, three jailers were convicted of assault, misconduct, and conspiracy to obstruct the investigation; two of them were sentenced to seven years in prison and a third received a five-year sentence (Smothers 1998: Welch 1997a).

As emphasized throughout this work, moral panic over immigrants in the early and mid-1990s has had a tremendous impact on the INS, most notably its policy of detaining increasingly more people for longer periods of time. Human rights advocates, however, insist that for most undocumented immigrants, asylum seekers, and refugees detention is costly, unnecessary, and unjust, especially considering that detainees are merely warehoused while their cases crawl through the vast bureaucracy of the INS (ACLU 2000e; Human Rights Watch 1998a). Adding to the controversy over INS detention are the deplorable conditions of confinement, obstructed access to counsel and the courts, inadequate medical care, and physical and sexual assault by staff. Lucas Guttentag, Director of the ACLU Immigrants' Rights Project, reminded us, "Immigrants awaiting administrative hearings are being detained in conditions that would be unacceptable at prisons for criminal offenders" (Sontag 1993: B1). This chapter examines recent shifts in INS detention policy along with the Kafkaesque nature of detention, harsh conditions of confinement, and brutality against detainees. To help explain why such problems remain out of sight and out of mind, the discussion begins by exploring the poverty of interest in INS detention centers.

The Poverty of Interest in INS Detention Centers

Problems at INS detention facilities fail to generate significant public concern for several reasons. First, the public generally is unaware that as of 2001 more than 20,000 undocumented immigrants were detained by the INS, nor does the public realize that most of those detainees were held in harsh conditions for prolonged periods. Second, undocumented immigrants confined to INS detention centers are subject to the criminalization process, and thus are portrayed as lawbreakers who have entered the United States illegally. From that punitive perspective, INS detainees commonly are viewed as being unworthy of compassion and even deserve harsh treatment for entering the country unlawfully. Finally, INS detainees are typically impoverished people of color whose plight does not often attract much sympathy from mainstream citizens (Welch 1997a, 1998, 2002a). Problems facing INS detainees are perpetuated further because authorities do not systematically inspect detention centers. Moreover, lawyers and advocacy groups have difficulty gaining access to detainees due to bureaucratic resistance by INS officials and jail administrators; as a result, detainees have few channels to make their complaints known (ACLU 1993, 2000e; Human Rights Watch 1998a; Lawyers Committee for Human Rights 1998b, 1999a).

The Policy Shift toward Increased INS Detention

Contributing to the process of criminalization directed at illegal immigrants are immigration policies that continue to draw from a larger criminal justice mandate pervasive in American society. More so now than at any point in its history, the INS boasts unparalleled authority coupled with all the resources of a criminal justice system. Whereas the INS operates under the canopy of the U.S. DOJ, it is unique because the agency has its own law enforcement personnel along with its own jail system, euphemistically referred to as "processing centers." Certainly, criminal justice activities in the INS always have been a prominent feature of the agency; however, nowadays the emphasis on law enforcement and detention has eclipsed the agency's commitment to service.

Borrowing from the crime control model dominating contemporary criminal justice, the INS has relied on detention as a means to deter illegal immigration. According to INS spokesman Russ Bergeron, "When people know they face detention if caught attempting to enter the country through international airports, they are much less likely to risk it" (Sullivan 1995b: B4). It is important to note that the INS is not planning to reduce the amount of detention space; rather, "Over the long term, we must replace the Elizabeth, N.J. [that closed following the riot] capability if we are to maintain a level of deterrence" added Bergeron (Sullivan 1995b: B4). Still, sharp questions have been raised about the INS's claim that detention deters illegal immigration. "Taken together, the critics say, the figures show the failings of a detention policy that is based more on available jail space than on how best to stop illegal immigration" (Sullivan 1995b: A1; see Chapter 8). The debate over whether detention deters illegal immigration also is complicated by competing interpretations of official statistics. INS officials offer one set of conclusions, largely supporting the deterrence hypothesis, whereas critics present an equally plausible interpretation of the statistics, thereby debunking assertions of deterrence (see Snowden 1995). Jeffrey Heller, an immigration lawyer, insists that undocumented immigrants fleeing persecution in their homeland are not likely to be put off by the prospect of detention in the United States. With that concern in mind, Judy Rabinovitz of the ACLU's Immigrants' Rights Project recommends that INS establish clear guidelines instead of implementing blanket detentions (ACLU 1993).

The push to detain increasingly larger numbers of undocumented immigrants for longer periods of time is driven by significant developments in INS policy. Prior to the 1980s, the INS enforced a policy of detaining only those individuals deemed likely to abscond or who posed a security risk (Marks and Levy 1994). By contrast, during the early Reagan years, the INS detention policy became more expansive, a shift prompted by the arrival of the Mariel Cubans and the Haitian boat people. At that time, INS officials believed that widespread detention would deter illegal immigration. Key legislation also contributed to the increased use of INS detention, namely, the Immigration Reform and Control Act of 1986, commonly known as the Simpson–Rodino law (Arp, Dantico, and Zatz 1990).

Due to that alteration in INS policy, not only has the detainee population grown dramatically, but detainees are also now subjected to longer periods of confinement. "Immigrants in INS detention may find themselves behind bars for years, essentially serving time in local jails with no known end to their sentences and little likelihood for parole. No exception is made for most asylum seekers, about whom the INS does not even keep accurate statistics or know their numbers in detention" (Human Rights Watch 1998a: 87). In 1981, the average stay in an INS detention facility was less than four days, increasing to 11 days by 1986. By 1990, detention had increased to 23 days, with many individuals detained for more than a year. In 1992, it had increased again to an average stay of 54 days by 1994 (Lawyers Committee for Human Rights 1998b). Still, critics insist that official statistics on length of detention are misleading because "those figures are skewed by the inclusion of thousands of Mexicans who are detained for a day or two before they are thrown back over the border" (Solomon 1995: 26). Human Rights Watch found that many detainees, including asylum seekers, are imprisoned for exceedingly long periods of time, even for as long as three or four years. In Vermilion Parish Jail in Louisiana, the chief of the jail said that the average length of detention for INS detainees in his facility was 14 to 16 months (Human Rights Watch 1998a: 87).

Principle 11 of the (UN) Body of Principles states, "a person shall not be kept in detention without being given an effective opportunity to be heard promptly by a judicial or other authority," a requirement extending to all held in detention, whether they are criminally accused or administratively detained. In their investigation, Human Rights Watch was surprised to find a number of INS detainees held for considerable lengths of time before being brought to immigration court, including those who wanted only to be deported back to their home countries.[2] Gregory Osnomi, a Nigerian detained at the Virginia Beach Correctional Facility, reported that he had been held by the INS for 19 months and had yet to appear in immigration court. Osnomi wrote, "I want you to know that I am not trying to fight deportation, on the contrary, am trying to be deported . . . so that I can be reunited with the family that I have been away from" (Human Rights Watch 1998a: 88).

The INS has struggled to contain its booming inmate population, which at more than 20,000 detainees has tripled since 1995. However, due to limited capacity in its 18 detention centers, the INS parcels out more than 10,000 detainees to a haphazard network of 900 private state prisons and county jails, including 250 facilities where it rents beds regularly (Casimir 2001; Sullivan 2000a). Such an ambitious detention project is indeed costly. Since the passage of the punitive immigration laws in 1996, spending on detention (and removal) has jumped from $367 million in 1996 to $878.6 million in 2001 (Sullivan 2000a). The INS estimated it pays an average of $58 per day to hold a detainee in a local jail; hence, it costs more than $10,000 for each detainee to be jailed for six months. As we shall explore further in Chapter 8, the INS has become a key player in the corrections–industrial complex in which local and private jails rely enormously on INS detainees for revenue. For example, at the Yamhill County Jail (Oregon), the $690,000 the INS pays each year is nearly half of the jail officers' salaries. "It's in the best interest of the Yamhill County taxpayers and us to have these folks here," Sheriff Norman Hand said of the INS detainees (Sullivan 2000a: EV7). Still, INS officials acknowledge that relying on local jails has significant drawbacks. Even though Congress has poured money into the INS in recent years, those funds have not been allocated to the construction of INS jails. David Venturella of the INS stressed the agency's needs: "We wanted our own facilities, and no one would give us the money to do it" (Sullivan 2000a: EV3). Venturella conceded that little will change until the agency gets more of its own sites.

Adding to the human rights advocates' concerns about the increased use of detention by the INS are allegations of racism in U.S. immigration policy, especially considering that most detainees are people of color. Among those most commonly detained by the INS are Central

Americans, Cubans, Haitians, and Nigerians. Critics further point out that whites seeking asylum in the United States typically face much less resistance by INS and rarely are detained indefinitely (Cook 1993; Marks and Levy 1994; Welch 1991, 1997a, 2002a).[3]

The Kafkaesque Nature of Detention

Especially for refugees and asylum seekers, being detained by the INS can be traumatic. Indeed, some observers describe INS detention as Kafkaesque, drawing on *The Trial*, a novel by Franz Kafka (1937) in which the main character fights a secretive criminal justice system that refuses to provide him with any information about his arrest or the status of his case. Over the years, many undocumented immigrants have been placed in what critics call "Motel Kafkas," which are literally motels that hire private security guards, raising serious questions of accountability. In several incidents, detainees have been held in a motel room for months, where they are deprived of fresh air and telephones, and in some cases they are shackled and sexually abused by the security staff ("Motel Kafka" 1993). According to the news article,

> In 1993, three teenagers—two boys and a girl—from Sri Lanka arrived at Kennedy Airport on a Northwest Airlines flight and requested asylum. Northwest detained them for about two months, footing the motel and security guard bills until the airline persuaded the city to arrange for foster care. During those two months, the teenagers' lawyer never knew where they were being held. And the young people weren't allowed to call him. They told him that they only were fed twice a day because the guard said there wasn't enough money for three meals (1993: 3).
>
> In 1992, Delta Airlines found itself with 13 TWOV [traveling without visas] passengers from China who requested asylum. Two escaped, a pregnant woman was paroled and Delta ended up housing, feeding and guarding the remaining 10 until INS arranged for them to get an asylum hearing. Delta shelled out $181,000 that included $9,800 in medical bills for a woman who broke her arm when she leapt from her hotel room in an attempt to escape (1993: 3).

Over the past several years, human rights organizations have found that little has changed at Motel Kafkas (ACLU 2000e; Lawyers Committee for Human Rights 1998b). As described in the previous chapter, asylum seekers arriving at airports are automatically apprehended, interrogated, strip-searched, shackled, and jailed pending the outcome of their cases.

Those arriving at Kennedy International Airport (NYC) are told that they will be sent to a hotel that actually is a Motel Kafka. Oleksiy Galushka, 32, of the Ukraine, has been at a Motel Kafka operated by Wackenhut, a private corrections company, for two years. He continues to fight his deportation order: "They tell me we send you to a place like hotel for approximately seven days. But this is not hotel—it is more like prison, but much worse. At least in prison you have a sentence. In prison you can move around, go to library . . . you can get fresh air" (Casimir 2001: EV1). Similarly, Philip Sesay, a 54-year-old asylum seeker who fled Sierra Leone after its elected government was overthrown in 1997, has been incarcerated at the Wackenhut jail for more than three years. At that particular Motel Kafka, Sesay and other detainees have witnessed men scrawling words on the walls with their own feces, and people staging hunger strikes, while others try unsuccessfully to commit suicide by hanging with threadbare sheets or swallowing analgesics and liquid detergent (Casimir 2001). The Kafkaesque reputation of INS detention is perpetuated further by unforgivable grave errors committed by the agency. While conducting an investigation of the Varick Street detention facility in New York City, the ACLU (1993) discovered U.S. citizens mistakenly detained by the INS. In one case, ACLU researchers assisted the release of a detainee who had been held for 14 months, long beyond the statutory release period; moreover, that particular detainee was confined despite incontrovertible evidence of U.S. citizenship. Also during the ACLU study at Varick, two other detainees had verified their U.S. citizenship but remained in confinement.

Traditionally, penologists have described jails and prisons as *total institutions*, because they force prisoners to lose contact with the outside world, especially their families who serve as a vital source of support (Goffman 1961). Nowadays, contemporary correctional facilities have become *less-than-total* institutions, allowing inmates to have much more contact with the free world (Farrington 1992; Welch 1996c). The exception to that trend is INS detention, in which detainees remain exceedingly isolated from their families, their lawyers, and the courts. Human Rights Watch describes the plight of detainees:

> Locked behind bars in criminal jails, limited in their English language ability and fearing possible deportation, immigration detainees are both physically and emotionally isolated. A key element in overcoming this isolation is communication with friends and family in the outside world. Outside sources not only provide critical emotional support, they also often provide the only

financial and logistical resources available to help the detainee obtain legal counsel. (1998a: 65)

Despite the crucial need for contact with family and attorneys, INS detainees are denied access to the kind of communication that those in outside world take for granted. Most local jails do not offer coin-operated telephones, and many such phones are equipped to make collect calls nationally but not internationally. That problem puts immigrants, especially asylum seekers, at an extreme disadvantage, since many detainees have no contacts in the United States and must rely on people in their home countries to send them money or to provide critical documents needed to corroborate their asylum claim (Human Rights Watch 1998a: 65). Compounding their isolation, the INS (as well as local jails and private corrections corporations that manage detention facilities) adheres to rigid and at times arbitrary institutional rules that limit and discourage visitation.

Frequent Transfers

In addition to being confined in local jails located hundreds of miles from their families and legal counsel, INS detainees also are frequently transferred, deepening their hardship. The INS often transfers its detainees from facility to facility and state to state to accommodate the logistics of court appearances, immigration case status, and availability (and cost) of bed space, but they rarely consider the location of families and lawyers. In fact, in many instances, neither families nor attorneys are notified when detainees are transferred. Many such transfers contradict Principle 20 of the UN Body of Principles that states, "if a detained or imprisoned person so requests, he shall if possible, be kept in a place of detention or imprisonment reasonably near his usual place of residence." For obvious reasons, Principle 20 was established so that detainees might receive crucial support from families and legal counsel. Moreover, many families have difficulty financing long-distance travel and accommodations. Despite those obstacles, some families go to great lengths to maintain contact with their loved ones. The family of Luis Cortez, a Cuban detainee, spent more than $2,000 traveling from California to Pennsylvania to see him, only to end up driving to six jails during a 10-day stretch in search of him. No one at any of the Pennsylvania jails could tell the Cortez family where to find Luis. Eventually authorities located him at the Snyder County Jail in Pennsylvania. The family was allowed one two-hour noncontact visit before they embarked on their long journey home (Human Rights Watch 1998a: 88).

Whereas INS officials contend that the agency transfers detainees in order to bring them closer to family and attorneys, many lawyers and families disagree, accusing the INS of using frequent transfers to cut costs and in some instances to punish detainees. Still, other observers insist that decisions regarding transfers are made without taking into consideration the special needs of detainees. Max Ogando, 28, a deaf native of the Dominican Republic who communicates only in Spanish sign language, was taken into INS custody in New York. Ogando had just completed a one-year prison sentence for assault, a misdemeanor in New York but an aggravated felony under the revised immigration law. In New York, Ogando has a child, a pro bono lawyer, and a Spanish sign language interpreter, the only person he understands in court proceedings. Two days after his attorney took the case, Ogando was transferred to the Etowah County Jail in Alabama and his case to an immigration court in Atlanta, making his problems all the more difficult. The Legal Aid Society of New York could not afford to send his lawyer to Atlanta, and Ogando could not communicate for telephone proceedings. Ogando appeared in court with no attorney and was ordered deported; he appealed, and the case is pending (Sullivan 2000a: EV9).

Lost in the System

Due to the enormous impact that the 1996 legislation has had on INS detention policies, the agency has grown faster than its ability to keep track of its booming detainee population. Consequently, it is not uncommon for the INS to lose its detainees. In one previously mentioned Kafkaesque incident, an asylum seeker was denied his appeal when he did not appear in federal court. Later the INS realized that he was still in its custody but that it had failed to locate him in time for his hearing. In a similar incident, a lawyer for a group of detainees suing over dangerous jail conditions wrote to the INS, desperately trying to find a member of the group who had been transferred from a Pennsylvania jail. Justice Department lawyers reported that the detainee had been deported; later, government officials notified immigration lawyers that the detainee had not been deported but had been moved to another jail within the vast detention network. And in a Los Angeles juvenile center, a Chinese youth was forgotten by the INS for more than a year until he initiated contact with his social worker to ask about the progress of his case (Tulsky 2000a).

In some instances, immigration lawyers have found INS officials to be uncooperative in locating detainees. Critics charge that the INS cannot or will not fully account for who is being held, even when ordered by the courts to do so. Recently, the INS refused to provide a list of detainees eligible for release to the federal public defender in Portland, Oregon, who discovered through a Catholic priest that dozens of detainees and asylum seekers were housed in Oregon jails. The INS resisted a court order to produce the list, and when the agency did finally provide it, it omitted some eligible detainees and misidentified others or their locations. In 1998, Congress ordered the INS to report exactly how many detainees are asylum seekers along with other important demographic data. As of 2002, the INS has yet to disseminate such crucial information (see Sullivan 2000a).

Being transferred from facility to facility creates other problems for INS detainees whose personal property (including legal documents) is simply lost or thrown away; in fact, jail authorities rarely make an effort to forward detainees' mail to their new destination, forcing them to lose greater contact with their families and lawyers. "You always have to leave everything behind when you are transferred," said one detainee who had been transferred five times in seven months of detention, adding, "You have to buy them at one place, leave them, then buy them again later" (Human Rights Watch 1998a: 62). Understandably, the loss of legal papers and other supporting documentation can have serious consequences for asylum seekers and other detainees fighting deportation. Due to frequent transfers, Harjinder Singh, an Indian Sikh who had been in INS detention for more than two years, was unable to receive critical documents from his family. After his lawyer failed to file an appeal, Singh decided to represent himself and solicited documentation from the Sikh Student Federation. The documents initially were sent to Krome Service Processing Center in Miami, but by then Singh had been transferred to Bay County Jail Annex in Panama City (Florida) and never received them. Later he was transferred to Monroe County Detention Center in Key West (Florida), where he asked his family in Canada to fax the documents again to him. More than a year later, Singh had still not received the documents; then he was returned to Krome (Human Rights Watch 1998a: 62).

Lack of Legal Representation

Compounding isolation and the Kafkaesque nature of detention, many detainees drift through the convoluted hearing process without the aid of an attorney. Even though detainees have the right to a lawyer (but not at government expense), many go unrepresented, because they cannot afford to pay legal fees and many others are simply not lucky enough to draw the interest of a pro bono organization that will prepare their case without charge. The consequences of not having legal counsel are particularly drastic for asylum seekers who risk being returned to their homeland where they face persecution: In no uncertain terms, final decisions on granting asylum are a matter of life and death. The Justice Department reports that one-third of asylum seekers go through the hearing process without an attorney, and applicants who have legal counsel are six times more likely to be granted asylum. Even officials at the INS and the DOJ are concerned about the lack of representation. Paul W. Schmidt, chairman of the Board of Immigration Appeals, which decides administrative appeals of immigration judges' rulings, notes, "The system is built on the premise that we have an adversarial process. But it is hard to have an adversary system if you don't have good advocacy" (Tulsky 2000b: EV1). Andrew I. Schoenholtz, director of law and policy studies at Georgetown University, concurred: "We have a substantially complex legal process. It is almost impossible that those not represented could understand the system well. And that can almost determine whether or not they are granted asylum" (Tulsky 2000b: EV2). In many instances, asylum seekers who manage to hire a lawyer find themselves poorly represented by incompetent lawyers who are unprepared to handle the complexities of the case, and even more tragically some are simply swindled by unscrupulous attorneys.

Even for detainees who do have legal representation, there remain numerous obstacles. For example, many lawyers complain that rigid institutional rules keep them from seeing their clients. Carol Kolnichak, a pro bono attorney, struggled to represent a detainee applying for political asylum: "It's easier to visit my clients on death row than it is to visit an INS detainee at Orleans Parish" (Human Rights Watch 1998a: 74). U.S. immigration law dictates that immigrants have a right to unobstructed access to their attorneys. For many detainees, however, access to counsel is usually compromised by being held in remote jails far from family who can locate and pay for lawyers. Frequent transfers, restrictive visitation policies, and limited telephone access also significantly undermine adequate representation (Taylor 1997).

Harsh Conditions of Confinement

While detainees agonize over the lengthy review process of their cases, they also must contend with the harsh conditions of confinement, which take their toll physically, psychologically, and emotionally. Indeed, many detainees are subjected to inhumane living quarters where adequate medical and mental health services are scarce, and these problems are compounded by language and cultural barriers. In some instances the pains of imprisonment become particularly tragic as detainees fall victim to physical and sexual abuse by custodial staff. For years human rights groups have challenged INS detention, insisting that for most undocumented immigrants and asylum seekers confinement is not only unnecessary but also unjust. According to the Lawyers Committee for Human Rights,

> Our experience in assisting and representing detained asylum-seekers has led us to have serious concerns about the conditions in which asylum-seekers are held. Our detained clients are held primarily at the large Wackenhut and Elizabeth detention facilities. They are often brought to the facility in handcuffs or leg restraints. Upon arrival, they are stripped of their possessions and dressed in prison attire. They are then given a bed in a large holding area where they will live with many other detainees for at least three months or four months, and perhaps for a year or more.
>
> At the Elizabeth facility, they will be shackled with leg weights during their credible fear interviews. Asylum-seekers at both facilities report that they are frequently hungry and that medical care is deficient. They have no meaningful access to the outdoors, as the "outdoor" recreation area is no more than a relatively small enclosed internal area without a roof. Some clients have reported that they have been insulted or mistreated by facility officers. Many have reported that they are placed in segregation unfairly, and other asylum-seekers have complained of the use of forced sedation. One of our clients was recently assaulted and injured by an officer at the Elizabeth facility. The incident is currently under investigation. (1998a: EV9)

It is important to keep in mind that detention in and of itself reinforces the criminalization process whereby undocumented immigrants and asylum seekers typically are viewed and treated no differently than those who have been jailed for committing criminal offenses. Whereas the criminalization of immigrants occurs in INS operated facilities, that form of degradation can be even more profound for detainees transferred to county jails. "Guards treat them [INS detainees] the same as their fellow inmates—the convicted criminals with whom they share cells. The detainees wear prison uniforms and eat prison food, and they are subjected to the same rules about visitors, contraband and even personal hygiene—generally, thrice-weekly showers—as all of the 'regular' prisoners" (Tebo 2000: EV1).

Under international refugee law, asylum seekers deserve special treatment because they are usually victims fleeing abusive governments; tragically though, under the care of the INS they face new kinds of abuse. INS detention records do not indicate which detainees are asylum seekers; consequently, they are simply mixed with other INS detainees and local jail populations. According to Kenneth Roth, executive director of Human Rights Watch, "In most cases, the INS should not be detaining these people at all, much less in jails. But they should certainly never be held in remote facilities, where they can't get access to legal counsel or psychological counseling services" (Human Rights Watch 1998c: 1; Sullivan 2000a).

In view of those issues, Human Rights Watch (1998a, 1998c) embarked on a comprehensive investigation into conditions and treatment at the jails used by the INS. They found that INS detainees in jails are subjected to physical mistreatment, are not provided with basic medical care, are often unable to communicate with jail staff due to language barriers, and are subjected to severe restrictions on contact with families, friends, and legal representatives. (See Note 2.) The report also documents other problems, including frequent, unexplained transfers; excessive or inappropriate discipline; commingling with accused or criminal inmates; and more dramatic charges, such as the 1998 incident during which guards at the Jackson County Correctional Facility in Florida allegedly used electrified batons and shields to shock detainees. Based on its findings, Human Rights Watch condemns detention practices of the INS, urging an end to the use of local jails to hold immigrants. Given the premium placed on government accountability, human rights groups criticize the INS for "abdicating responsibility for people under its care" (Roth, quoted in Human Rights Watch 1998c: 1).

Whereas the criminalization of INS detainees is pervasive in county jails, similar degradation also occurs in INS operated facilities. At the Krome Detention Center in Miami, detainees "wear orange uniforms, and the guards on the grounds are armed, and the intimidating sound of gunfire can echo through the camp from a nearby target range where I.N.S. officers practice" (Rohter 1992: E18). When asked why Krome looks so much like a jail, Richard Smith, INS regional director, answered, "That's because it is a jail, albeit a minimum security jail. The sign outside may say that it's a processing center, but that's just semantics" (Rohter 1992: E18; Welch 1997a, 1998).

Deplorable Living Conditions

According to Article 10(1) of the International Covenant on Civil and Political Rights, "All persons deprived of their liberty shall be treated with humanity and with respect for the inherent dignity of the human person."[4] While even INS operated facilities have had difficulty ensuring the humane treatment of its detainees (ACLU 1993, 2000f; Lawyers Committee for Human Rights 1998b), that responsibility is strained further when the agency relies on local jails. Because local jails are designed to hold accused and convicted criminals on a short-term basis, they usually do not offer educational programs or work opportunities, leaving detainees absolutely idle for months or years at a time. To pass the time, many INS detainees simply sleep and watch television. Libraries are limited or nonexistent, and few facilities have reading materials in the languages of the detainees. Detainee complaints about the physical environment of jails range from cigarette smoke filling the air to cockroaches and vermin sharing their cells. In the words of one INS detainee, "I am locked in a cage twenty-four hours a day. The food is very little. There is no light in my cell. There is no law library. The place is filthy. It looks like a dog pound" (Human Rights Watch 1998a: 54).

Fabio Díaz, an INS detainee from the Dominican Republic, described the conditions at the Stone Park City Jail (Illinois):

> The jail had no heat and it was thirty-five degrees outside. Six INS detainees were put in a room originally meant for two people—another room meant for two had four people in it. The room is never cleaned, and there are no clean sheets. One time I purposely spilled water on my blanket so that I could get one that didn't stink so badly. From Friday to Monday we can't shower. We are just in our cells all weekend long. We are not allowed to bring any property, and there is no radio, no TV, no games, no books. (Human Rights Watch 1998a: 55)

When Díaz asked jails officials for a grievance form to complain about the conditions, he was told that the facility did not have grievance forms (Human Rights Watch 1998a: 55). Some of the most disturbing and pervasive complaints of deplorable conditions have come from detainees at Orleans Parish Prison in Louisiana, where the jail complex has 10 buildings and holds more than 6,000 individuals, approximately 500 to 600 of whom are INS detainees. "My first time here, I thought I'd gone to hell," one detainee recalled upon arriving at the Central Lock Up (CLU) section of the jail. "We spend eighteen hours in the cell and are allowed out only between 12 and 6 p.m. When I arrived I wasn't given any bedding. Later, I got a wool blanket that made me very hot [in August]" (Human Rights Watch 1998a: 56). Numerous detainees at the Orleans Parish Prison reported that cockroaches and mice were ubiquitous, and to pass the time they constructed traps to catch the mice. One Cuban man who spent five months in detention claimed that in one night he and his friends caught 10 mice in a homemade trap. Many units of the Orleans Parish Prison have no air conditioning; the jail relies on two old fans that are insufficient to cool the humid Louisiana summer air. "Even in your underwear you sweat. You can't sleep at night," said one detainee (Human Rights Watch 1998a: 56). A common complaint among detainees held at various jails around the country is that they are seldom or never allowed outdoor recreation time or that recreation often depends on the whims of the correctional officers on duty on any particular day. "We never get to go outside. There is a weight room, but you have to sign up and share it with other, criminal inmates" noted a Vietnamese detainee confined in the Dallas County Jail. At Clark/Frederick/Winchester Adult Detention Center in Virginia, jail officials explained that their policy restricts inmates from outdoor exercise when the temperature is lower than 55 degrees, because the jail did not want to have to provide outerwear (Human Rights Watch 1998a: 59).

Language Barriers

When detainees from the far reaches of the globe, such as Pakistan, China, Ecuador, or Afghanistan, find themselves in local jails around the United States, communication between jail officers and detainees is often impossible. Indeed, many jails holding INS detainees are located in rural parts of the country where staff may rarely have encountered non-English speaking people before the INS began paying them to hold its detainees (Human Rights Watch 1998a: 63). Language barriers make everything from receiving medical attention to understanding jail rules extremely difficult. Without proper translation, detainees cannot understand legal services lists, call attorneys, or make requests or file grievances, all of which contribute to their isolation. In one particular case, a Sri Lankan asylum seeker who does not speak English was held at the

Orleans Parish Prison for more than three years. For a while, another Tamil speaking detainee translated for him, but once the other detainee was deported, he had no way of communicating with jail staff or other detainees (Human Rights Watch 1998a: 64).

Inadequate Medical Care

In doing business with local jails, the INS requires only that they provide 24-hour emergency care for detainees. In fact, those jails are not required to have a doctor, nurse, or medical unit on staff, nor are they required to conduct an initial health screening, even for infectious diseases. Due to the absence of guidelines, a host of problems persist, including lack of prompt treatment, inadequate diagnosis, and inappropriate treatment (Florida Immigrant Advocacy Center 1997; Human Rights Watch 1998a: 67). Although Principle 24 of the UN Body of Principles provides that "[medical] care and treatment shall be provided free of charge," many INS detainees in local jails are required to pay a fee for each visit to the doctor to reduce frivolous visits (Human Rights Watch 1998a: 68). Local jails also subject INS detainees to serious health risks. In the Orleans Parish Prison, a Vietnamese detainee held for 28 months expressed fear and concern over the treatment he was receiving:

> I myself have full-blown AIDS, my "T" cell count is way below 200, I fear for my life daily due to insufficient medical care and a diet negligent of the basic vitamins and minerals needed to stabilize my health and condition. . . . [The medical tier] is a very cramped, unhealthy place. This place is designed to hold twenty-one patients, but on any given occasion there are thirty to thirty-five patients sleeping on the floor! (Human Rights Watch 1998a: 68)

In another case, a Honduran detainee held at DuPage County Jail in Illinois was discovered to have active tuberculosis. The jail notified the INS that it did not have proper facilities to keep someone with this disease and recommended that the INS transfer him to another facility. Because the INS could not locate another facility that would take custody, the infected detainee was simply released. Remarkably, the INS dropped the detainee off at a local homeless shelter without any medicine and without notifying public health officials. The INS also never notified the detainee's attorney of his client's release, "instead allowing the young man with an active infectious disease to wander off with no resources" (Human Rights Watch 1998a: 69). Although the warden at DuPage County Jail later said, "the Health Department finally tracked him down at a local hospital," his lawyer, who has not heard from his client again, wonders: "For all I know, he could be dead" (Human Rights Watch 1998a: 69).

Inadequate Mental Heath Services

Given the stress of the immigration review process, compounded by deplorable jail conditions and protracted periods of confinement, INS detainees endure excruciating psychological and emotional strain, often manifesting as deep depression and even suicide attempts. Especially for asylum seekers who have experienced past persecution or torture, long-term detention can be particularly debilitating:

> For asylum seekers in local jails, waiting in detention can be psychologically devastating. Post traumatic stress disorders, lack of language skills, ignorance of legal rights, lack of access to lawyers, fear of government authorities, and a criminal environment where they may be housed with convicted criminals all combine to exact special suffering on asylum seekers. While in detention there is little to do but sit and worry if you will ever get out of jail or if you will be deported back to a situation you fear. (Human Rights Watch 1998a: 87)

Article 22(1) of the UN Standard Minimum Rules states that at every institution at least one medical officer should be knowledgeable of basic psychiatric protocol. Moreover, Article 25(2) requires the medical officer to "report to the director whenever he considers that a prisoner's physical or mental health has been or will be injuriously affected by continued imprisonment or by any condition of imprisonment." To the dismay of human rights advocates, the INS does not require local jails to adhere to international standards regarding the mental health of its detainees, not even for asylum seekers who have been victims of persecution (Human Rights Watch 1998a: 70).

Human Rights Watch has chronicled the anguish that harsh confinement has had on INS detainees. Guy Mbenga-Mondundou, an asylum seeker from the former Zaire, held in the Berks County Jail (Pennsylvania), said that he attempted suicide by hanging himself after he learned that his wife had miscarried while he was detained. In a letter to Human Rights Watch, Chen Sie En, a detainee at the Orleans Parish Jail, wrote, "I have become depressed. I can't stand it any more. I don't care if I am sent back to China or released on bail. I just have to get out." An Indian asylum seeker at Krome Service Processing Center (Florida), who had been detained more than two years at the time of the interview, pleaded desperately: "I want deportation. No more jail—if I die, then I die. Fine" (Human Rights Watch 1998a: 71).

Finding that stark conditions were causing detainees to become suicidal, federal public defenders asked a judge to move or release all long-
term detainees from the new regional jail in The Dalles (Oregon). The
jail does not allow televisions or newspapers. There is no commissary
and no bilingual officers. For most INS detainees, there is no work and
very little recreation. Detainees are kept indoors 23 hours a day. "It's a
no-frills jail," said Captain Larry Lindhorst. "I wouldn't say jail is an en-
joyable stay; I wouldn't want to be here either. But we try to make them
comfortable when they're here, and we're still just getting going" (Sullivan 2000a: EV8). The INS defended the jail, which passed all state and
INS inspections. But after the federal public defender in Portland complained in court, the INS immediately moved almost all long-term detainees to INS detention in Seattle (Sullivan 2000a: EV8; see Welch and
Gunther 1997a, 1997b).[5]

Brutality against Detainees

Criticism over the warehousing of INS detainees has sharply intensified
as undocumented immigrants and asylum seekers fall victim to physical
or sexual abuse, a problem that is more likely to occur in local jails
(Casimir 2001; Dow 2001a; Sullivan 2000a). Indeed, fear of victimization is pervasive among INS detainees. "Here, our lives are in constant
danger where there is no classification of inmates. I'm mixed with murderers, sexual molesters, armed robbers, and the mentally disturbed,"
said one asylum seeker held in the Ayovelles Parish Prison (Louisiana;
Human Rights Watch 1998a: 51). Still, for the truly unfortunate detainees, their fears are realized. INS detainees at the Pike County Jail (Pennsylvania) have persistently complained of excessive disciplinary sanctions
and physical abuse by guards. Ramón Medina reported being placed in
"the hole" (solitary confinement) after telling correctional officers that
he was going to file a complaint against them. According to Medina, he
was brought to the solitary confinement cell with his hands and feet
handcuffed and was hit and kicked in the head and arms by four correctional officers. Medina said that one of the officers, Brian Bain, took
off his uniform and yelled at Medina, "We can do this as men," before
proceeding to beat him with the three other officers present. "I was hit
in the eye and head and am in a lot of pain. I can't sleep at night. I also
have a bone sticking out of my left hand"(Human Rights Watch 1998a:
83). While in "the hole," Medina was kept naked without a mattress, using toilet paper to keep warm. Medina issued a complaint against Offi-

cer Bain, who was subsequently dismissed from the jail. A Pike County Jail official explained that Officer Bain was dismissed due to "burnout"; previously, jail administration officials twice ordered him to undergo counseling (Human Rights Watch 1998a: 83).

At the Tensas Parish Detention Center (Louisiana) in 1996, an argument broke out involving INS detainees and local inmates. When guards intervened, they ordered Enrique Rodriguez and five other Cuban detainees to strip naked; one at a time, the men were beaten with a pipe covered with tape. "I heard the metal pipe drop and I thought, my god, they're going to kill me," said Rodriguez (Human Rights Watch 1998a: 93). Rodriguez reported that three correctional officers, one of whom he identified as Captain Benjamin Britton, beat him in front of the jail's warden, injuring his head and hand:

> I was crouching down to block my head. Another guy had his thumb broken. The beating lasted three or four minutes. Afterwards, they put all of us and one American in lockdown while we were still naked. The isolation room they put us in had two beds for six people, and for the first twenty-four hours we had no blanket or mattress. No medical attention was given to any of us, and it was not until seven days later that they brought us to medical services because there were no marks or bruises that looked so bad at that time. (Human Rights Watch 1998a: 84)

In 1998, three Tensas Parish deputies who were implicated in the 1996 incident pleaded guilty to two counts of civil rights violations of county inmates. One of the three who entered a guilty plea was Deputy Benjamin Britton, whom Rodriguez identified as having beaten him. Sheriff Jeff Britt was also indicted on separate charges of beating a local inmate with a blackjack (a leather-covered bludgeon) and lying to the FBI. Britt's trial ended in a hung jury ("Tensas Sheriff Indicted" 1998; "Sheriff's Beating Case" 1998).

Whereas many of the jails contracted by the INS have histories of violence, human rights advocates insist that one of the most notorious institutions is the Orleans Parish Prison in New Orleans, where beatings by guards are commonplace (Hedges 2001b; Human Rights Watch 1998a). Shi Cheng Qin said that in 1999 he was beaten for more than 20 minutes by five guards who stopped only when Qin began coughing blood. Qin said that during the beating he threatened to call a lawyer or the FBI. A guard then responded: "How are you going to contact them if you are in segregation without a phone, envelope, writing pad or writing pen?" (Hedges 2001b: EV1). Other detainees have complained of brutality, and in 1999 a lawsuit filed by 13 Asian detainees against the facility documented a pattern of abuse, including gladiator contests in which INS detainees were pitted against county inmates. Several Asian detainees said the inmates beat them until they were bloody. In a deposition, Tin Huu Pham, a detainee, gave an account of the beating of Chau Van Cong: "I saw Mr. Van Cong was unconscious on the ground. He got blood where his mouth and nose at, and the rest of the Asians, they just sit down. And it was a horrible sight. And I was weak, real weak. And Sergeant Verrett asked me to slip Mr. Van over on his side so he wouldn't choke on his own blood, but I was so weak, I was bleeding myself, and I couldn't do it" (Hedges 2001b: EV2). In 2000, after the case was tried but before the judge rendered a decision, the Orleans Parish Criminal Sheriff's Office settled the lawsuit, agreeing to pay an undisclosed amount to the 13 detainees, who were later released under what Russell Bergeron, director of media relations for the INS, said were "routine release procedures" (Hedges 2001b: EV2).

Similar problems persist in detention centers operated by the INS. Among its most troubled facilities is the Krome Detention Center in Miami, whose notorious reputation gained national attention beginning in the early 1990s when three educational specialists were dismissed after reporting incidents of physical and sexual abuse (LeMoyne 1990). During that controversy, INS officials at Krome denied allegations of violence and human rights abuses. Constance K. Weiss, an INS administrator at Krome, begged the question, "Why would we want to run a place where we beat the hell out of people?" To that question, refugee advocates replied in a two-part answer: "To discourage other potential refugees and because it is easy to get away with. Detained immigrants are a powerless group . . . without recourse to normal political or legal channels" (Rohter 1992: E18; also see DePalma 1992).

Despite national headlines, an FBI investigation, and several lawsuits against staff members, human rights advocates were astonished to find that 10 years later abuse against INS detainees continues (Human Rights Watch 1998a; see Dow 1998). Having learned that some of the INS officers implicated in abuse incidents in 2000 also were identified in her report 10 years earlier, Cheryl Little, executive director of the Florida Immigrant Advocacy Center, said, "We feel so helpless. How can this be happening in the United States of America?" (Sullivan 2000a: EV10). In 2000, 90 female detainees held at Krome were transferred to a county-operated jail—a move intended to protect them—as federal agents continued their investigation of sexual abuse at the facility (Chardy 2000a). Authorities had already charged Lemar Smith, a corrections officer, with sexually assaulting a male-to-female transsexual detainee. The victim, an asylum seeker from Mexico, said she was raped in an isolation cell a second time after she reported the initial assault to three INS supervisors. Since then, at least a dozen detention officers have been removed from duty at Krome or reassigned to jobs amid a widening sex and bribery scandal (Sullivan 2000a). Indeed, the problems at Krome highlight the fact that the INS struggles to protect its detainees not just at local jails, but also at the facilities it operates directly or through contracts with private corporations.

Human rights advocates applauded the move to protect the women, but also expressed concern about moving the detainees to a county jail. Attorneys for the detainees recommended that the women be released into the community or supervised at shelters. However, Robert A. Wallis, the INS District Director, insisted that the agency would transfer the women "to a full service, state of the art facility that would ensure those detainees the most safe, secure and humane detention conditions possible"(Tulsky 2000c: EV2). Cheryl Little expressed concern over the transfer: "No question about it: It's a jail. It would be highly inappropriate to move the women to local county jails. None of the women at Krome are serving criminal sentences" (Chardy 2000a: EV2). Wendy Young of the Women's Commission for Refugee Women and Children, which issued a blistering report on the conditions facing women at the INS detention center, added, "County prisons and hotels are not acceptable alternatives to Krome. Conditions are harsh and very punitive. INS detainees are second-class citizens at county jails because they don't get their constitutional rights like the other inmates" (Chardy 2000a: EV3; Women's Commission for Refugee Women and Children 1998a, 2000). Acknowledging the ironies of immigration control inherent in INS detention policy, Young remarked, "Where else in the United States do you jail the people who were sexually abused rather than the people who committed the abuse" (Tulsky 2000c: EV1). Cheryl Little agreed: "Clearly, we didn't want females at Krome exposed to abusive officers. But in trying to solve one problem, they created another. They are, in some ways, punishing the victims" (Tulsy 2000c: EV2).

Tragically, the INS plan to protect the detainees by transferring them to a county jail failed. Two days after being admitted to the Miami–Dade County Jail, a number of the women allegedly were "flashed" by a male inmate, and in a separate incident that same day, another female inmate was allegedly the victim of a sexual attack by a male prisoner, which triggered an internal investigation at the facility. Critics of INS detention practices were infuriated, noting that the women were supposed to be segregated from male inmates and supervised only by female officers. "The irony is not lost on these women. The women were supposedly transferred for their own protection, and they're telling me they're every bit as vulnerable as they were at Krome. The women are being unduly punished and victimized," said Cheryl Little (Chardy 2000b; Ross 2001: EV1; for other recent incidents of sexual assault on INS detainees see Egelko 2000; Grossman 2000; Human Rights Watch 1998a; Women's Commission for Refugee Women and Children 1998a, 2000).

Conclusion

Since the passage of the reformed immigration laws in 1996, the INS has stepped up its reliance on detention, but due to limited capacity at their own processing centers, the agency has had to send its detainees to county jails, federal prisons, and private lockups. There, INS detainees typically are subjected to protracted periods of confinement along with harsh institutional conditions. To make matters worse is the fact that some of them are beaten or sexually abused. Human rights groups have harshly criticized the INS for it inattention to the care of people it detains. Allyson Collins of Human Rights Watch describes INS detention as "cold storage. . . . They treat people as things they have to store rather than treating them as people" (Christensen et al. 2000: EV1). In many instances basic human dignity eludes the INS and the correctional facilities with whom it does business. At the Liberty County Jail (Texas), a female detainee complained: "The jail took away my shoes because they were a different color. I walk around barefoot. The jail does not give us underwear or a bra—even when we have our period. I just have to sit around when I am using a maxi pad" (Human Rights Watch 1998a: 60).

For years, the INS has not always done its best to release undocumented immigrants and asylum seekers who even the agency contends do not belong in detention. "To its credit, the INS recognized eight years ago the need to develop a program to parole asylum-seekers out of detention. To its great discredit, the INS still has not fully implemented the resulting program. This failure of implementation is a result of pervasive lack of accountability and responsibility" (Lawyers

Committee for Human Rights 1998b: 11). Recently, 13 federal courts around the country have chastised the INS for not exercising its discretion for parole detainees. When federal judges appointed federal public defenders in the Northwest district to represent people who could be released because they posed no flight risk or threat, more than 80 percent of those eligible were set free, including asylum seekers who had no criminal history yet had been held for years. "The process was not working fairly at all. They were slow, incredibly rigid and harsh," said Federal Public Defender Steven Wax (Sullivan 2000a: EV4). Jay Stansell, also a federal public defender, noted that such problems stem from a system that is immune from the courts: "That's the danger you get when you put an agency charged with locking people up, without a judge or jury involved, also in charge of deciding when the person is going to get out" (Sullivan 2000a: EV4). Still, INS officials counter that their agency will be blamed as soon as someone who is released offends again. "You're damned if you do and damned if you don't," said Charles DeMore, INS district director in San Francisco (Sullivan 2000a: EV4; also see Acer and Guerrero 2001; Lawyers Committee for Human Rights 1998b).

Recognizing the need to reform the INS, Commissioner Doris Meissner, as one of her final acts before resigning in 2000, ordered agency officials to exercise more discretion in the use of detention (and removal), and, equally important, she introduced new standards for confinement. Meissner seemed genuinely interested in softening the impact of the 1996 immigration laws. Under new detention standards that are being phased in at local jails, the rights of INS detainees (e.g., access to counsel and the courts as well as ending the practice of strip searches before and after visits from attorneys) are emphasized along with improved institutional services (e.g., food, health care, access to telephones; INS 2000b). Whereas the new guidelines and standards suggest a change of heart toward INS detainees, human rights experts are skeptical. As far as its overall policy is concerned, the INS new guidelines have skirted the enduring controversy over the law's court-stripping provisions since the INS does not relinquish its prosecutorial discretion, allowing the agency to enforce the law as it sees fit (Schiller 2001).

Also in light of persistent institutional problems, immigration attorneys have their doubts about meaningful reform. According to immigration specialist Ira Kurzban, "That sounds like a Band-Aid approach to a bigger problem: the ability of the INS to detain people for substantial periods of time. The INS doesn't have the resources or the ability to provide long-term detention, and consequentially they do a poor job of it. That often leads to the mental and physical abuse of detainees" (Martinez 2001: EV2). Penny Venetis, associate director of the Rutgers Constitutional Litigation Clinic, added, "A big problem is with the whole set up, and they didn't address it. They should not be sending people [INS detainees] to local and county jails" (Burke 2001: EV2). Immigrants' rights advocates also say that the new guidelines have "no teeth" and point out that the INS and local jails face no penalties for ignoring the standards (Amon 2000b). Revealingly, the INS requested from Congress funds that would employ 80 officers charged with monitoring the more than 1,000 jails under contract. Lawmakers, however, approved only enough to hire 10, thus substantially limiting the degree of scrutiny ("INS Standards Need Teeth" 2001). Already administrators at county jails that house INS detainees have balked at the new standards. Captain William Mullanaphy of the Passaic County (New Jersey) Sheriff's Department noted, "When they're in our facility, they have to operate under our rules and regulations" (Burke 2001: EV1).

All things considered, it is important to recognize the slippery slope facing INS detainees. Simply put, reformers could win the battle and lose the war. ACLU attorney Judy Rabinovitz explains: "We could lose by winning. They [INS] could build a giant facility that's clean and has a fully stocked library and plenty of outdoor recreation—[for instance] in Oakdale, Louisiana where detainees are out of the public eye, and away from family and attorneys. The goal is not to have beautiful, wonderful detention centers, but to make detention at most a last resort" (Solomon 1995: 30; see Kerwin 1997, 2000).

7

Neglecting Unaccompanied Children

I think of [the staging area] as being a kind of warehouse. We have shipping and receiving. Only it's human beings in the warehouse.

Narcisco Leggs, the Los Angeles juvenile coordinator and the official in charge of the B-18 staging area

He would beg me, "Please figure out a way to get me out of here."

A relative of 15-year-old Angel Avila, who was held for three months in the Los Angeles Central Juvenile Detention Center

The INS thus remains free to violate children's rights in flagrant disregard of U.S. laws and international human rights standards.

Human Rights Watch

At the age of 15, Angel Avila, who was abandoned as a baby, embarked on a lonely and treacherous journey from Honduras to Mexico's border with the United States, struggling to find food and sleeping along roadsides. After swimming across the Rio Grande River to enter the United States, Angel hitchhiked to New York City in search of relatives and better life. Despite his optimism, however, Angel endured more hardship. He was arrested for shoplifting, and although a city family court judge dismissed the charge, the INS took him into custody to be deported. In 2000, after four months in a New York children's home, Angel was abruptly transferred to the notorious Los Angeles Central Juvenile Detention Center, where he scuffled with gangs, was pepper-sprayed by staff, and forced to spend days in solitary confinement. Angel realized his New York relatives, immigrants themselves, could not afford a lawyer or even airfare to visit him, deepening his sense of isolation. Immigrants' rights advocates vowed to fight for Angel's release and residency, but he elected to return to Honduras because throughout the lengthy hearing process he would still remain a prisoner at the Los Angeles juvenile jail (Montero 2001; Sullivan 2000b).

Tragically, for many unaccompanied immigrant children, Angel's painful experiences in INS detention are all too common. Unlike Elian Gonzalez, who was rescued at sea after a botched boat escape from Cuba that claimed his mother in 2000, most unaccompanied children in the INS are not showered with toys and trips to Disney World. And, while the news crews covered Elian's every move, much of the mainstream media has consistently ignored the plight of children held in INS detention (Becker 2000). Michael Bochener, a lawyer with the Human Rights Watch, said, "Too many kids across the country are being locked up for too long, and what's more, they're being held in restrictive, jail-like settings" (Montero 2001: EV2). In 2000, the INS apprehended 4,600 undocumented youths, many of whom had been separated from their parents during the dangerous border crossings or arrived at U.S. airports seeking asylum after fleeing persecution in their homeland. On average, the INS has 500 youths in its custody each day, but due to limited detention space, the agency ships many of them to juvenile centers and in some instances to adult jails.[1] The fact that those youth are subjected to a criminalization process inherent in INS detention has not escaped human rights groups. "INS policy is caught up in the criminalization of anything associated with arriving in the U.S. without proper papers," said Alicia Triche of the Los Angeles CLINIC (Montero 2001: EV2). Moreover, the criminalization of undocumented children is met with detention practices amounting to little more than warehousing.

To the dismay of human rights advocates, the detention of immigrant children stems from a criminal justice agenda guiding immigration policy; further, such practices reflect prevailing trends in the contemporary juvenile justice system in which authorities have resorted to greater reliance on incarceration rather than enlightened alternatives (Welch 1999b). In this chapter, various facets of INS detention and its impact on children are explored, including another glimpse at the conflict caused by the INS's commitment to law enforcement over service, court-ordered reform for the INS, and the enduring institutional problems of the INS. While addressing bureaucratic ignorance and resistance, controversies over the conditions of confinement in facilities located in Los Angeles, Arizona, and Pennsylvania are examined in depth. Because INS detention policies and practices ought not be viewed apart from existing international standards on the treatment of children, the discussion begins with an overview of human rights concerns.

Children in INS Detention: A Human Rights Perspective

Many children in INS custody entered the United States to escape extreme poverty, natural disasters, civil war, or human rights atrocities in their homeland. Indeed, child refugees are no longer mere bystanders in adult conflicts. In China, Kosovo, Sierra Leone, and other countries around the world, children are the deliberate targets of human rights abuses, including infanticide, conscription as a child soldier, bonded labor, and sexual servitude (see Drinan 2001). As civil war ripped through Sudan in the late 1980s, thousands of so-called lost boys were driven from their homes and out of the country. Many of those boys who were five years old at the time had witnessed their parents being killed. While girls were taken in by other families or forced into marriage, the boys embarked on a momentous exodus, walking for weeks and covering thousands of miles. Many boys did not survive; some drowned in rivers while others were attacked by animals or succumbed to starvation. The lucky ones reached Ethiopia, but then their fate changed once again as authorities there forced them out in 1991. Along with streams of other refugees, the boys journeyed to a camp in neighboring Kenya, eventually capturing the attention of human rights organizations. In 2000, 50 of the Sudanese boys arrived in New York and in 2001 an additional 350 resettled in the United States under the auspices of the UNHCR and a State Department-brokered program. That year organizers from 10 charitable agencies resettled 3,600 boys, relying on foster homes located throughout the nation (Corbett 2001; Moore 2000).[2]

In Central America, where governments provide few social services, discarded youths fear "social cleansing," a term used to describe death squad tactics employed by police and vigilante groups. In Honduras alone, more than 340 homeless children have been killed since 1998

(Bucio 2001; Sanchez 2001). Consider the case of 16-year-old Santos Ramon Zepeda Campos, a homeless shoeshine boy who was beaten numerous times by police in Nicaragua, once so severely that he was hospitalized for two weeks. To protect himself, Santos slept in trees; still, he feared for his life. Acting on a strong sense of survival, Santos escaped the brutal streets of his homeland by walking to the United States. After a 13-month journey, Santos reached Arizona, where the INS apprehended him. Fortunately, INS inspectors found his story credible, concluding that Santos risked further persecution should he be returned to Chinandega. Santos was granted asylum in the United States in 2000 (Bucio 2001: EV1).

Particularly in developing nations, many parents struggle to safeguard their children, but others are complicit in that persecution. For example, female genital mutilation generally is conducted at the behest of a young girl's parents. And according to the Lawyers Committee for Human Rights, "In a number of traditional societies, girls are targeted as the victims of honor killings for opposing their subjugation to demeaning social roles. One of our clients was held captive in her father's home and regularly beaten for resisting his authority to marry her off against her will" (2000a: 3). Without question, unaccompanied children who must make their way to safety without the assistance of their parents are particularly vulnerable. In recognizing those uniquely difficult circumstances, the international community on numerous occasions has declared that child refugees deserve special consideration:

> Along with the 1959 *UN Declaration on the Rights of the Child*, the *UN Convention on the Rights of the Child* calls on all nations to ensure that refugee children are guaranteed protection and affirmative humanitarian assistance under the *Refugee Convention*. Although the United States has not yet ratified this *Convention*, it certainly has endorsed the *Convention*'s approach to refugee children through its accession to the *Declaration on the Rights of the Child*. In any event, given the near universal acceptance by States of the Convention, these norms arguably have achieved the status of customary international law. (Lawyers Committee for Human Rights 2000a: EV3)

Despite a global consensus on human rights, the United States continues to neglect the fundamental rights afforded child refugees. Jacqueline Bhabha, director of the Human Rights Program at the University of Chicago, reminds us that the United States has isolated itself from international practices prohibiting the detention of child refugees: "No other country in all the Western countries that receive unaccompanied minors does this" (Sullivan 2000b: EV2; see Women's Commission for Refugee Women and Children 1998b; Young 1998). Experts agree that it is especially traumatic for children fleeing persecution and requesting asylum in the United States to be placed in INS detention. Human rights organizations have harshly criticized the INS for its detention practices involving children, citing violations of international law, the U.S. Constitution, and numerous statutory provisions, regulations, and court orders (Human Rights Watch 1997; also see Amnesty International 1997). According to international law, children should be detained only as a last resort; furthermore, such detention must not be under prison-like conditions so as to preserve the "best interests of the child" (*United Nations Convention on the Rights of the Child* 1989, Art. 3; UNHCR 1995, 1996).

Until recently, the INS did not have an established set of guidelines for detaining children. Typically such matters were left to the discretion of local INS administrators or municipal, county, and state law enforcement authorities. As a result, strategies for dealing with unaccompanied children have been varied and inconsistent. While some children are placed in foster family settings, others are sent to county juvenile correctional facilities (prisons for criminal minors) or, even worse, in county jails with adult inmates. The absence of guidelines also produces little or no accurate data about the number and status of children detained by the INS system; likewise, there is not much reliable information about the conditions or length of confinement. Therefore, "it is impossible to determine what happens to these children while in the hands of the INS" (Human Rights Watch 1997: 41; also see Amnesty International 1997; Gamboa 2000).[3]

Dual Mandate and Conflict of Interest

As discussed in previous chapters, the INS is a unique agency operating according to a dual mandate comprising law enforcement and service. Given the criminal justice agenda driving U.S. immigration policies, however, service often takes a backseat to enforcement. Quite often the INS loses sight of its role as a service provider, instead structuring its professional identity around law enforcement. In the frank words of David Tally, of the INS Western Region counsel's office, "We're here to deport people, if they're deportable" (Human Rights Watch 1997: 41). Terminology prevalent within the INS reveals the agency's law enforcement culture. When interviewing INS officials about policies and practices, human rights groups are distressed by the frequent use of the term "prisoner" to refer to administrative detainees, including asylum seekers and even child refugees. Adding to the controversy over detaining children, in some cases the INS separates children from their parents: Recently, an 8-year-old Czech girl was taken from her mother, who was trying to enter the United States with fraudulent papers. The girl was held for two days at Los Padrinos while her mother was held in another INS facility (Sullivan 2000b). Human rights investigators also found that few INS officials questioned the practice of keeping unaccompanied minors in prison-like conditions, prompting advocates to stress once again the importance of safeguarding children in government custody:

> More than any other group of aliens, unaccompanied children suffer as a result of this attitude, for it creates a grave conflict of interest for the INS. Unlike adults, unaccompanied children cannot simply be left to fend for themselves while their immigration status is being adjudicated. Both United States law and international standards reflect an awareness that children require special protection and care. (Human Rights Watch 1997: 42)

In addition to requiring medical care, counseling, and education, children in INS custody need legal representation. Their young age, the complexity of immigration proceedings, and lack of English skills make it exceedingly difficult for them to obtain a fair hearing without the assistance of a lawyer. According to human rights organizations, rather than being held in INS detention, those children ought to be placed in the care of agencies capable of protecting the their rights and interests (Amnesty International 1997; Human Rights Watch 1997: 42). Indeed, detention perpetuates the criminalization process whereby children in INS custody are subjected to treatment commonly reserved for those charged with criminal offenses. In 2000, a 15-year-old Central American girl was apprehended by the INS at the Los Angeles airport. The girl was fleeing her abusive father, who she says raped and beat her. Although her mother and stepfather were living in Los Angeles and willing to care for her, the INS booked her into Los Padrinos, a juvenile jail where she was detained for six weeks (Sullivan 2000b). Inside such facilities, child detainees are required to wear jail uniforms and usually spend long periods of time in locked cells; compounding their frustration, visits and telephones calls are closely monitored by jail staff. Some of the more unfortunate children are housed with criminal offenders, subjected to body searches, and disciplined with pepper spray. However, unlike those charged with crimes, INS detainees are not furnished lawyers at government expense, and because they are too poor to hire an attorney, few enjoy the privilege of legal counsel (Lawyers Committee for Human Rights 2000b; Sullivan 2000b).

Court-Ordered Reform

Over the years, there has been considerable legal activity aimed at reforming the INS policies and practices involving the detention of unaccompanied children. In 1985, the detention conditions for children held in the Western District of the INS became so deplorable that attorneys filed a class-action suit against the agency, a case that eventually became known as *Flores* v. *Reno* (1993).[4] *Flores* remains significant because it challenged the region's use of blanket detentions, a practice that failed to release children who could have been cared for in the community; equally important, it brought judicial scrutiny of the prison-like conditions in which children were detained. The suit proved effective to the extent that two major changes were instituted. First, the INS developed a national policy for the detention and release of unaccompanied children, allowing many youths to be released to a parent, legal guardian, close adult relative, or an unrelated adult designated by the minor's parents. Second, *Flores* contributed to an agreement governing the conditions of confinement, a settlement that stemmed from a 1987 consent decree obliging the INS to place detained minors in nonsecure shelter care settings rather than in juvenile prisons. Under the terms of the consent decree, the INS is not permitted to hold children in county detention facilities for more than 72 hours, except in emergencies. Additionally, the consent decree included a set of requirements for detention facilities (known as the "*Flores* requirements"). Although the consent decree applied specifically to the Western District of the INS, the agency adopted most of the *Flores* requirements as its national policy (Human Rights Watch 1997).

To satisfy the *Flores* requirements contained in the Alien Minors Shelter Care Program, the INS contracted with private and nonprofit organizations to provide shelter care facilities for detained minors, a move intended to reduce drastically the agency's reliance on correctional facilities. The program proposed to deliver services to unaccompanied children in a manner sensitive to culture, native language, and the complex needs of those youth. Much like international standards and U.S. statutes governing the treatment of minors, the program reflects an awareness of the vulnerability of unaccompanied children in INS custody. According to the *Flores* requirements, the facilities under contract with the INS must provide those children with "an integrated and structured daily routine which shall include, but not be limited to: education, recreation, vocational experience or chores, study period, counseling, group interaction, free time and access to legal or religious services" (Alien Minors Shelter Care Program 1987: 6). The regulations also require the following:

- "Program rules and disciplinary procedures must be written and translated into a language understood by the minor. These rules must be provided to each minor and fully understood by each minor."
- "Each minor is to enjoy a reasonable right to privacy."
- Facility staff must provide minors with "information regarding the availability of free legal assistance . . . the right to be represented by counsel at no expense to the government[,] . . . the right to a deportation or exclusion hearing before an immigration judge . . . [and] that they may apply for political asylum or request voluntary departure in lieu of deportation."
- Facility staff must ensure that minors have the opportunity to go on frequent field trips: "All minors shall be afforded opportunities for escorted visits to the surrounding communities for leisure activities at least twice each week." Staff must also respect the religious needs of minors: "Whenever possible, minors are to be afforded access to religious services of their choice." (Alien Minors Shelter Care Program 1987: 9–11, 18–24)

Years after the *Flores* requirements in conjunction with Alien Minors Shelter Care Program had been instituted, however, human rights organizations have complained that the INS frequently has failed to comply with the consent decree. In particular, Human Rights Watch conducted an investigation that "revealed consistent and widespread violations of all of these regulations" (1997: 16; also see Amnesty International 1997; Lawyers Committee for Human Rights 2000b).

The Persistence of Institutional Problems

Despite long-term efforts to reform the system, Human Rights Watch found that "children in INS detention are invisible: they have slipped through the cracks in America's legal system" (1997: 2). Regrettably, the

INS has failed to articulate a policy for determining whether a minor requires detention in a secured facility; as a result, the INS continues to place many unaccompanied children in highly restrictive settings, a significant breach of the *Flores* requirements. Much like adults in INS custody, children also are subjected to the Kafkaesque experience of detention. Rarely are the children furnished with adequate information about their legal rights in a language they comprehend. Many of them are frequently transferred from one facility to another, a clear violation of the UNHCR rule that states, "In order to ensure continuity of care and bearing in mind the best interests of the child, changes in residence for unaccompanied children should be limited to a minimum" (UNHCR 1996, Section 7.2). Such transfers usually occur without advance warning to their relatives and attorneys, and much like their adult counterparts, children quite often get lost in the system. In the words of immigration lawyer Judy London of the Central American Resource Center (CARECEN):

> Usually I get a panicky call, not from the kids, but from a relative, saying, "My kid is held somewhere in L.A." So I make twenty calls over two days. Eventually I figure out where the kid is, if I have the name, but it's hard. And if you just want to find out, in general, how many kids are where, it's impossible. We're filing a class action suit about detention conditions, and [the INS] is now under court order to reveal names and locations of class members. We'll see if they do it. Usually the problem is, you never get this information, you just can't get anyone to tell you where the kids are. (Human Rights Watch 1997: 23)

Even worse, the immigration attorneys accuse the INS of using frequent transfers as retaliation against those who make complaints regarding institutional conditions. Carlos Holguin, a lawyer with the Center for Human and Constitutional Rights, said, "You start kicking up a fuss about conditions for kids in one spot, the INS just moves them to another. You complain about [Los Padrinos] and they move the kids to Arizona. You complain about Arizona and they transfer them to Texas" (Human Rights Watch 1997: 23). Most children in INS custody, however, do not have legal representation, and with only limited access to telephones it is difficult for them to maintain ties with relatives and human rights advocates who could marshal support for them (see "Access Denied" 2001). Because unaccompanied children are not eligible for release after posting bond (as is the case with adults in INS custody), many remain in detention for months on end, isolated, bewildered and frightened.

Detained in the City of Angels

Whereas the conditions of confinement for children in INS custody vary, overall they are so poor that they violate international law, the U.S. Constitution, U.S. statutory provisions, INS regulations, and the terms of court orders. Immediately following the *Flores* settlement, conditions at the Los Angeles facilities improved for a time but have since deteriorated. Some children are still being sent to county jails, where they are detained along with convicted juvenile offenders. Even worse, some children are illegally housed with a general jail population that includes adult offenders. When detention space in county facilities is unavailable, occasionally children sleep for several nights in offices in the federal building (Human Rights Watch 1997: 35).[5]

Given the high security of the Los Angeles facilities, all of which are surrounded by barbed wire, children in INS custody essentially are confined to institutions that resemble prisons rather than holding centers. They are required to wear institutional uniforms and not permitted to keep their personal belongings. Sharon Lowe, a member of the Los Angeles County Probation Board, points out that those children are supposed to be detained: "But basically they are incarcerated. The INS doesn't call it that, but that's what it is" (Human Rights Watch 1997: 33). Although the UN Rules for the Protection of Juveniles Deprived of Their Liberty prohibit the use of solitary confinement for child detainees, the facility at Los Padrinos often punishes children who have violated institutional rules by placing them in "the box," a windowless isolation chamber containing a metal cot, a sink, and a toilet.

Since most children in INS custody do not speak English, their detention is marked by even greater confusion and isolation. Whereas children from Latin America usually find staff members who speak Spanish, those from other regions of the world rarely encounter anyone who speaks their language. According to Gilbert Fung, an immigration lawyer who represents Chinese children,

> Chinese kids get herded around like sheep. Staff can't communicate with them, so they basically just push and pull the kids to get them to go somewhere. The education is meaningless for these children—they just sit and listen, but have no idea what's going on. Even the food is a problem—they don't know what American food is. They're used to rice and noodles, and they are given food that's too salty, too rich. . . . Most get sick in their first week in detention, but they don't know how to ask for doctors. (Gilbert Fung quoted in Human Rights Watch 1997: 34)

Advocates also are disconcerted by the absence of mental health professionals needed to offer counseling and support. Lorena Muñoz, a legal aid lawyer, told Human Rights Watch about one of her clients: "I had a Pakistani kid who spoke no English, and he was so scared and depressed, he was suicidal. We got an interpreter and we had him observed, and the psychologist said yes, he was suicidal. We told the INS, and so they evaluated him—*in English!* And they said he was fine" (Human Rights Watch 1997: 34).

Other forms of neglect abound. The chief source of recreation is watching television—often in a language they do not understand. They rarely receive visitors and leave their living quarters only to go to court hearings, which are demeaning since the children must remain in prison uniforms and regularly are transported in shackles. "Kids get brought in at weird hours, like three in the morning," said Judy London. "It's just whenever the INS feels like transporting them. So they miss breakfast because they're being transported, and they miss lunch because of the hearing" (Human Rights Watch 1997: 35).

Contributing further to their isolation, children struggle to maintain contact with their relatives, a problem compounded by inadequate access to telephones. A 15-year-old girl told human rights investigators, "We get access to a phone sometimes every other day . . . but phone use is withheld as a privilege. I'm not sure if I can receive calls. I want to call my relatives in Acapulco, but I have no money, and they can't take a collect call because there is only a pay phone in the village" (Human Rights Watch 1997: 21). Trying to request permission to use the telephone is difficult enough for those who do not speak English, but for Asians the task is nearly impossible: "Some of these kids have never used a phone before. They come from tiny villages, and they don't even understand what the different numerals represent. Staff won't help, or they can't, because they don't speak the children's dialect" (Gilbert Fung quoted in Human Rights Watch 1997: 21).

Detained in the Desert

Although the Alien Minors Shelter Care Program was intended to provide alternatives to correctional institutions, conditions in some of the new shelter-care facilities are just as harsh as county jails. In Arizona, children are kept in a private secure facility operated by a Texas-based company called Southwest Key, which specializes in running juvenile detention centers.[6] The facility opened in 1996 specifically to meet the

Flores requirements and has space for 48 children;[7] curiously, it does not appear much different from a high security correctional institution. The structure stands surrounded by a tall wire fence, and children are not permitted to leave the grounds. In fact, the children can only leave the locked building while under close supervision, a privilege they enjoy only for one hour a day for supervised physical education. The director of the facility explained that the children's time outdoors is limited because the intense desert heat might be harmful to them; however, that explanation has been contradicted by children, who said that they are sometimes forced to work outside as punishment for rule violations (Human Rights Watch 1997).

Except for court hearings, it is not uncommon for the children to be held for months without a single trip off the premises, a breach of the Alien Minors Shelter Care Program, which states, "All minors shall be afforded opportunities for escorted visits to the surrounding communities for leisure activities at least twice each week" (1987: 22). The staff told Human Rights Watch that children are taken on one field trip every six weeks; while this in itself violates INS regulations, children there reported even less frequent field trips. Moreover, the staff uses field trips as rewards for good behavior, but the children say that even those who abide by the rules are often kept inside the facility for several consecutive months. In the words of detainee Yung Chi, "You're allowed to go on a field trip if you have enough points. Most of us have enough points, but [still are not allowed to go out]" (Human Rights Watch 1997: 36). In further violation of the Alien Minors Shelter Care Program, the facility does not provide access to clergy on site or allow the children to attend services in nearby towns (Human Rights Watch 1997).

The Alien Minors Shelter Care Program also requires that detainees have access to public libraries, but in Arizona the children have never visited a library in the community. And the facility does not have its own library. Villa, a 15-year-old, said, "There are no books or magazines to read. The only reading we do is in class" (Human Rights Watch 1997: 36). Still, many of the reading materials distributed in class are written in English, thus perpetuating the cultural gap between staff and non-English speaking children. Human rights investigators contend that the facility is operated with an astonishing degree of cultural insensitivity. Occasionally, Spanish speaking children, as punishment, are forced to attend class and meals with the Chinese detainees. Li Zhen said staff instructs the Chinese children "to behave like Americans, not like Chinese.

They tell us to act like good Americans, not like bad Chinese" (Human Rights Watch 1997: 37). Although INS policy requires staff to provide students with a written explanation of rules in a language they can understand, many non-English speaking children drift through detention without ever fully understanding the process by which rewards and punishments are distributed. Compounding their frustration, many children were denied privileges they had earned through good behavior.

The children are kept in crowded conditions where they have little personal privacy and few opportunities to use telephones. Shiao-Yun, 17 years old, reported that staff does not let her call her uncle, even though he has repeatedly phoned her. Staff members routinely tell children that if their relatives want to talk to them, "They'll call you, you don't need to call them" (Human Rights Watch 1997: 29). Compared with the children detained in Los Angeles County, those held in Arizona have even less access to attorneys in large part because the facility is located in a remote town between Tucson and Phoenix. The region has few immigration lawyers who represent indigent clients, and due to inflexible and arbitrary rules dictating visitation, local attorneys experience difficulty meeting with their clients; likewise, lawyers have been denied opportunities to make presentations informing children of their legal rights. Not only are the children isolated from attorneys, advocates, and relatives who could offer valuable support, but they also suffer from the lack of personal privacy. Children are herded around in groups and kept under constant supervision, never allowed to be alone in their rooms to read or think. Reacting to the oppressive form of institutional management, one boy said, "Every day is a kind of punishment, to be imprisoned here" (Human Rights Watch 1997: 37).[8]

Detained in Pennsylvania

After Human Rights Watch (1997) issued its report on INS detention in Los Angeles and Arizona, the agency made efforts to improve its policies and practices. Specifically the INS developed an extensive training program for more than 1,500 officers nationwide and increased the number of shelter beds from 130 to 350. Because Human Rights Watch was concerned about other facilities holding children in INS custody, the group expanded its investigation. In 1998, Human Rights Watch conducted a site visit at the Berks County Youth Center (BCYC) in Leesport, Pennsylvania, where the county administers a secure detention facility along with two shelters.[9] Despite improvements in dealing with children in INS detention, Human Rights Watch found that many problems persisted, including its reliance on secure detention centers for juvenile offenders, where more than one-third of children in INS custody are housed (Sullivan 2000b). In those punitive environments, children are detained along with adolescents who have committed violent offenses. At the BCYC, human rights investigators found children in INS custody are held in penitentiary-like conditions:

> For six months, Xiao Ling [15 years old] lived in a small concrete cell, completely bare except for bedding and a Bible in a language she could not read. Locked up in prison-like conditions with juveniles accused of murder, rape, and drug trafficking, Xiao Ling said that she was kept under constant supervision, not allowed to speak her own language, told not to laugh, and even forced to ask permission to scratch her nose. Bewildered, miserable, and unable to communicate with anyone around her, she cried every day. (Human Rights Watch 1998d: 1)

Much like children detained in facilities in Los Angeles and Arizona, those held at the BCYC undergo a criminalization process usually reserved for those charged with criminal offenses, including strip searches and other degrading treatment. When children are transported to court, they are commonly handcuffed from the time they leave the facility until their return, a period lasting more than eight consecutive hours, and often they are forced to skip meals. Ann Carr, an immigration attorney, complained about the practice and described meeting with an 11-year-old client who was "so small, the handcuffs were practically falling off his hands" (Human Rights Watch 1998d: 4). When questioned about the use of handcuffs, the INS insisted that practice was within its rights as a security measure: Under INS enforcement standards, the use of restraints during transportation was at the officers' discretion. However, international guidelines stipulate that handcuffs be used only under exceptional circumstances; furthermore, the practice should not cause humiliation or degradation and should be restricted to the shortest possible period of time (Article 64 of the UN Rules for the Protection of Juveniles, contained in *United Nations Convention on the Rights of the Child* 1989). Until recently, children in INS custody were also transported to court together with adult inmates, in direct violation of the *Flores* agreement (also see Becker 2000; Young 1998).

Inside the BCYC, staff uses restraints and isolation as a last resort for dealing with children exhibiting aggressive behavior. The primary form of discipline is rigorous physical exercise. Children complained that the physical exercise had become excessive and demeaning. One child indicated that even if children were sick or unable to complete the exercise, the staff "would keep on fucking with them until they do it" (Human Rights Watch 1998d: 5). Paul, 16, reported that another detainee had been forced to perform 400 disciplinary pushups during the course of a single day. In another instance, a detainee who suffered from severe asthma was required to run numerous laps until she collapsed, and even then staff continued to harass her. Many times disciplinary action was taken against detainees whose only transgression was their inability to comprehend staff directions. Miguel, a 16-year-old, said, "When you come here, they make you learn English and say everything to you in English. But if you are from El Salvador, and don't speak English, they don't give you time to understand. . . . A lot of times, staff don't give time for translation and make us do pushups" (Human Rights Watch 1998d: 5). The imposition of pushups and other physical exercise as disciplinary measures violates international standards when such punishment compromises the physical or mental health of a child (UN Rules for the Protection of Juveniles, Article 67, contained in *UN Convention on the Rights of the Child* 1989).

Often the children do not receive adequate legal assistance from those who can explain in a language they comprehend the intricacies of the hearing process; consequently, many of them languish in detention for months without a clear understanding of what is happening to them and why.[10] Fernando, a 16-year-old Salvadoran, said, "when I came here, they gave us a paper and told us to read it. They told us about the rules here, and about showers, classes, etc. But no, they didn't give me a list of lawyers, or anything about court or a judge" (Human Rights Watch 1998d: 3). Although the BCYC employs Spanish speaking staff, until recently there were no staff who could communicate with the Chinese speaking children, who represent the majority of those detained at the facility. Language and cultural barriers contribute tremendously to children's fear and confusion over the detention. According to Human Rights Watch, "The intake process for the secure facility can be frightening for any child. However, one can only imagine that being brought in handcuffs and leg irons into a facility surrounded by a fifteen-foot razor-wire fence and then being strip searched without any explanation in a language a child can understand, could be terrifying" (1998d: 4).

The United Nations Convention on the Rights of the Child, the United Nations Rules for the Protection of Juveniles, and the UNHCR have issued declarations providing for education for children in detention to prepare him or her for return to society. While the BCYC offers children several hours of classes per day, non-English speaking children are often simply given books or worksheets to work on individually. Until recently, the BCYC had no English-as-a-second-language program, which severely hampered the ability of children to adapt to their environment or to benefit from other instruction. In one instance, a Chinese youth who had been detained at the facility for more than two years still could not speak English. Investigators found that much of the instruction was compromised by staff language deficiencies. One boy told Human Rights Watch, "We didn't know what she was saying, and she didn't know what we were saying" (1998d: 4).

Like those at other INS detention facilities, children at the BCYC are subject to frequent transfers, often without notice. Not only do such transfers create unnecessary confusion and anxiety for detainees but also for their families and attorneys who are at the mercy of an impersonal bureaucracy when they are trying to locate children. Moreover, transferring children in INS custody without notice to their attorneys violates the agency's regulations, most notably the *Flores* requirements. Similarly, release procedures and family reunification often are delayed without reasonable excuses. For three months, four Pakistani children remained in detention even though each had a close relative in New York with guardianship papers. While the INS waited for the documents to be authenticated, the children were kept in a high security unit, deprived of phone contact and visitation with relatives. Only after their attorney, Ann Carr, protested was contact reestablished.

Use of the high security wing at the BCYC continues to raise concerns from human rights advocates, in particular the enforcement of rigid rules for conduct that among other things prohibits INS detainees from speaking their native language. Like other facilities, investigators found that at BCYC decisions to place children in secured cells often were arbitrary (see Becker 2000; Young 1998). Making matters worse, staff routinely defied international standards and INS regulations that guarantee certain rights for children in confinement, including the right to wear their own clothes and the right to have access to information in their own language, appropriate educational services, and meaningful activities and programs promoting their development and health. Even though international standards and INS regulations prohibit commingling, the BCYC staff not only allows it but also claims that it has a "positive effect on both populations by enabling the INS children to pick up English and giving culturally enriching interactions to the juveniles charged as delinquents" (Human Rights Watch 1996d: 5; see United Nations Convention on the Rights of the Child 1989; UNHCR 1995, 1996; *Flores* v. *Reno*).

Bureaucratic Ignorance and Resistance

Human rights organizations concede that there is much they do not know about how the INS processes and detains unaccompanied children, and perhaps even more bewildering, there is much that the INS does not know either. While Congress continues to invest funds and resources in the INS, the agency struggles to maintain records of its activities, leaving huge gaps of information. The INS does not keep comprehensive statistics on children in its custody, making it difficult to know precisely the number of children who were ultimately deported, successfully filed asylum claims, and who were released to family members living in the United States. Elizabeth Herskovitz, an INS detention and deportation officer in Washington, D.C., noted that the INS does not track dispositions in juvenile cases: "In our statistics, we don't separately track juveniles and adults. It would present tremendous data-gathering problems, and we have never had a reason to keep those statistics. To us, a deportation is a deportation, whether it is an adult or a juvenile" (Human Rights Watch 1997: 90). Without reliable data at its disposal, the INS perpetuates bureaucratic ignorance insofar as its personnel and administrators remain uninformed about some of the agency's operations, a problem that raises grave questions about government accountability.

In its investigation of the INS, Human Rights Watch found astonishing levels of ignorance among top INS officials. In Los Angeles, Rosemary Melville, the INS acting district director, told Human Rights Watch, "We have a very open environment with local attorneys. They're given policy changes and everything, and have lots of access to the kids. . . . We're all concerned with the welfare of the kids. . . . As far as we know, all our facilities are up to the *Flores* standards. . . . Access to phones and representation is no problem for the kids" (Human Rights Watch 1997: 39). However, when asked specifically about INS policies pertaining to children, Melville seemed uninformed of basic legal requirements. Melville did not know the legal procedure governing deportation hearings for children under the age of 16. Melville was "unsure whether or not minors held in Los Angeles County detention centers are always kept separate from convicted offenders, and equally uncertain about whether the INS had any policy about separation from offenders" (1997: 40).[11] Melville also was unaware of the circumstances under which minors might be released to area shelters or to foster families rather than placed in INS detention: "I don't know. Again, I'm not an expert on this" (1997: 40). John Salter, the Los Angeles INS District Counsel, insisted that children could only be released to immediate relatives, "without a directive from Washington. A home-study would be required, and it would be up to Washington" (1997: 40). To the contrary, Human Rights Watch pointed to INS regulations that permit children to be released to shelters, lawyers, or foster families at "the discretion of the District Director"—who was, in this case, Rosemary Melville, who appeared unfamiliar with that particular release option (1997: 40).

Advocacy groups have long been troubled by the extent to which INS officials exhibit bureaucratic ignorance, but just as important they are disheartened by a cavalier attitude toward unaccompanied children. When Human Rights Watch asked Melville whether she would consider planning alternatives to detention (e.g., foster care and release to local shelters), she said that she had "no plans to look into anything like that" (1997: 41).[12] Melville explained, "our priority is dealing with the immigration business at hand. You don't understand how busy this place gets. Kids make up only a few of our detainees and we can't spend all our time worrying about minor procedural things" (1997: 41).[13] Bureaucratic ignorance greatly undermines efforts to reform INS detention. Making matters worse, human rights investigators at times are stonewalled by INS officials who refuse to disclose information about the children the agency has in its custody. That form of bureaucratic resistance reaches the point of hostility when human rights researchers are deliberately fed misinformation:

> If INS officials in Los Angeles were characterized by ignorance and indifference towards detained children, officials in Arizona distinguished themselves by what often appeared to be overt ill-will towards detained children and their advocates. In Los Angeles, we did encounter some difficulties in gaining access to facilities and in having confidential discussions with children, but the difficulties seemed a matter of passive resistance. In Arizona, however, we met with active hostility. INS officials and their agents at the detention facility seemed determined to prevent us from gaining access to accurate information about the children in their custody. We encountered everything from

the standard forms of bureaucratic resistance to transparent and deliberate
falsehoods, along with a wide variety of blatantly obstructive behavior. (Human Rights Watch 1997: 41)

Officials at the Arizona facility, for instance, falsely told Human Rights
Watch that all the children in its custody had legal council, and even
went so far as to release a list of attorneys; however, when investigators
tried to verify that information, the lawyers contacted said that they did
not represent the children. Other problems surrounding the disclosure
of information persist at the Arizona facility. Upon their request for a
copy of the institution's written policy on access to courts and legal information (the existence of which is required by INS regulations), Human Rights Watch (1997) initially was told that no such policy existed.
Eventually, Melissa Jenkins, then-director of the facility, conceded that
she had a copy but refused to share it with Human Rights Watch. Such
hostility appears to characterize the relationship of Southwest Key and
the INS with other concerned groups. Tucson Ecumenical Council Legal Assistance (TECLA), the only local organization that offers legal
services to indigent detained minors, and the Women's Commission for
Refugee Women and Children repeatedly have been refused access to
the facility to present the children's rights to them. Bureaucratic ignorance and resistance not only hinder attempts to reform INS detention,
but as a result, unaccompanied children in INS custody, an exceedingly
vulnerable group, also are denied fundamental rights under international agreements, the U.S. Constitution, and statutory law. In particular, those children are deprived of due process, access to legal representation, humane living conditions, personal privacy, and basic information
about what is happening to them and why (Amnesty International 1997;
Human Rights Watch 1997).

Conclusion

Public criticism over INS processing and confinement of unaccompanied children has not been completely ignored by the agency. Recently,
adopted guidelines for INS detention centers have included provisions
for training more than 15,000 staff and hundreds of nonprofit and jail
workers in children's rights (May 2001; Sullivan 2000b).[14] Still, critics
insist that unaccompanied children should not be detained; rather, they
should be placed in the custody of social service agencies that are committed solely to caring for children. Given the emphasis on law en-

forcement at the INS, service is sorely compromised; consequently, un-accompanied children are more often treated as prisoners rather than vulnerable minors in dire need of protection. Ironically, Amnesty International states, "with regard to children, the INS presumes to look out for the 'best interests' of the very individuals it seeks to remove from the United States and forcibly return to countries where their lives and freedom may be in danger" (1997: 2).

Recently, a Chinese girl, 15, and five Chinese boys spent eight to 12 months with violent offenders in the Multnomah County (Oregon) juvenile jail waiting for their asylum cases to be heard. Even after she was granted asylum, the "girl who cries," as she was called by other inmates, remained in jail for more than seven weeks. INS officials said that paperwork and difficulty locating an uncle delayed the girl's release. However, documents filed in federal court by Portland INS staff members and the Oregon congressional delegation later revealed that the agency failed for six months to find the uncle, never told the girl whether she would be released, and misled members of Congress about the circumstances of the other teens being detained. Oregon political leaders demanded that the INS remove the children from the county jail. Ten days later, the girl was transferred to a foster home; similarly, one of the boys was released to an uncle and the four other children were sent to detention centers in California and Arizona (Sullivan 2000b: EV3; also see Sanchez 2001).

According to the UNHCR, all unaccompanied children should have a guardian or adviser appointed from an independent and formally accredited organization in each country. "The guardian or adviser should have the necessary expertise in the field of child caring, so as to ensure that the interests of the child are safe-guarded, and that the child's legal, social, medical and psychological needs are appropriately covered"(1996, section 5.7). The United States lags far behind many countries that comply with international standards by separating the care-taking agency from the agency charged with the prosecution of unaccompanied children.[15] Human rights groups urge the INS to transfer unaccompanied children in its custody to child welfare authorities, an option that already is being practiced in some of its districts. For example, in the Chicago area, an agency called the Heartland Alliance is under contract to the INS to provide shelter care for unaccompanied children. In contrast to Southwest Key, the private company that operates the detention facility in Arizona, Heartland Alliance is not in the corrections business;

rather it plays in integral role in the local social service network. And unlike the Southwest Key institution and those in Los Angeles, Heartland Alliance has earned the respect of human rights groups for its commitment to children. Still, there are problems, most notably in the realm of legal representation. Given the dearth of local attorneys able to provide pro bono services, many children proceed through immigration hearings without counsel (Human Rights Watch 1997). The lack of legal assistance for unaccompanied children in INS custody remains a problem that many political leaders have ignored. In 2000, Congress proposed three laws requiring the INS to furnish more legal advice to detained children; none passed (Sullivan 2000b). Human rights organizations suggest that indigent children who remain in INS detention while their immigration status is being resolved be assigned government appointed lawyers (Fagen 2001; Human Rights Watch 1997; Sanchez 2001).

Even under the best conditions, being confined to a facility is detrimental to those in INS custody, particularly unaccompanied children. As an alternative, child advocates strongly recommend that the INS improve its efforts to release unaccompanied children to unrelated adult friends or to local foster families. That release option is not only more humane but also makes good financial sense. Whereas the expense of keeping a child in detention is more than $100 a day, there is no cost in releasing them to unrelated family friends.[16] Overall, the problem of unaccompanied children in INS custody is indeed solvable, especially considering their relatively small numbers (estimated between 200 and 300; Human Rights Watch 1997). In closing, Daniel Shanfield, of the Lawyers Committee for Human Rights, reminds us, "We must uphold the important principle that children are part of the human family and have an independent right to protection from harm and the enjoyment of fundamental rights" (Lawyers Committee for Human Rights 2000a: 4).

8

The INS Detention Industry

As the economic system intrudes further into matters of law, justice, and punishment, the picture that may emerge may be one of the "business of law and order" being run by "merchants in justice and punishment" whose only interest lies in the law of the free market (profit).

J.R. Lilly and M. Deflem

This may prove to be the most lasting impact of the movement to translate societal problems into profit-making opportunities.

Marc Mauer, The Sentencing Project

The tremendous profits accruing to the prison-industrial complex demonstrate that the free market works best when people aren't free.

Kevin Pranis, Grassroots Leadership/Prison Moratorium Project

ike so many other local jails that contract with the INS, the Wicomico County Detention Center in Maryland knows the financial rewards of detaining undocumented immigrants and asylum seekers. The Wicomico facility draws $50 a day for a bed that costs the county only $17.89 to maintain, clearing $32.11 every day for each detainee it holds. That simple profit multiplies exponentially, producing revenue at rapid pace; in 1999, the jail earned $2.7 million from the INS. With the irresistible prospects of doing long-term business with the INS, the county issued plans for constructing a new facility

149

that would rake in $4 million a year, a timely proposition considering that county voters have rejected new taxes. Residents and county administrators have come to realize that the jail is a veritable "cash cow" since it is not only self-sufficient but also creates a surplus capable of bailing out the county during an economic crunch. According to the warden, "Five years ago, the county needed to raise $65,000 in 30 days. I picked up the phone and called the INS and said, 'Send me 70 inmates.' And it was done" (Montgomery 2000: EV2).

For those unfortunate enough to be confined at the Wicomico jail, life in detention can be harsh. The jail's financial success is due in large part to its thrift; the facility spends less on its inmates than any other jail in Maryland, and it shows. Recently, more than 80 INS detainees signed a letter complaining that they "sleep on the floor with cockroaches," eat "baloney [sic] 2 and sometimes 3 times a day," and receive a single set of clothes, forcing them "to walk naked when they washed" (Montgomery 2000: EV2). There are complaints of inadequate medical care and allegations of excessive force and improper use of a restraint chair, a plastic device draped with straps in which detainees are immobilized for 24 hours or longer. Indeed, when it comes to maintaining institutional order, the warden dispenses rough justice. Should INS detainees get out of line, they are tossed into a cell with 30 American thugs, for a little "attitude adjustment." The warden also freely admits, "We do use dogs. I will turn dogs loose on a pod of inmates if they're raising hell. Dogs are ideal jailers. They have no conscience. They're colorblind. And they don't care who they bite" (2000: EV2). The Wicomico County Detention Center has a curious relationship with the U.S. Department of Justice (DOJ). The jail receives generous fees from the INS while simultaneously being investigated by the DOJ for civil rights violations against detainees. In the face of controversy, the warden stands his ground, insisting that his jail is tough but constitutional. However, when immigrants' rights groups have requested a site visit, the warden refuses to let them step inside the gate. Without apology, the warden said, "Basically, I will push the legal envelope to the limit. I'm not going to let anybody be abused. But I don't want anybody looking over my shoulder, either" (2000: EV2).

Operations at the Wicomico County Detention Center reveal unsettling contradictions in INS detention practices, most notably the reliance on unnecessary and costly confinement that generates income for facilities renting their cells. In doing so, the INS abdicates its custodial responsibilities to local jails and private corrections companies, which the agency and concerned groups have difficulty monitoring. Despite cries from human rights groups, the business of detaining undocumented immigrants and asylum seekers has produced a vast network of more than 900 jails nationwide, all eager to cash in on lucrative INS contracts, which usually pay twice the cost of housing inmates charged with criminal offenses (Casimir 2001). Local jail administrators have taken comfort in the fact that Congress remains deeply committed to its fight against illegal immigrants. In 2000, the budget for the INS totaled $4.27 billion, an 8 percent increase over the previous year; by 2001, federal lawmakers increased the INS budget once again to $4.8 billion, an 11 percent increase. More significantly, the INS detention budget jumped from $800 million in 2000 to $900 million in 2001 (INS 2001; see Burke 2001; Hedges 2001a). Although the INS has allocated funds to improve service, the lion's share of the budget is devoted to "strengthening its successful multi-year strategy to manage the border, deter illegal immigration, combat the smuggling of people, and remove criminal and other illegal aliens from the United States" (INS 1999: 1), all of which funnels more money into detention. The INS spends more than a third of its $900 million detention budget on renting cells, mostly in remote rural counties where there are low costs and beds to spare. INS detainees are the fastest-growing segment of the nation's correctional population: In 1997, 8,200 detainees were held by the INS, and by 2001 that figure leaped to more than 20,000 (Burke 2001; Hedges 2001a; INS 2001).

The INS policy shift toward detention and away from parole has not occurred in a vacuum. For the past two decades, the INS has been responding to key ideological and market forces driving the uncritical acceptance that greater law enforcement activities coupled with fewer social services not only are rational and legitimate but lucrative as well.[1] This chapter demonstrates that the INS is not merely imitating the U.S. criminal justice machinery but also is operating under the same canopy of social control. In concert with other components of the criminal justice system, the INS is responding to economic cues from the corrections–industrial complex, an enterprise that commodifies lawbreakers as well as undocumented immigrants. The discussion begins with an overview of the new penology, an emerging paradigm that continues to transform criminal justice into an apparatus of social control committed to managing certain segments of the surplus population. As we shall see, the new penology contributes to the campaign against illegal immigrants, which in turn feeds the corrections industry.

Social Control and the New Penology

The INS's reliance on detention conforms to the larger pattern of incarceration in the United States. With only 5 percent of the world's population, the United States holds 25 percent of the world's prisoners. Since 1990 America's correctional population has doubled and currently swells by 1,000 inmates every week. In 2000, there were 1,931,859 federal, state, and local prisoners, a 3 percent increase from the previous year. Massive increases in prisoners, however, contradict crime rates, which have dropped by 16 percent since 1995 (Bureau of Justice Statistics [BJS] 2001; see Hallinan 2001; "Record Number Held" 2001). In describing the government's commitment to imprisonment, criminologists Feeley and Simon (1992) shed light on an emerging trend in social control, one they identify as the *new penology*. Whereas traditional penology stems from criminal law and criminology and emphasizes punishing and correcting individual offenders, the new penology represents a significant departure in the way lawbreakers are viewed by authorities. The new penology adopts an actuarial approach in which specialists assess risks of specific criminal subpopulations (e.g., drug offenders) and recommends strategies designed to control those aggregates. In particular, incarceration as a form of incapacitation and containment has become the preferred measure for controlling so-called dangerous and high-risk groups.

With a staunch commitment to imprisonment, the new penology raises serious concerns for crime control policy. Because the new penology does not intervene or respond to either the individual offender or adverse societal conditions, it fails to address the sources of (street) crime: "It does not speak of impaired persons in need of treatment or of morally irresponsible persons who need to be held accountable for their actions" (Feeley and Simon 1992: 452). Instead, the new penology concentrates on maximizing social control, utilizing prediction tables and population projections to streamline the criminal justice system. Since the new penology takes an actuarial approach, it emphasizes efficiency, management, and control rather than individualized justice and attempts at reform. Simply put, the criminal justice system recycles human beings from one form of custodial management to another without attempting to impose justice or reintegrate offenders into society (Feeley and Simon 1992; also see Clear 1994; Platt 1994; Welch 1996b, 1999b).

Perhaps the most distressing contradiction of the new penology is that its actuarial tenets strive to improve public safety without attempting to reduce crime. According to Feeley and Simon, "The new penology is neither about punishing nor about rehabilitating individuals. It is about identifying and managing unruly groups. It is concerned with the rationality not of individual behavior or even community organization, but of managerial process. Its goal is not to eliminate crime but to make it more tolerable through systemic coordination" (1992: 455). The new penology also has unfortunate repercussions for those marginalized by poverty, most notably people of color. Given that impoverished minorities are disproportionately unemployed and undereducated, they generally are perceived as a dangerous class who pose a threat to the social and economic order (see Gordon 1991). Therefore, according to principles of the new penology, that so-called dangerous and high-risk group must be tightly controlled by the criminal justice apparatus. The social consequences of the new penology are difficult to overlook. For decades there have been sharp increases in the incarceration of impoverished and minority offenders, evidence that the actuarial impetus of the new penology, and its emphasis on prison warehousing, overrides individualized justice (Adler 1994, Spitzer 1975; Welch 1994, 1999b).

In his book *Search and Destroy: African American Males in the Criminal Justice System* (1996), Jerome Miller chronicles the ever-rising black population in American prisons: In 1930, the rate of incarceration for black people was three times that of whites; in 1950, the rate increased to four; in 1960, the rate climbed to five; and in 1970, the rate surpassed six. More recently in 1989, the rate of incarceration for blacks reached seven times that of whites and in 1996, the rate has jumped to eight. Similarly, in 1990 the Sentencing Project found that almost one in four (23 percent) black men in the age group 20–29 was either in prison, jail, on probation, or parole on any given day; furthermore, the black correctional population is greater than the total number of black men of *all* ages enrolled in college (Mauer 1990). Astonishingly, that figure had increased to one in three by 1995 (Mauer and Huling 1995). It has been said rather bluntly, "not only has the prison system gotten bigger, but it also has gotten blacker" (Christianson 1991: 62–63; also see Tonry 1998). In 2000, 791,600 black men were in prison, the most ever in U.S. history (BJS 2001). Feeley and Simon lament the emergence of the new penology since it pushes "corrections even further toward a self-understanding based on the imperative of herding a specific population that cannot be disaggregated and transformed but only maintained—a kind of waste management function" (1992: 469–470).

By emphasizing enforcement and confinement rather than service and alternatives to detention, the INS embraces the new penology, marking an important transformation in its management of undocumented immigrants. Over the past two decades, the INS has resorted to processing large aggregates, particularly groups of specific nationalities (e.g., Central Americans, Cubans, Haitians, and Nigerians). As a case in point, an executive order instructed the INS to detain all excludable Cubans arriving in the United States effective September 14, 1994 (Sale 1994). Similarly, during the 1980s the U.S. Attorney General targeted Salvadorans by granting the INS authority to make arrests without warrants, leading to the detention of hundreds of Salvadorans (see *Orantes-Hernandez* v. *Meese* and *Orantes-Hernandez* v. *Thornburgh*; see Chapter 9).

The actuarial approach complements further an INS detention policy that values efficiency, management, and control. Adhering to bureaucratic and rational-legal imperatives, the INS relies on specialists, experts, and technicians to classify aliens (i.e., excludable and deportable aliens) as well as to predict and forecast immigration trends. In doing so, immigration specialists apply actuarial methods to assess the costs of immigration (e.g., establishing financial estimates related to health care, education, and other social services; see Chapter 2). In line with the new penology, specialists in the INS are assigned the task of managing aggregates, meaning that groups—and not individuals—become the units of analysis. Consequently, emphasis is placed on the management of groups of people rather than on accommodation, equity, and other positive social transformations of individuals.

Under the new penology, the INS detention policy does not facilitate the reintegration of immigrants into community; on the contrary, it often resists such assimilation. As discussed in Chapters 5 and 6, the INS has been sharply criticized for not implementing available parole options that would reduce its detention population. In 1998, after human rights groups issued a raft of scathing reports about INS detention (see Lawyers Committee for Human Rights 1998b), INS Commissioner Doris Meissner vowed to increase the use of parole for undocumented immigrants and asylum seekers who pose no threat to the community.

Two years later, however, advocates say there has been little progress: "An INS initiative to review the cases of criminal detainees held for more than six months produced 1,800 paroles, but the INS still counts 2,700 people who have been in custody longer than six months. And that doesn't include noncriminal foreigners" (Montgomery 2000: EV3).

Consider also the controversy surrounding the Asylum Pre-Screening Officer (APSO) Program, an initiative designed to use detention space more judiciously and expand the use of the Pilot Parole Project. Even though the Pilot Parole Project contributes to the formulation of a humane detention policy and is supported by officials from the UNHCR, the DOJ, Amnesty International, and the Lawyers Committee for Human Rights, there are reports of noncompliance in certain districts. Marks and Levy found "that the district directors in Harlingen and New York have rejected a significant number of positive parole recommendations" (1994: 10). Marks and Levy discovered "The New York district director's action in this regard particularly troubling in light of evidence that aliens are denied parole in New York solely because of their national origin. In particular, we are concerned about reports that Nigerian asylum seekers face a presumption against parole solely because they are Nigerian" (1994: 11). In response to those findings, allegations of discrimination and institutionalized racism in the New York district were brought to the attention of the New York City Commission on Human Rights; subsequently, that agency issued a letter of concern to the INS district director. Because the INS detention policy appears to be aimed at immigrants of color, parallels to the new penology should not be dismissed as trivial. As we discuss further, the new penology serves as an administrative model by which the economic potential of the corrections–industrial complex is realized, especially considering that INS detainees are treated as raw materials benefiting the corrections business.

Raw Materials for the Prison Industry

Among the key contradictions facing capitalism is its proliferation of wealth, an economic pursuit that marginalizes a large segment of society from which deviance and crime is produced. Because those marginalized are significant in both sheer numbers and their perceived threat to the social order, the state invests heavily in law enforcement and prisons. In doing so, the criminal justice system provides social control functions for the political economy by protecting the prevailing form of capitalism (Barnett and Cavanaugh 1994; Spitzer 1975; Welch 1999b). In light of the growing corrections–industrial complex, however, it is clear that those operations of social control themselves have the capacity to accumulate capital, thus compounding the ironies of the criminal justice apparatus. Consider, for example, the criminalization of drugs, a strategy that escalates rather than reduces the drug trade. That is, the imposition of higher penalties serves to increase the risk of selling illegal drugs, making the activity more lucrative, and in the end, recruits an endless supply of peddlers who already have been marginalized economically. When drug offenders are incarcerated, they subsequently become raw materials for the corrections industry, an economic enterprise considered legitimate by many proponents of a free market (Welch et al. 1999; Welch, Wolff, and, Bryan 1998; Wilkins 1994).

The war on drugs and its commodification of prisoners sheds light on the equivocal nature of the criminal justice machinery given that relatively harmless lawbreakers are treated as if they were menacing and dangerous (Adamson 1984; Spitzer 1975; Welch 1999b, 2000a, 2000b). The net-widening tendencies of the criminal justice system are accentuated by the economic imperatives of the corrections industry that demands a greater supply of prisoners, even if those offenders are nonviolent. In 1997, New York Governor George Pataki announced that an additional 7,000 prison beds (priced at $635 million) were needed to handle what he claimed to be a growing number of violent offenders. Pataki's proposal was squarely contradicted by statistics showing that New York's crime rate was dropping; in fact, 60 percent of those sentenced to prison in 1996 were convicted of nonviolent offenses. Pataki, along with other mainline politicians, was accused of grandstanding on the crime issue and placating upstate legislators who see corrections as economic engines for their districts ("New York's Prison Building Fever" 1997; also see Thomas 1994a). Manufacturing false claims and manipulating fear of violence are common strategies that government officials rely on to generate funding, thereby expanding the corrections–industrial complex (Donziger 1996a; Irwin and Austin 1994).[2]

To return to the issue of race inherent in the new penology and the war on drugs, a special issue of *Social Justice* noted that blacks constitute 14 percent of the nation's drug users, approximately the same percentage as their representation in the general population. However, blacks account for 35 percent of drug arrests, 55 percent of drug convictions, and 75 percent of admissions into state prisons (2000: 1).

Again, a crucial function of the war on drugs, and other "tough on crime" initiatives—including anti-immigrant campaigns—is its production of mass quantities of prisoners, or raw materials, for the corrections industry. That economic-punishment nexus is reinforced by lengthy sentences (especially mandatory minimums) that ensure profitability since long-term occupancy in prison translates into a handsome financial per diem. A trade publication geared toward investors, *The Cabot Market Letter*, compares a private corrections facility to "a hotel that's always 100% occupancy . . . and booked to the end of the [20th] century" (Bates 1998: 13; also see James 2002). On Wall Street the booming corrections industry has created a bull market, further evidence that crime does indeed pay. Tremendous growth in the prison population coupled with generous increases in expenditures have spawned a lucrative market economy with seemingly unlimited opportunities for an array of financial players: entrepreneurs, lenders, investors, contractors, vendors, and service providers. In 1995, the American Jail Association promoted its annual conference with advertisements reeking of crass commercialism, "Tap Into the Sixty-Five Billion Dollar Local Jails Market" (see Donziger 1996b). The World Research Group organized a 1996 convention in Dallas that was billed "Private Correctional Facilities: Private Prisons, Maximize Investment Returns in This Exploding Industry."

Without much hesitation, corporate America has caught the scent of new public money; indeed, representatives from AT&T, Merrill Lynch, Price Waterhouse, and other golden logo companies attended the meeting in Dallas. Similarly, the prison industry has attracted other capitalist heavyweights, including the investment houses of Goldman Sachs and Salomon Smith Barney, who compete to underwrite corrections construction with tax-exempt bonds that do not require voter approval. Defense industry titans Westinghouse Electric, Alliant Techsystems, Inc., and GDE Systems, Inc. (a division of the former General Dynamics), also have entered the financial sphere of criminal justice, not to mention manufacturers of name-brand products (e.g., Dial soap) currently cashing in on the spending frenzy in corrections (Burton-Rose 1998; Elvin 1994/1995; Parenti 1996, 1999; Teepen 1996).

As the INS remains faithfully committed to law enforcement and detention, its organizational links to the corrections–industrial complex have become increasingly evident. The INS, in terms of its governmental affiliation, is located in the DOJ, where other law enforcement and corrections agencies reside, including the FBI, the DEA, U.S. Marshals Service, Organized Crime and Racketeering (OCR) Section, and the Federal Bureau of Prisons (BOP). Although the INS is directed by a commissioner, ultimately all policies and practices are instituted and supervised by the U.S. attorney general, the chief administrator of the DOJ. Correspondingly, the National Institute of Justice (NIJ), the research arm of the DOJ, commissions evaluation studies intended for policy consideration, including prison construction and privatization, both of which are instrumental to the corrections industry. For the record, the NIJ has long supported additional prison construction and courted private interests in the corrections market. In 1987, the NIJ submitted a press release to the Associated Press and United Press International (the nation's largest conduits for print media) about a study claiming that society spends an average of $25,000 a year to incarcerate an offender, whereas it costs $430,000 for that person to remain free to commit crime. Criminologists quickly dismissed those figures as blatant exaggerations; however, the report already had influenced prison policies. California Governor George Deukmejian cited the study in his 1989 address justifying the state's $1.5 billion corrections budget. Assistant Attorney General Richard Abell referred to the report in a mass-mailing to policymakers throughout the country. And director of the NIJ, James K. Stewart, had previously publicized his support for private corrections in a *New York Times* op-ed, "Breaking Up Government's Monopoly on Prison Cells" (Stewart 1985; also see Lilly and Deflem 1996; Lilly and Knepper 1993).

Those developments in correctional policy have prompted criminologists to look deeper at the structure of the corrections–industrial complex, a term reminiscent of the military–industrial complex popularized initially by President Dwight D. Eisenhower and later by sociologist C. Wright Mills. In his critically acclaimed work, *The Power Elite* (1956), Mills presented evidence of an integrated collective of politicians, business leaders (i.e., defense contractors), and military officials who together determined the course of state, economic, and military policies. Taking their cue from Mills, researchers discovered a similar cohort existing in the corrections–industrial complex, comprising politicians, business leaders, and criminal justice officials (Adams 1996; Christie 1994; Donziger 1996a; Ethridge and Marquart 1993; Irwin and Austin 1994; Nuzum 1998). The corrections–industrial complex embodies the iron triangle of criminal justice, where subgovernment control has been established (Thomas 1994b). Operating well below public awareness, influential players in the corrections subgovernment determine the course of policy and spending, including (a) private corporations eager to profit from incarceration (e.g., Corrections Corporation of America, Correctional Services Corporation, Wackenhut Corrections), (b) government agencies anxious to secure their existence (e.g., Bureau of Justice Assistance, NIJ), and (c) professional organizations (e.g., the American Bar Association, the American Correctional Association). The iron triangle of criminal justice siphons power from each of these sectors, producing a formidable alliance, one that critics contend is a pocket of displaced influence over government (Lilly and Deflem 1996; Lilly and Knepper 1993; see Chevigny 2000; "Critical Resistance" 2000).[3]

The INS and the Corrections–Industrial Complex

Strapped for housing space, the INS creates significant financial opportunities for local jails and private corrections companies, where 60 percent of agency's detainees are confined (Firestone 1999). Whereas the current wave of INS detention is driven by the 1996 laws aimed at cracking down on illegal immigrants and criminal aliens, the emergence of the INS as a key participant in the corrections–industrial complex is traced to 1987. At that time, the INS began using local jails to hold long-term detainees after they rioted and destroyed much of the prison in Oakdale (Louisiana), an institution built specifically for Mariel Cubans. Because those Mariel Cubans were being detained indefinitely and could not be deported, the INS grouped them into cliques of 30 detainees and dispersed them to local jails (Hedges 2001a). As mentioned previously, the INS has in its custody approximately 1,000 indefinite detainees (most of them Cuban), most of whom are housed in local jails and federal prisons (Indefinite Detention Project 2001: Chapter 5). The Mariel Cuban experience sheds critical light on the INS and its role in the corrections–industrial complex. It seemed that from the time of their arrival, many Mariels were destined to become another form of "human rabble" eligible for state-sponsored warehousing (see Irwin 1985; Welch 1994). By claiming—albeit falsely—that many of the Mariels posed a threat to the American communities, the INS justified its indefinite detention of several thousand Cuban men. With implications to the new penology, the Mariel phenomenon proved lucrative for the INS as it strengthened its ties to the emerging corrections– industrial complex. The Mariels represented another aggregate with promising potential as raw materials, and the INS wasted little time in commodifying them for financial gain. Before the Mariel exodus, the INS was a relatively obscure agency in the DOJ, but its low profile soon changed. Congress rewarded the INS handsomely for its plan to detain thousands of Mariels, and by 1988 the INS budget soared to $2.2 billion, a 100 percent increase over six years (Hamm 1995). As mentioned, by 2001, the INS budget mushroomed to $4.8 billion with $900 million earmarked for detention, one-third of which is allocated to the renting of jail cells in local and private jails (Burke 2001; INS 2001; Welch 2000c).

Revenue for the Public Sector

At an average cost of $58 per day per detainee, the INS spends nearly a half-million dollars each day to house its detainees in local jails. That arrangement provides a valuable source of income for local governments; in some cases, county debts have been paid and taxes reduced due to revenue from the INS (Casimir 2001). Whereas "not in my backyard" used to be a popular reaction by local residents protesting new jails and prisons, nowadays communities welcome such institutions, especially in regions hit hard by economic downturns. More than 900 local jails have joined the vast network of facilities eager to house INS detainees, and like many communities, the Wicomico County Detention Center has come to rely heavily on the financial windfall from the INS. The warden continues to lobby county administrators to bring even more INS detainees to Wicomico, boasting, "Renting beds is a lucrative business. If I built 500 beds, I could rent them all tomorrow morning" (Montgomery 2000: EV3).

In Farmville, Virginia, sustained profits from detaining those in INS custody have made the Piedmont Regional Jail entirely self-supporting (Montgomery 2000). In Passaic County (New Jersey), the INS compensates the local jail $77 per detainee per day, compared with the $58.50 the state pays. The cost of feeding and housing an inmate costs the jail $32 per detainee per day, and the difference fills county coffers, adding $1.42 million to the county treasury in 2000 (Burke 2001; Morley 2001). In neighboring Bergen County (New Jersey), local officials recently expanded the Hackensack jail, but in 2000 its revenue dropped by $1.2 million because the state corrections department housed fewer inmates there. As a plan to boost revenue to pay for the $62.4 million jail expansion, the Sheriff's Department cut a deal with the INS to hold criminal aliens awaiting deportation. Sheriff Gordon Johnson spoke frankly about the corrections industry: "This contract will allow us to recapture some of the money that goes into running the facility" (Morley 2001: A1, A4). The INS has agreed to pay the local jail at least $65 per inmate per day, and if the 64-bed housing unit remains full, the facility can earn as much as $1.5 million a year.

Whereas many local jails have just recently discovered the financial benefits of holding INS detainees, others have been cashing in for more than a decade. In the 1980s, the York County Prison in Pennsylvania began doing business with the INS; still, it was the passage of the 1996 immigration laws that brought in a greater volume of detainees and revenue. On average, the York County Prison houses more than 200 asylum seekers and more than 750 deportable criminal aliens at a fee of $60 per detainee per day. In 2000, York County earned $16.5 million from the INS. York County's President-Commissioner Chris Reilly recognizes that the arrangement is mutual; the facility helps the INS meet its high demand for beds, and by housing detainees the county has found a way to pay its bills ("Alleged Mistreatment" 2000). With a seemingly detached view of the controversy over holding INS detainees for profit, Commissioner Reilly said, "We're not in the policy business. So we're just, you know, providing a decent place for them to stay while their case is being heard here in the United States. But there's no doubt about it that the prison program has been enormously helpful in keeping our taxes low" ("Alleged Mistreatment" 2000: EV2). York County has one of the lowest property tax rates in the state, and has not raised taxes in seven years; in fact, the newest addition to the jail built exclusively for INS detainees funded a substantial property tax cut. INS revenue helps pay for county services such as the court system and a nursing home. With the prospect of earning future income from the INS, the county is preparing to enlarge its facility, marking the third major expansion in eight years (Montgomery 2000; "Alleged Mistreatment" 2000).

Much like the facility in York County, the Orleans Parish Prison in Louisiana has remained one of the most often used jails in the INS detention network. To describe the Orleans Parish Prison as big is an understatement. The facility has capacity for 6,448 inmates and always has space available for the INS, usually holding more than 200 of its detainees on any given day. The Orleans Parish Prison also is cheap, charging only $48 per day per INS detainee, compared with $165 per day in New York City; still, the jail earns twice as much from INS detainees than it does from state prisoners. Even by charging lower fees, the

Orleans Parish Prison pulls in a healthy profit because it budgets only $19.65 per day to house each detainee (Hedges 2001a).

Along with the Orleans Parish Prison, the state of Louisiana has the distinction of holding more INS detainees than any other state. Since the INS has limited space at its Oakdale facility, the agency farms out many of its detainees who are held indefinitely because the government in their homeland refuses to accept them. More than 500 indefinitely detained inmates, mostly Mariel Cubans, are housed in parish jails scattered throughout Louisiana. Like the Orleans Parish Prison, parish jails remain committed to the INS because the agency pays double the going rate. Human rights groups have been critical of the detention industry that prompts local jails to rent their cells to the INS. Joe Cook, director of the ACLU Louisiana chapter, said he was not surprised Louisiana prisons house more detainees than other states: "If there's a way to make a dollar off of someone else's misery, the public officials in Louisiana will be lining up to get their share" (Clendenning 2000a: EV2; see Burton-Rose 1998; Solomon 1995). As we mention again later, it has been widely reported that INS detainees are mistreated and subjected to deplorable conditions at jails in Louisiana and elsewhere.

Profit for the Private Sector

In previous chapters, we referred Motel Kafkas, where detainees are subjected to various forms of abuse at the hands of private security guards. At first glance, the use of motels and residential hotels for detention purposes appears highly unusual—certainly not representative of the larger correctional enterprise. But a closer look at that practice reveals that a link between hotel and correctional industries is fast becoming emblematic of how prisoners, residents of halfway houses and welfare hotels, and undocumented immigrants are warehoused. The story of ESMOR (see Chapter 6) illustrates that hotel administrators have successfully infiltrated the corrections–industrial complex despite long histories of abuse and mismanagement. In the wake of the riot at its privately operated detention center in Elizabeth, New Jersey, ESMOR rebounded nicely even after losing its contract with the INS. The company quickly reorganized, renaming itself Correctional Services Corporation (CSC), then continued its development as a dominant vendor in the detention of undocumented immigrants (as well as state prisoners from various jurisdictions). From its inception, ESMOR/CSC became one of the most lucrative private contractors to enter the correctional sweepstakes, winning a bidding war created by the government's willingness to abdicate its responsibility of overseeing the supervision of prisoners and detainees. Since 1989, ESMOR/CSC has secured 11 contracts in four states, managing more than 1,900 prisoners in various detention and correctional facilities; by 1994, ESMOR/CSC revenues increased 72 percent to $24.27 million (Sullivan and Purdy 1995).

Interestingly, before ESMOR/CSC formed into a private correctional company, its partners—James Slattery and Morris Horn—were managers for the Sheraton Hotel in Washington, D.C. When the homeless population surged in the early 1980s, Slattery and Horn made the lucrative transition to public housing, earning a profitable contract to manage one of New York City's most notorious welfare hotels, the Brooklyn Arms (a single residence occupancy [SRO] hotel). In short order, the Brooklyn Arms became synonymous with crime, vermin, and horrific conditions. According to Steven Banks, a Legal Aid Society attorney who sued the city for the inhumane conditions at the welfare hotels, the "Brooklyn Arms had dark hallways, peeling paint, rodents and a shortage of beds. . . . It was nothing but a warehouse for desperate families that allowed the ownership to reap substantial profits by providing minimal services" (Sullivan and Purdy 1995: 28).

In 1989, New York City officials were forced to acknowledge the inhuman conditions at the Brooklyn Arms: Its 600 housing code violations persuaded city managers to reconsider its reliance on SROs. Subsequently, Slattery and Horn, each without correctional expertise, moved on to the next housing emergency: prisons, halfway houses, and INS detention centers. ESMOR was contracted to operate the Brooklyn Community Corrections Center in 1989. And in 1991, ESMOR was awarded a contract from the BOP to open an 84-bed halfway house at the LeMarquis Hotel in Manhattan. Controversy erupted at both facilities. In Brooklyn, residents initially protested the opening of the Brooklyn Community Corrections Center, but opposition was quelled after Slattery hired William Banks, the campaign manager for Edolphus Towns, a powerful Brooklyn lawmaker. Banks embraced the task of lobbying the neighborhood and its political leaders, a service that brought him a salary of $222,000 from ESMOR in 1993 and $238,000 in 1994; at that time, ESMOR's president and chief executive officer, James Slattery, was paid $197,633 in salary and compensation (Sullivan and Purdy 1995).

Conflict also followed Slattery and ESMOR to the halfway house at the LeMarquis Hotel in Manhattan, where the BOP found numerous problems in the conditions, including vermin, electrical code violations, and insufficient services. Salaries for staff at the halfway house were dismal, contributing to turnover as high as 100 percent in one year; federal inspectors found that in 1992 there were 30 percent fewer employees than required in the contract. More disturbingly was the lack of food. Managers conceded that there were often 30 meals available to feed 100 inmates, thereby forcing them to compete, and sometimes fight, for food. To cut costs and increase profits, ESMOR also relied on inexpensive laboratories to process drug tests on inmates. Lab tests were often bungled, leading to falsely indicting inmates for illicit drug use. During that period, 12 inmates were returned to federal prison when their drug tests results showed incorrect positive results, according to the BOP. Additionally, staff members at the LeMarquis were accused of various forms of corruption, such as accepting bribes from prisoners (Sullivan and Purdy 1995).

Despite a lengthy history of institutional problems at several locations, ESMOR continued receiving government contracts while federal officials simply ignored a well-documented pattern of mismanagement. In 1993, ESMOR earned a $54 million contract to operate the INS detention facility in Elizabeth, New Jersey. Competitors for the contract argued that ESMOR's bid was insufficient to operate the facility safely and adequately. ESMOR underbid its closest competitor, Wackenhut Corrections Corporation, by a whopping $20 million. Wackenhut warned INS that ESMOR would be jeopardizing the safety of the facility and its detainees by gutting its operational costs. Wackenhut's caveat proved prophetic: The ESMOR facility erupted in mayhem in 1995. Upon investigation, the INS found that ESMOR hired guards who did not meet the requirements of the contract or were only marginally qualified. Investigators also reported that ESMOR demonstrated a continuing cycle of contract violations (INS 1995). Carl Frick, a veteran jail warden who was the first administrator of ESMOR's detention center in Elizabeth, remarked after the riot that the company's executives "don't want to run a jail. They want to run a motel as cheaply as possible. . . . Money, money, money. That's all that was important to them" (Sullivan and Purdy 1995: A28; see also Purdy and Dugger 1996).

After restructuring its image by changing the company's name, ESMOR, now called CSC, has continued its expansion in privatized corrections, profiting from locking up federal, state, and local prisoners. CSC became a publicly traded company in 1994, and by 1999 it had significantly increased its share of the private corrections market. Despite losing its INS contract for the Elizabeth facility, CSC has surged further into the corrections–industrial complex. CSC's durable financial portfolio indicates that its stock is gaining confidence among stockholders, attracting even more new investors (Welch 1999b; also see Yeoman 2000).

Industry analysts expect future growth for CSC and other private corrections companies contracted to house various segments of the correctional population, including INS detainees. Wackenhut Corrections Corporation, a Florida-based company, is one of the world's largest private jailers, operating 55 correctional facilities in North America, Europe, Australia, South Africa, and New Zealand, with a total of 39,522 beds. In Queens, New York, Wackenhut has a five-year, $49 million contract with the INS to operate a jail with capacity for 200 detainees (Casimir 2001). In 2001, Wackenhut opened its Val Verde Correctional Facility in Del Rio, Texas, a huge state-of-the-art facility designed to house 720 federal prisoners (including INS detainees) and 60 county inmates. Acknowledging the company's involvement in the corrections–industrial complex, Don Houston, central regional vice president of Wackenhut, said, "This private-public partnership with Val Verde County, U.S. Immigration & Naturalization Services, U.S. Marshal Service and Border Patrol is an important relationship to further expand WCC's position in the correctional services market in the Central Region of the U.S." ("Wackenhut Corrections Opens" 2001: EV2). For Wackenhut, the comprehensive management contract is estimated to produce annual revenues of approximately $13.5 million. In Miami, the firm announced plans to build a low security prison for criminal aliens, mostly nonviolent drug offenders. Cloid Shuler, a vice president at Wackenhut, assured residents that the facility would have "positive economic contribution" to the community, including the creation of 300 full-time jobs, with the pay scale for prison guards starting at $36,000 a year (Ross 2000: EV2).[4]

On the business side of detention and incarceration, there is considerable speculation that privatization will continue to flourish, thus fulfilling its enormous potential by generating significant capital and handsome dividends. The economic formula is simple. Investors in private corrections are anticipating more prisoners to be incarcerated for longer periods of time; consequently, chief executive officers and other financial players expect to profit opulently from the prison enterprise. Michael Blumberg, warden of the privately operated Citrus County Detention

Facility in Lecanto, Florida, which houses 29 indefinitely detained Mariel Cubans, appreciates the financial opportunities afforded by the INS: "We've got 400 beds here, and those extra inmates fill the beds" (Firestone 1999: A22). By 2005, industry analysts project the private share of the prison market to more than double (Bates 1998a; also see Parenti 1996, 1999). Evidence of current—and future—financial gain in private corrections is another blunt reminder of the economic forces driving correctional policy. Although many corporations and their investors benefit financially from the privatization of corrections, the downside has tragic human consequences, including the unjust detention of undocumented immigrants and asylum seekers who, in effect, become raw materials for the corrections business.

Contradictions in the INS Detention Industry

The INS detention industry involves the public sector, who rents local jails to the INS, as well as the private sector, who offers privatized corrections as an alternative to government operated facilities. Still, both types of facilities create contradictions for INS detention practices, including the controversy over profiting from detention, lack of accountability and monitoring, and the reluctance to spend money on institutional services for detainees. Generating revenue from INS detention raises ethical concerns because it reduces the processing of undocumented immigrants and asylum seekers to the accumulation of capital at the expense of programmatic and humanitarian ideals. Critics of the detention industry oppose the farming out of INS detainees to other facilities, especially penal institutions, on the grounds that the INS should not retreat from its responsibility of caring for those the agency takes into its custody. Kathleen Lucas, an immigrants' rights advocate, insists, "These folks have not committed a crime. They fled from their home countries because they were being persecuted or because they were about to be persecuted or killed. They come to the United States and we put them in prison. Now if you need to detain an asylum seeker, fine. Detain them somewhere, but not in a prison. I just think that's absolutely wrong to be profiting from the pain and suffering of other human beings" ("Alleged Mistreatment" 2000: EV2).

Opponents of INS detention practices also contend that the safety of undocumented immigrants and asylum seekers hangs in the balance when local jails and private correctional companies assume custody. As discussed in previous chapters, many INS detainees have been subjected to physical and sexual abuse (see Chapters 5, 6, and 7). Despite formal complaints and lawsuits filed against the INS over abuse and neglect, it continued sending its detainees to facilities known for their mistreatment and deplorable conditions of confinement ("Alleged Mistreatment" 2000; "Prison Guards Charged" 2000).

- In 2000, INS detainees held in county jails in Louisiana issued affidavits that guards beat and verbally abused them. The detainees complained that there were no job training or school programs and reported being fed a monotonous diet, usually consisting of lukewarm grits for breakfast, rice and beans for lunch, and sandwiches for dinner. The detainees did not have access to a law library, a crucial problem since the majority did not have lawyers and handled their own cases. Most detainees merely sat locked in their cells at least 18 hours a day.
- In 2000, 13 INS detainees filed a suit against the Orleans Parish Prison accusing corrections officers of beating them during disciplinary hearings.
- In 2000, two dozen INS detainees from the Hudson County Jail (New Jersey) sent a letter to the INS saying they were held in cells where "human waste was clearly visible over the floors and toilets" and explained that they were prevented from filing a lawsuit because they did not have legal representation. Additionally, they complained of frequent transfers that forced them to miss crucial court appearances, virtually ensuring that they would be deported. When the detainees attempted to file grievances, jail officials refused to sign them, keeping the formal complaints from being processed.
- In 2001, a suit filed by INS detainees at the Passaic County Jail (New Jersey) alleged an array of abuses, including overcrowding, lack of working showers and toilets, and inadequate medical care. INS detainees at the San Pedro Jail (in Los Angeles) filed a similar suit, which was recently settled out of court with the INS.
- Suits have also been filed from jails in Chicago and the INS detention centers in Elizabeth, New Jersey, as well as at Krome (Miami), where accusations of sexual abuse are being investigated by the U.S. Justice Department. (Hedges 2001a: EV3–4; also see ACLU 2000e; Amnesty International.1999a; Florida Immigrant Advocacy Center 1997; Human Rights Watch. 1998c; Lawyers Committee for Human Rights 1998b; Solomon 1999; Spoto 1998; Women's Commission for Refugee Women and Children 1998a, 2000).

Such despicable detention practices also raise the issue of the lack of accountability, a problem compounded by the absence of systematic and routine monitoring. Human Rights Watch warns, "It is a difficult enough task for the INS to screen and monitor its own thousands of agents, over whom it has direct control. When detainees are farmed out to local law enforcement agencies whose officers the INS has had no involvement in hiring, training or monitoring, they are placed in an unnecessarily vulnerable situation" (1998a: 84). Quite often the INS has exhibited a hands-off attitude when it comes to monitoring jails with which it does business. Even as the U.S. DOJ investigates civil rights abuses against detainees held at the Wicomico County Detention Center, INS officials said they have no reason to question the warden's management practices: "It's his facility," said Chris Bentley, spokesperson for the INS Baltimore District, "What he says goes" (Montgomery 2000: EV2).

It is important to note that within the INS detention industry local jails operate according to the same economic principles adhered to by private corrections companies. That is, they strive to house as many INS detainees for as long as possible; during which time they keep spending on basic services for detainees to a minimum so as to not disrupt the finely calibrated economic formula that protects their profits. Resorting to cheap warehousing reinforces an industry-wide view of INS detainees as raw materials rather than vulnerable people with many personal needs. In marketing his company's correctional expertise, the cofounder of the Corrections Corporation of America boasted, "You just sell it like you were selling cars or real estate, or hamburgers" (Bates 1998a: 12). That perspective is shared by an increasingly growing number of local and private jails attracted to the detention industry by the prospects of long-term revenue. According to one CCA warden, "I don't think we have to worry about running out of product" (Bates 1998a: 18).

In the face of numerous reports documenting the mistreatment of INS detainees in local and private facilities, the INS recently issued a set of standards designed to provide better health care and psychological services, ample recreation time, cleaner sheets and uniforms, and improved access to the outside world, including free phone calls, law libraries, and presentations explaining detainee rights. To meet the new standards, facilities will be pressured to devote more funds and resources to institutional services for detainees. Such spending, however, promises to be costly and thus detrimental to the profit margin; consequently, many facilities will either ignore the guidelines or demand more money from the INS. At the Wicomico County Detention Center, the warden said that even allowing detainees to go outside every day, as stipulated by the new standards, would hike costs from $50 per detainee per day to $80 due to the expense of increased supervision (Burke 2001; also see Hedges 2001a; Montgomery 2000).

Overall, the detention of undocumented immigrants and asylum seekers contributes to wasteful spending since funds allocated by Congress to the INS are swiftly siphoned into local governments and private corrections companies. The most reasonable and humane alternative to costly and unnecessary confinement is to release INS detainees to family, friends, and advocates capable of providing shelter and support, thereby relieving the financial burden to the INS and federal government. Moreover, money saved by substantial reductions in detention can then be allocated to services, a sorely needed function of the INS.

Conclusion

While critics question the tortured logic of increasing expenditures in criminal justice at the expense of vital social services, the corrections industry continues to generate an ideological and financial windfall for politicians, corporations, and a growing cast of opportunists. Curiously though, the corrections industry rests upon an inverted set of economic assumptions insofar as the supply-and-demand principle operates in reverse. According to Adams, "More supply brings increased demand. Industry insiders know that there are more than enough inmates to go around" (1996: 463). That economic principle explains the continued commodification of lawbreakers in American capitalist society, augmented by the war on drugs and other "tough on crime" initiatives, including anti-immigrant campaigns. Indeed, investors are betting that the incarceration business will remain prosperous because its raw materials—prisoners and INS detainees—are in constant supply (Burton-Rose 1998; Parenti 1999).

Ample evidence shows that the economic–punishment nexus portends grave consequences for prisoners as well as American society. As discussed previously, a corrections enterprise geared toward accumulating capital does so by slashing operating costs, most notably skilled labor (i.e., professional, well-trained staff) and much needed programs and services (e.g., education, medical care, substance abuse treatment):

The end results are neglect, abuse, and violence against those behind bars (see Dow and Greene 2001). At the societal level, heavy reliance on incarceration, whether to create social control, profits, or both, undermines democracy by shifting even greater power to the state and the corporate class. In its wake, the impoverished and racial minorities are left vulnerable to an overzealous, overfinanced criminal justice machine. With those problems in full view, the American correctional system has been referred to as the regressive socialism of the conservative right because it is the only expanding public housing and the only growing public-sector employment ("Prison Boom" 1995).

Due to its economic and organizational links to the corrections–industrial complex, the INS does not merely mimic recent developments in criminal justice, it has also become a fixture in the sprawling apparatus of social control aimed at exclusion and detention rather than integration and assimilation. The prevailing coercive and commercial facets of INS detention policy are shaped further by the new penology whereby aggregates, most notably immigrants of color, are herded and managed according to actuarial principles. Those developments are increasingly evident within the INS, given that the agency allocates greater resources to its police and prison functions while neglecting service. Consequently, the mistreatment of INS detainees, coupled with harsh conditions and protracted periods of confinement, is conveniently overlooked by legislators and policymakers who cater to the crass financial imperatives of the corrections business, resulting in repressive warehousing in lieu of humane processing of undocumented immigrants and asylum seekers (see Welch 2000c; also see Welch, Weber, and Edwards 2000).

9

Reforming the System

The 1996 law is probably the most anti-American law I've ever seen. It eliminated all legal protections. We had people arrested in the middle of the night, and families didn't know where their fathers or brothers or sons were. Hard-working people who were paying their taxes, had kids in college, have had their families now thrown into poverty.

Representative Bob Filner (D–California)

With the harsher treatment given to undocumented aliens, and other immigrants, we're now at risk of creating a new underclass. The last time we had that it was called Jim Crow. And it has taken us years to undo the damage.

Bishop Thomas Wenski of the Archdiocese of Miami

All asylum applicants, future Americans or not, are entitled to humane treatment as a matter of justice.

Senator Sam Brownback (R–Kansas)

n 1999, Donovan Williams traveled to Jamaica to honor his recently deceased mother. Upon returning to the United States, an INS officer at the airport ran a routine background check on him. Because Williams, a 25-year legal resident who had lived in the United States since age 12, had been convicted of a drug violation in 1986, the INS immediately took him into custody. The INS then placed him in detention at the Krome Detention Center, where he spent Christmas, separated from his family and still grieving his mother's death. In so many ways, his case is typical of those also explored in this book. Williams is a long-term legal resident who was convicted of a nonviolent offense involving drugs for which he served an eight-month jail term. Since that infraction, Williams has lived as a model citizen, working and raising a family. Because the 1996 immigration reforms are applied retroactively, Williams faces deportation, a penalty that imposes irrevocable damage to his children and their mother (Benjamin 2001).

Critics of the 1996 immigration laws point to the harm extended to families and communities, particularly in cases in which so many people depend on the person detained. Together Williams and his longtime girlfriend, Millicent Drummond, are raising their four children. Still, Drummond concedes, Williams served as the family's center: "Sometimes I don't know what I'm going to do. Donovan was the one who looked after the kids. He loved spending time with them. They used to confide in him, not me. I never had the patience. Now I feel like I must be going crazy or something" (Benjamin 2001: EV4). Howard, his 13-year-old son, bursts into tears when asked about his father: "I wish my dad was here. It's wrong what they're doing. He's been living here 20-something years. They should just let him go" (2001: EV4). Williams's family struggles financially while he remains helpless in detention. Shortly after his arrest, the family car was repossessed, and without his $1,600 income each month Drummond has had enormous difficulty keeping ahead of household bills. To compensate, Drummond, a home health aide, works extra nursing shifts but often is called home to attend to the children's needs, even missing two weeks of employment when Donovan Jr., 10, broke his leg while riding a bike. Others have witnessed the pain inflicted on Williams and his family. "I went up to him during our weekly greeting and he seemed depleted, like he wasn't alive," said Pastor Sidney Edwards of the Words of Faith and Praise Ministry in Lauderdale Lakes. "It's been difficult for the whole family since [Williams] has been gone. He was a big support for the children" (2001: EV4). U.S. Representative Alcee Hastings, one of the few lawmakers who opposed the revised immigration laws in 1996, acknowledged, "As should have been expected, individuals who are an asset to their communities have been deported. And strong, viable families have been torn asunder" (2001: EV4).

Like so many other people in INS custody, Williams was unaware that by traveling abroad he risked deportation. Grappling with the

Kafkaesque nature of his ordeal, Williams said, "I lived basically my whole life in this country. I was raising a family. Things were going great. Now they are telling me all those years are worth nothing?" (Benjamin 2001: EV2). Apparently those years are not worth anything, at least from the standpoint of immigration judge Neale Foster, who ordered Williams deported, stating that he did not have enough "equity" in the United States. Williams appealed that ruling but remains in INS custody, and since the process is assured to be a lengthy one, he was transferred to a county jail 320 miles from his home, making it all the more difficult for him to maintain contact with his family. Even if his family does make the six-hour trip, the Clay County Jail does not permit contact visits or visits from people under age 18. "Me back in county jail? It doesn't make sense," he said during an interview, sitting in a courtroom with his ankles snared in jangling chains and his wrists handcuffed. "I paid my debt to society many years ago. What have I done to be brought back here now?" (2001: EV2)

In the Clay County Jail, conditions of confinement are as harsh as a maximum-security penitentiary. Detainees are allowed only three hours of outdoor recreation per week. Williams usually skips his recreation privilege because the staff requires that inmates be placed in handcuffs and leg irons while being moved to the recreation yard and other areas including the church. Williams also has had problems with legal representation. Initially, Drummond hired a lawyer for $1,500 who dropped the case after she could not make additional payments: "They wanted another $6,000. I just didn't have it" (Benjamin 2001: EV2). Fortunately, he received pro bono assistance from the Florida Immigrant Advocacy Center, but being housed in a remote county jail has obstructed his access to counsel. Whereas some INS processing centers allow detainees to call their attorneys free of charge, many county jails do not; as a result, Williams must rely on mail and an occasional collect call. Like other INS detainees at the Clay County Jail and elsewhere, Williams complains of lack of privacy, inmates services, and health care, and being confined with criminal offenders. "There are many times when I fear for my life here. It scares me. There is a lot of fighting. Many times I sit up all night because it's like you have to be constantly watching," said Williams (2001: EV2).

As discussed throughout this work, the 1996 legislation rushed into law by a wave of moral panic has inflicted unnecessary pain and suffering on thousands of immigrants, their families, and communities. Indeed, the crackdown has produced a punitive campaign so expansive that it snares even legal residents who have had minor brushes with the law along with those fleeing persecution in their homeland. We have given sociological explanations in previous chapters of what has gone wrong with recent immigration policy. Rather than adopting a humane model to manage immigrants, Congress and the INS have turned to the prevailing criminal justice agenda as a means to control unpopular immigrant groups, especially those who are poor and non-White. In doing so, those people have been criminalized, pathologized, marginalized, and scapegoated. Compounding matters, once in INS custody, they are merely warehoused, a form of institutional neglect that is profitable for local and private jails that have discovered the benefits of the detention industry. Whereas numerous remedies and alternatives to INS detention have been explored throughout the book, this chapter takes a final look at current activities aimed at reforming the system. In particular, we shall revisit the ongoing debate over due process as it competes with the punitive model of immigration control; similarly, recent developments in the courts and Congress are examined. Entering into the new millennium, we consider key changes at the INS and recommend that immigration policies be formulated by compassionate logic rather than prejudice fueled by racism and classism.

Due Process versus Assembly Line Justice

To the dismay of immigrants' rights advocates, the 1996 immigration policies have adopted the rigid tenets of the conservative criminal justice agenda. From that perspective, the criminal justice process emulates the new penology, an assembly line conveyor belt down which moves an endless stream of criminal cases. This model stresses efficiency, reliability, and productivity as measured by increases in arrests, convictions, and incarcerations. Under ideal circumstances, assembly line justice is mechanical and routine (Packer 1964, 1968; Welch 2002b). Opponents of the assembly line model, however, insist that the criminal justice process rarely is smooth. Furthermore, the assembly line, manned by an array of police and prosecutors, is susceptible to human error and the frailty of authority under pressure, not to mention blatant abuses of power. In the face of those problems, due process was developed as a fair and reasonable alternative to the assembly line because it adheres to rules of criminal procedure inherent in the U.S. Constitution along with a host of protections for those arrested (Silver 1974; Skolnick 1994).

As noted in Chapter 4, foreigners do not have the legal right to enter the United States, but once here, the U.S. Constitution protects them from arbitrary treatment by the government. Specifically in deportation proceedings due process ensures that key procedural safeguards are observed: a hearing before an immigration judge and review, in most cases, by a federal court; representation by a lawyer (but not at government expense); reasonable notice of charges and of a hearing's time and place; a reasonable opportunity to examine the evidence and the government's witnesses; competent interpretation for non-English speaking immigrants; and clear and convincing proof that the government's grounds for deportation are validated (ACLU 1997: 2). The benefits of due process afforded noncitizens stem from significant judicial activities in the early 1960s when the U.S. Supreme Court under Chief Justice Earl Warren broke new ground in jurisprudence by taking seriously the possibility of error committed by actors in the criminal justice system. Drawing on the Bill of Rights, the Court strengthened procedural rights of the accused within the arrest-through-trial stages of the criminal justice process.[1] Law enforcement officials and their conservative allies accused the Warren Court of burdening police with a lot of unnecessary rules that interfere with their efforts to control crime (Cox 1968). As a backlash to the due process movement, the High Court in the 1970s and 1980s, under the tutelage of Chief Justice Warren Burger, reinvigorated a conservative agenda in criminal justice. As a result, assembly line justice contained in the crime control model gained prominence throughout the remaining years of the twentieth century. Several rulings by the Burger Court contributed to a criminal justice apparatus predicated on managerial efficiency and a commitment to crime control rather than a system overly concerned with the rights of the accused.[2]

Assembly line justice received continued support from the U.S. Supreme Court under William Rehnquist, who became Chief Justice in 1986 when Warren Burger retired.[3] Since that time, assembly line justice not only has had the backing of the judiciary but also legislators embarking on ambitious law enforcement platforms. In addition to allocating unprecedented resources to the wars on crime and drugs, lawmakers set out to empower further police. The Violent Crime Control and Law Enforcement Act (1994) added 100,000 new police officers over a six-year period and expanded the number of federal capital offenses from two to 58. The crime bill also adopted a "three strikes and you're out" provision that imposed lengthy sentences for repeat offenders. Given its popularity among crime control advocates, the "three strikes" rule was adopted by many states, producing a booming prison population. Other legislation further enhanced the criminal justice machinery by diminishing the rights of the accused and prisoners. As discussed previously, the Anti-Terrorist and Effective Death Penalty Act (1996) sharply limited defendants' rights and more significantly for noncitizens, the statute unleashed the controversial provision allowing secret evidence in deportation proceedings. Also that year, Congress voted to stop funding the Post-Conviction Defender Organizations that have played a vital role in representing death row inmates; similarly, lawmakers enacted the Prison Litigation Reform Act, curtailing significantly prisoners' rights (Robertson 2000; Welch 1999b).

By the late 1990s, the excesses of assembly line justice prompted a reexamination of the goals and means of the criminal justice system. Controversy over racial profiling (in which law enforcement officials consider a person's race or ethnicity in making traffic stops and conducting searches or other investigations) used to improve the efficiency of police work has raised concerns over due process and individual rights (Parenti 1999; Sachs 2001). Liberals insist that tough law enforcement campaigns undermine democratic ideals of justice, especially given that assembly line tactics target people of color and the impoverished, who do not have the resources to defend themselves adequately in court. With executions becoming more frequent than at any other time in U.S. history, serious questions have been raised about the number of errors committed by criminal justice officials, particularly in light of newly discovered DNA evidence that has overturned the convictions of hundreds of innocent prisoners. Even some conservatives concede that assembly line justice has produced grave problems for the criminal justice system. In 2000, Illinois Governor George Ryan, a "law and order" Republican, became so concerned that innocent persons risked being put to death in his state that he ordered a moratorium on executions until he was confident that sufficient safeguards had been instituted. Recently, other conservative politicians also have tempered their enthusiasm for the death penalty and other "tough on crime" initiatives, including the war on drugs (Welch 2002b).

Even lawmakers who enthusiastically boarded the bandwagon in 1996 have begun to take a second look at immigration policies patterned on the conservative crime control paradigm, including assembly line justice and the new penology. Immigrants' rights advocates are cautiously optimistic about such reevaluation, especially since several repressive mechanisms of immigration control have drawn the attention of the judiciary as well as some key legislators.

Recent Court Rulings

During the summer of 2001, the U.S. Supreme Court handed down rulings that carried profound implications for immigrants' rights, specifically *INS* v. *St. Cyr* (2001), *Calcano-Martinez* v. *INS* (2001), *Zadvydas* v. *Underdown* (1999), and *Ma* v. *Reno* (2000). In *INS* v. *St. Cyr* (2001), Enrico St. Cyr, a Haitian, entered the United States legally in 1986, but in 1996 he pleaded guilty to a drug violation. The Second Circuit decided that a federal district court judge in Bridgeport, Connecticut, had properly granted a writ of habeas corpus to St. Cyr. Furthermore, the Second Circuit ruled that there was no clear evidence that Congress intended to make retroactive the provision barring discretionary waivers to deportable aliens (*INS* v. *St. Cyr* also included a separate appeal by three natives of the Dominican Republic, Mexico, and Guyana who were ordered deported for drug crimes in New York state; see Asseo 2001a, 2001b; Greenhouse 2001a; Shaw 2001). In resolving the dispute, the U.S. Supreme Court found that immigrants who pleaded guilty to crimes in the years before harsh new provisions of federal immigration law took effect in 1996 do not face automatic deportation, and are permitted to seek exemptions under old rules that gave relief to more than half the people who applied. The 5-to-4 decision was an important statement by the court that judicial scrutiny should remain part of the checks and balances on matters of deportation. Moreover, the court determined that Congress did not have the authority to strip the federal courts of jurisdiction to review the way in which the attorney general administered immigration law (Greenhouse 2001b).[4]

The U.S. Supreme Court also reviewed a similar case challenging the court-stripping provisions of the 1996 laws. In *Calcano-Martinez* v. *INS*, Deboris Calcano-Martinez, 32, a native of the Dominican Republic and a mother of four children (all U.S. citizens) who has lived in the United States legally since she was three years old, pleaded guilty to selling an illegal drug in 1996. The next year, the INS determined that her offense was severe enough to justify deportation. However, the U.S. Court of Appeals for the Second Circuit, in New York, rejected the government's view that Congress, in passing the Illegal Immigration Reform and Immigrant Responsibility Act and the Anti-Terrorism and Effective Death

Penalty Act in 1996, had eliminated virtually all avenues of legal review. Moreover, the court ruled that lawmakers "had not wiped out a district court's ability to issue writs of *habeas corpus*, the traditional means of federal court review over official action depriving someone of liberty" (Schmitt 2001: 16). Marking another chief victory for immigrants' rights, the Supreme Court affirmed the ruling (*Calcano-Martinez* v. *INS*; Greenhouse 2001b).

The controversy over the INS's use of indefinite detention also has reached the U.S. Supreme Court. As mentioned in Chapter 5, the Fifth Circuit Court of Appeals, in *Zadvydas* v. *Underdown* (1999), decided that it was not a violation of due process to detain indefinitely a person with a final order of removal. Conversely, the Ninth Circuit ruled in *Ma* v. *Reno* (2000) that it was unlawful to detain persons with final removal orders for more than a reasonable period of time, a decision welcomed by immigrants' rights advocates. The High Court agreed to settle a split between the lower courts by reviewing *Ma* (currently *Ma* v. *Ashcroft* together with *Zadvydas* v. *Underdown*; see Clendenning 2000b; Gearan 2001; Indefinite Detention Project 2000). In 2001, the High Court concluded that immigrants who have committed crimes in the United States cannot be locked up indefinitely simply because the government has no place to send them. The ruling affects more than 3,000 deportable immigrants whose home countries either will not accept them or no longer exist; all were convicted of serious crimes, have served their sentences, and are now in legal limbo (Margasak 2001). Constitutional experts and advocates for immigrant's rights hailed the Supreme Court's actions:

> Despite the promise of the Statue of Liberty, noncitizens have rarely been treated as constitutional equals in this country. Yet in two surprising decisions the Supreme Court has come close to recognizing that immigrants are persons entitled to the same basic constitutional protections that apply to citizens. In doing so, the court broke from its own ignoble history of slighting immigrants' interests and may well have embarked on a new era in immigrants' rights. (Cole 2001: WK13)

Also in 2001, a federal appeals court ruled that the government must stop deporting immigrants with drunken-driving convictions, overturning an INS policy believed to already have removed thousands of people from the United States, including more than 500 arrested during a much-publicized 1998 roundup dubbed Operation Last Call. The decision by the Fifth Circuit Court of Appeals ruling also could enable those already deported to return to Texas, Louisiana, and Mississippi, the states under the court's jurisdiction. The three-judge panel rejected the government's argument that DWI (driving while intoxicated) offenses are crimes of violence, like assault, rape, and murder, because intoxicated motorists rarely intend to use force. Immigrants' rights groups welcomed the ruling, but restrictionist lawmakers, including Congressman Lamar Smith (R–Texas) who until recently oversaw the House immigration subcommittee, accused the court of abandoning prudent policy. Likewise, activists against drunken driving opposed the decision. "When you break the laws, you should be deported," said Bette Berns of Mothers against Drunk Driving (Robbins 2001: EV2). Immigration advocates, however, insist that DWI violators must be punished but not deported since that penalty far outweighs the severity of the offense (*U.S. v. Chapa-Garza* 2001; see Tagami 2000b).

The courts also have examined other disputes over the scope of the 1996 immigration law. The Ninth Circuit Court ruled in 2001 that provisions used to summarily deport illegal immigrants cannot be applied to people who sneaked back into the country before the law took effect in 1997, a decision that could affect as many as 22,000 undocumented immigrants summarily expelled from the United States without the benefit of a hearing or access to an attorney. The court determined that Congress did not intend for the law to be applied retroactively to those who had been deported and had returned before the law went into effect. Additionally, the court invited a constitutional challenge of some provisions of the sweeping immigration statute, suggesting that INS's enforcement of the law likely violates due process guarantees (*Castro-Cortez v. INS* 2000). Marc Van Der Hout, a lawyer with the National Immigration Project of the National Lawyers Guild, said, "This is an important decision and a victory for these clients. The [INS] has been acting like a bunch of cowboys, rounding 'em up and shipping 'em out with little regard for anything" (Carter 2001: EV1).

In protecting abuse victims, Ninth Circuit Court of Appeals significantly broadened the interpretation of grounds for political asylum when it ruled against deporting Rosalba Aguirre-Cervantes, who said she would be abused by her father if she were forced to returned to Mexico. The court allowed the 19-year-old to stay in the United States because of her past mistreatment, her well-founded fear of future abuse, and the fact that Mexico is unable or unwilling to interfere with that persecution. Aguirre-Cervantes reported being beaten regularly since infancy by her father who wielded a horsewhip, tree branches, a hose, and his fists, and refused to allow her to seek medical treatment (*Aguirre-Cervantes* v. *INS* 2001). Human rights advocates praised the decision because it expands the right to political asylum for victims of domestic violence in nations where the crime is ignored or even tolerated (McDonnell 2001).[5]

Recent Legislative Initiatives

Whereas the courts are instrumental in striking down unfair provisions contained in the immigration statutes, ultimately lawmakers have the authority to correct legislation by passing new laws. Over the past several years, human rights groups have tried diligently to persuade political leaders to revise the 1996 immigration laws. Fortunately, recently the social, economic, and political climate has begun to favor immigrants. Public opinion polls show that Americans were much less hostile toward immigrants in 2000 than during the early and mid-1990s when moral panic was evident. Particularly regarding their economic impact, attitudes toward immigrants have undergone a remarkable turnaround. In 1994, 63 percent of the public saw immigrants as "an economic drain on the country," and by 2000, that number had dropped, with 38 percent holding an unfavorable view of immigrants (Rosenblatt 2001: EV1). Moreover, as the Hispanic population in the United States continues to grow, so does their political clout, a development that has not been lost among those campaigning for office (Sengupta 2001a). Perhaps one of the most significant acts of Congress benefiting immigrants in recent years was approving the 245(i) waiver that allowed those who have been in the United States illegally to adjust their status by paying a $1,000 fee, thus permitting them to remain in the country without fear of deportation. Congress passed the program in 2000, and immigration officials estimated that more than 600,000 people might be eligible. To apply, an immigrant must be sponsored by an employer or by a close relative who is a U.S. citizen or legal permanent resident. The status adjustment allows them to move toward permanent residency and eventually citizenship under this law (Dewan 2001; Janofsky 2001).[6]

In 2000, the Senate Subcommittee on Immigration, under chairman Senator Sam Brownback (R–Kansas), publicly conceded that many members of Congress have second thoughts about the sweeping changes made in 1996. Lawmakers have been pressured to respond to well-publicized abuses of asylum seekers along with complaints from families being broken up by the harsh deportation statute. Daniel Kozuba has been fighting for years to keep from being deported to Canada. Kozuba, who has lived in the United States since he was five years old, served time for a drug-related conviction years before the 1996 law was passed. In 2001, his wife and about 40 members of her organization went to lobby Congress, as they have done every year since 1997. "By meeting with them [members of Congress] and being persistent, I feel we are starting to have an effect," Mrs. Kozuba said. "We take those families directly affected by these laws to their offices, and here they see people whose lives this legislation is destroying"(Malone and Trejo 2001: EV3).

Human rights organizations are hoping that pro-immigration forces will continue to shape future legislation. Recently, there has been scattered legislative activity that could alter how the government deals with immigrants. Acknowledging that many of the components in the 1996 immigration law are fundamentally unfair, Congress has initiated several key modifications to the statute. In 2000, the House of Representatives approved repeal of the retroactivity provision so that the law would only apply to those who had been convicted of aggravated felonies since 1996, thus sparing thousands of persons who had committed even minor offenses before the statute was passed. The measure, supported by INS leadership, has been stalled but is expected to be reintroduced in 2001. Another bill in the House would reduce the number of crimes requiring deportation, and Representative John Conyers (D–Michigan) has proposed eliminating mandatory detention, a 1996 provision that requires the INS to jail automatically people who have committed crimes, undocumented workers, and some asylum seekers who arrive in the United States without papers. In challenging the statute's court-stripping provision, Senator Patrick Leahy (D–Vermont) continues to lobby his colleagues to alter the 1996 law, arguing that it gives too much power to the INS, which has the authority to detain and deport without a judge's review (ACLU 2000a; "Fixing the INS" 2000; Schmitt 2001: 16).

Still, lawmakers expect a fight from those committed to the campaign against illegal immigrants and criminal aliens. Mark Krikorian, director of the Washington, D.C.–based CIS, insists, "There can be no justification for an immigration policy that did not actively screen out criminals. Otherwise why have an immigration policy? The American people are not for the immigration of criminals. We shouldn't have any criminal aliens at all here. The old saw among immigration lawyers used to be, 'It ain't over until the alien wins'" (Benjamin 2001: EV5). Although many politicians—including those who voted for the 1996 reforms—realize the consequences are not what they intended, others have told Marisa Demeo, regional counsel for the Mexican American Legal Defense and Education Fund, that they "are hesitant to change the policies out of fear they'll be accused in elections of allowing criminal immigrants to remain in the country" (Gamboa 2000: EV2). Billy Weinberg, a Congressional staff member, agrees: "I think we have a ways to go in convincing the rank-and-file [members of Congress] that this is not only a piece of legislation that contains flaws, but something they need to take steps to correct" (Malone and Trejo 2001: EV3). Despite the risk of political fallout, some elected leaders have courageously voiced their opposition to current immigration policies.

Adding to the movement for revamped immigration policies and practices, in 2000, the U.S. Commission on Civil Rights began taking a closer look at the 1996 laws and the effects they have on civil rights of immigrants. Chairperson Mary Frances Berry announced that the eight-member panel will visit detention centers, scrutinize immigration procedures, monitor enforcement, and hold hearings with immigration officials called as witnesses. "This nation's immigration policies and the way that they are implemented have obvious civil rights implications involving race, national origin and religious discrimination issues," Berry said. In particular, the commission will examine the nation's treatment of asylum seekers. "Unfortunately asylum seekers have not only suffered under an oppressive regime in their native countries, but they may also be subjected to racial, ethnic, religious and gender bias upon their arrival in America," Berry said (Gamboa 2000: EV1).

Concerned with the harshness of the 1996 immigration law and the manner by which it processes asylum seekers and refugees, the Senate introduced the Refugee Protection Act (S. 1940) in 2000. In that bill, Senators Brownback and Leahy admitted they were deeply troubled knowing that the INS turned away asylum seekers because they fled without proper documents. In many such cases, the government that they are fleeing stripped them of their documents. The proposal intended to roll back provisions of a 1996 immigration law that mandates immediate (expedited) removal of aliens arriving at U.S. ports of entry without valid papers or with fraudulent papers unless the arriving alien demonstrates a fear of return to their home country. Moreover, the measure would correct current policy allowing a low-level immigration inspector to make the removal decision, a determination that cannot be appealed to a judicial officer. The Refugee Protection Act has had the ardent support of human rights groups:

Because persons fleeing persecution are least likely to have proper papers from the very government that is oppressing them, they are vulnerable to expedited removal. Most vulnerable are victims of torture, including women who have been raped or otherwise sexually assaulted. Experience with such victims shows us that they are often afraid or even unable to talk about what has happened to them, especially to men in government uniforms. These people are most at risk of being wrongly turned away at our borders. (Amnesty International 2000c: 1; also see ACLU 2000a; Lawyers Committee for Human Rights 2000b)

In 2001, the Senate Judiciary Committee's subcommittee on immigration held public hearings on treatment of asylum seekers, inviting testimony from immigration advocates along with those holding restrictionist views. Eleanor Acer, senior coordinator of the asylum program at the Lawyers Committee for Human Rights, told the panel, "Expedited removal is a system designed to fail those we most want to protect. It lacks the very procedural safeguards that are necessary to ensure that legitimate asylum seekers are not mistakenly returned to face persecution" (Vekshin 2001: EV1). Conversely, Dan Stein of FAIR opposes major changes to the 1996 law and testified that asylum often is abused, calling it a backdoor route to gain entry into the United States. Stein believes that current asylum laws put the country in the role of the "international nanny—of a nation trying to ensure that no person encounters the vexations of life's misfortunes" (Vekshin 2001: EV2). Senator Brownback took issue with Stein's testimony and reminded him, "We are turning back now a number of people. We know they are going back to tough conditions" (Vekshin 2001: EV2; see "U.S. Religious Leaders" 2001).

As emphasized throughout the book, moral panic over immigrants is fueled by economic anxiety, in particular the perception that scarce jobs are being taken by foreigners. During periods in which work is plentiful, however, policies to import labor often emerge without public resistance. Indeed, as unemployment remained low during the first few months of the George W. Bush presidency, his administration had to respond to proposals that would bring into the United States more guest workers from Mexico to fill the needs of various industries and agriculture. Congress continues to mull the details of a recently expanded guest worker program that could give up to 8 million undocumented Mexicans in the United States the same rights as American workers. Senate Banking Committee Chairman Phil Gramm (R–Texas), who headed a delegation to Mexico City, said a law probably could link the numbers of Mexican workers who could be admitted to the U.S. unemployment rate, reducing immigrant workers when unemployment rose and allowing more in when jobs were plentiful. "I think we have a once-in-a-lifetime opportunity to get this done," Gramm said, noting that both countries have new presidents and congresses (Thompson 2001: EV1). Gramm's venture for an expanded guest worker program has drawn fire from many immigration advocates. The Congressional Hispanic Caucus insists that any such plan would be unacceptable unless it eventually led to permanent residency for guest workers, a provision that Gramm opposes (Dillin 2001). Also Mexican President Vicente Fox would like to see a new American program that would offer legal status and eventual citizenship to millions of undocumented Mexican migrants who are currently in the United States. Similarly, the American Federation of Labor and Congress of Industrial Organizations (AFL-CIO) in 2001 said it will press Congress to grant amnesty to the nation's 6 million to 11 million undocumented immigrants, an extreme about-face for the labor movement, which throughout its history has "shunned undocumented workers, characterizing them as people who brought down wages, broke strikes, and stole jobs from 'real' Americans" (Rodriguez 2001: EV1).

Gramm argued that the expanded guest worker program would reduce illegal immigration to the United States by removing the "magnet" of illegal employment. Perhaps unconsciously alluding to the ironies of immigration control, Gramm added, "The bottom line is we have millions of people who are working illegally in America; they do not have legal protections. They are vital to our economy, yet they are violating our laws" (Thompson 2001: EV2). A public opinion poll shows that by a narrow margin, 39 percent to 38 percent, Americans oppose creating a new guest worker program with Mexico; still, another 23 percent were undecided (Dillin 2001: EV2). Whereas widespread hostility against immigrants had waned along with economic worries, there remain serious reservations about importing labor from Mexico. William Smith, who lives in Youngstown, Ohio, rejected a new guest worker program: "Pretty soon all we're going to have are low-paying jobs and these jobs must go to Americans first. We have to take care of ourselves" (Dillin 2001: EV3). Glover Ledford, a retired General Motors employee in Livingston, Tennessee, another opponent of the guest worker idea, remarked, "We've got too many people." To stem the flow illegal immigration, Ledford said boldly that he would "build a high fence all around America" (Dillin 2001: EV3).

The INS in the New Millennium

When Doris Meissner stepped down as head of the INS in November 2000, she left behind an agency that has grown tremendously not only in sheer size but also in social significance. During the 1990s, immigration issues contoured political and economic discourse over America's changing racial and ethnic composition, and the INS was caught in the middle of heated battles between pro-immigration forces and restrictionists. Quite frequently, Meissner drew criticism and praise from both camps. Still, there remain disagreements over what Meissner considered to be one of her major accomplishments, namely, keeping the INS intact despite enormous pressure to split the agency into two, one devoted to service and the other to enforcement. In 2001, President Bush, who supports dividing the INS, named James Ziglar to serve as the INS commissioner. Attorney General John Ashcroft applauded Ziglar's nomination: "Jim Ziglar has my full confidence. His post is a crucial one, because while we must guard our nation's borders with vigilance, we must also remember that the greatness of our nation comes from generations of immigrants" ("Bush Names Immigration Head" 2001: EV1).

Activists on all sides of immigration policy, however, reacted with skepticism over Ziglar's nomination. Despite his reputation for fairness and solid management skills, Ziglar was criticized for his lack of experience on immigration issues, a concern that is particularly relevant considering that Bush intends to overhaul the INS. Jeanne Butterfield of the AILF said, "I don't think you'd put someone in charge of the IRS who doesn't know tax law, or someone to head the SEC [Securities and Exchange Commission] who doesn't know securities law. This is a potentially distressing signal to the people who most depend on immigration services" (Davies 2001: EV1). Restrictionists were equally concerned about the appointment of Ziglar. David Ray of FAIR insisted, "We're looking for a manager who can hit the ground running. Immigration is out of control and this agency is in crisis. We just hope he has the management experience to do the job" (Davies 2001: EV2).

As the INS forges into the new millennium, it appears imminent that it will undergo major reorganization. Bush intends to create different agencies for service and enforcement, a plan that has substantial support among congressional Republicans who claim the Clinton administration attempted to use the naturalization program to benefit Democrats. House Judiciary Committee Chairman James Sensenbrenner (R–Wisconsin), who is expected to direct congressional efforts to divide the INS, has called it a "dysfunctional agency" whose "drastic restructuring" will be "a top priority" ("Ashcroft Visits INS" 2001: EV1).

Even with significant transformations, the INS, along with legislators, should work to reconcile glaring contradictions in the 1996 immigration laws, especially the expanded register of aggravated felonies that are applied retroactively as well as the use of mandatory detention, indefinite detention, expedited removal, court-stripping provisions, and secret evidence. Human rights groups are hoping that crucial changes in the immigration policy will accompany other reforms of current detention practices, most notably the reliance on county and private jails that subject undocumented immigrants and asylum seekers to deplorable conditions while obstructing their access to counsel and the courts. Whereas it is unrealistic and impractical for the INS to abandon completely its use of detention, immigrants' rights advocates strongly urge that confinement be used only as a last resort and only as long as necessary. In closing, if U.S. immigration policy is to be more enlightened and humane, then it must become less politicized. By doing so, policymakers will be able to formulate rules and regulations according to compassionate logic rather than moral panic.

Epilogue

September 11, 2001, and the Challenge Ahead

Life is going to get a little more difficult for immigrants. The attacks, combined with rising unemployment, will erode public sympathy toward immigrants in the country illegally.

Steven Camarota, Center for Immigration Studies, a Washington, D.C., group in favor of restrictions

There are people and governments in the world who believe that in the struggle against terrorism, ends always justify means. But that is also the logic of terrorism. Whatever the response to this outrage, it must not validate that logic. Rather, it must uphold the principles that came under attack yesterday, respecting innocent life and international law. That is the way to deny the perpetrators of this crime their ultimate victory.

Human Rights Watch

In the wake of the terrorist attacks on the World Trade Center and the Pentagon on September 11, 2001, the nation's immigration system has undergone intense scrutiny and criticism. In response, government officials and lawmakers recommended sweeping changes for immigration policies so that they might meet the needs of national security. Less than two months after the attacks, Congress announced plans for

187

the Patriot Act of 2001, a law that would grant the federal government expansive powers in dealing with immigrants and those suspected of criminal activities, especially terrorism. However, as we discuss, recent measures to combat terrorism at home by zeroing in on immigrants greatly concerns civil libertarians and immigrants' rights groups, particularly in light of racial profiling and scapegoating, mass detentions and mistreatment, and the government's refusal to disclose information about those detained.

Reshaping the Political Debate over Immigration

As Americans and their political leaders were left wondering how suicide hijackers could have struck without any apparent warning and caused such enormous death and destruction, sharp questions were aimed at the nation's immigration system. Investigators soon determined that at least 15 of the 19 terrorists involved in the September 11 attack entered the country legally on some form of temporary visa (i.e., tourist, business, or student; Sheridan 2001). With those facts in store, wholesale changes in policy would be inevitable, thus altering the course of the debate over immigration. Lamar Smith (R–Texas), former head of the immigration subcommittee in the House of Representatives, noted, "If it hasn't turned it 180 degrees, it has turned it 90 degrees" (Francis 2001: EV1). Previously, discourse over immigration centered on economics, specifically the use of immigrants for low-wage labor. Since the attacks, however, emphasis remains on national security and the role of the INS in protecting the United States from foreigners intent on committing acts of terrorism. Public opinion supports that shift in priority. Weeks after the attacks, a Zogby International poll, conducted for the CIS in Washington, found that virtually all segments of American society overwhelmingly (77 percent) felt the government was not doing enough to screen those entering the nation (Hegstrom 2001).

Adding to a sense of uneasiness is the perception that government officials were asleep at the switch. Two of the men who commandeered the plane that crashed into the Pentagon, Khalid Al-Midhar and Nawaq Alhamzi, were on a U.S. government watch list of suspected terrorists. Likewise, Mohammed Atta, who masterminded the attacks on the World Trade Center and the Pentagon, was on the State Department's terrorist watch list, "but no one was watching as—like all the conspirators, apparently—he entered the United States legally and crisscrossed the country by airplane and rental cars under his own name" (Shapiro 2001: 22; Sheridan 2001). Astonishingly, crucial information about a plan involving an attack on the World Trade Center uncovered by the police in Hamburg (Germany), where Atta and five other hijackers lived, never made it across the turf boundaries of U.S. law enforcement agencies (Shapiro 2001). Members of Congress stridently called for an immigration policy that would contribute to national security. "The defense of our nation begins with the defense of our borders," announced Representative Tom Tancredo (R–Colorado), who heads the Congressional Immigration Reform Caucus (Francis 2001: EV1).

As discussed in the previous chapters, the immigrants' rights movement had recently earned several key victories, but after September 11 many of those advances have been shelved. Amnesty for illegal immigrants for which Mexican President Vicente Fox negotiated as recently as August 2001 appears on hold, perhaps permanently:

> And that's only the beginning. After moving toward extending more rights and benefits to immigrants, Congress and local leaders now seem set to reverse the trend. Beyond closing the border, they talk of taking away driver's licenses, restricting access to education and even using local police to help track down visa violators—all areas where liberals have won recent important victories. (Hegstrom 2001: EV1)

Congressman Tancredo speaks for many of his colleagues when he said, "There has been a tectonic shift in thinking" (Hegstrom 2001: EV1). Still, advocates remain determined not to lose ground in their push for immigrants' rights. Eliseo Medina of the Service Employees International Union in Los Angeles, who is organizing an effort to legalize undocumented immigrants, is optimistic that his campaign will succeed because he believes that Americans can distinguish between hardworking immigrants and those who come here to cause harm. Moreover, Medina argues that legalizing undocumented immigrants makes it easier for the INS to keep track of them, thus contributing to national security (Hegstrom 2001; Lester 2001).

Exactly how the debate over immigration plays out during the next few years promises to remain politically significant in large part because the Republican party has been trying to win support among Hispanics, and few issues are more important to them than immigration. "I believe it's going to complicate the Republicans' outreach to the Latino community," said Antonia Hernandez, president and general counsel of the Mexican American Legal Defense and Educational Fund. "With immigration, you hit a home run" (Lester 2001: EV3). As we shall see in the next section, recent antiterrorist legislation has deep implications for immigrants and their rights.

Political Responses to Terrorism

The political responses to the September 11 attacks stressed greater law enforcement for immigration control. Within days of the attacks, Representative George W. Gekas (R–Pennsylvania), chairman of the House immigration subcommittee, said that illegal immigration already had been a major concern and predicted that there would be more enforcement of the existing immigration laws as well as tightening of the borders (Sheridan 2001). Regrettably, however, some lawmakers resorted to hyperbole in characterizing current immigration control. In calling for more legislation aimed at reforming immigration and visa rules, Senator Dianne Feinstein (D–California) quipped, "Our nation's borders have become a sieve" (Vlahos 2001: EV1). Adding to that anxiety, Senator Byron Dorgan (D–North Dakota) pronounced, "The only thing[s] keeping the bad guys out of the United States late at night in some remote areas are orange traffic cones" (Vlahos 2001: EV1).

Eight days after the attacks, Attorney General John Ashcroft asked for broad authority to detain for an indeterminate length of time individuals his agency believes pose a threat to national security (Povich 2001). Ashcroft further proposed to limit appeals of those detentions and put all such cases under the jurisdiction of the federal court in the District of Columbia. Further bolstering his law enforcement agenda, Ashcroft asked for sweeping powers to eavesdrop on electronic communications by suspected terrorists, to eliminate the statute of limitations on terrorism cases, and to track suspicious movements of money. With historical lessons at hand, advocates for civil liberties urged political leaders to exercise caution in passing new legislation:

> In past crises during this century—from the anarchist-communist scares of 1917–18 to the Oklahoma City bombing in 1995—Congress has responded by enacting major expansions of state police powers over the objections of civil libertarians. During World War I, Congress passed the Espionage and Sedition acts, which were used to arrest more than 1,500 people, many of whom were deported. In 1996, after Oklahoma City, Congress enacted antiterrorism and immigration control legislation that severely curtailed the ability of defendants in death penalty cases to appeal their sentences and that

allowed federal officials to use secret evidence in deportation cases. (Pianin and Edsall 2001: EV1)

Senator Edward Kennedy (D–Massachusetts) voiced similar concerns about sections of Ashcroft's proposals that would limit judicial appeals of detentions or deportations and would set up a new legal standard for detention that requires only a "reason to believe" that someone is associated with terrorism (Povich 2001). Soon lawmakers backed away from the administration's request to detain immigrants indefinitely; still, new antiterrorist legislation was poised for congressional approval (Hudson and Boyer 2001).

On October 26, 2001, President George W. Bush signed into law the USA Patriot (Utilizing and Strengthening America by Providing Appropriate Tools Required to Intercept and Obstruct Terrorism) Act. The following are some of the statutes' key provisions:

- Make it a crime to knowingly harbor a terrorist.
- Let the U.S. attorney general hold foreigners considered suspected terrorists for up to seven days before charging them with a crime or beginning deportation proceedings. The administration had initially sought to be able to hold them indefinitely, but Congress refused and limited such detention to seven days.
- Permit federal authorities to obtain court orders for "roving wiretaps," which would allow them to tap any phone a suspected foreign terrorist might use rather than a single phone.
- Make it easier for U.S. criminal investigators and intelligence officers to share grand jury, wiretap, and other information.
- Give the U.S. Treasury Department new powers to target foreign countries and banks deemed as money-laundering threats.
- Authorize funds to triple the number of Border Patrol agents along the U.S. northern border and to triple the number of INS inspectors at each port of entry along the northern border.
- Allow law enforcement to obtain a subpoena to get from Internet providers records about the electronic mail transmissions of suspected terrorists.
- Increase the statute of limitations as well as the punishment for many terrorist crimes.
- Limit the wiretap and surveillance provisions to four years ("Bush Signs" 2001: EV1).

Whereas the Patriot Act received overwhelming bipartisan support, civil liberties and immigrants' rights organizations worry that the new law will have unfair consequences not only for immigrants but also for U.S. citizens (Hentoff 2001; Shapiro 2001). While lawmakers and political leaders have their sights fixed on tracking down terrorists in the United States, numerous difficulties complicated the early stages of that law enforcement campaign. Chief among those concerns are scapegoating and racial profiling, as well as mass detention, abuse and mistreatment, and the government's refusal to disclose information about those they detain. Indeed, those recent developments greatly frustrate advocates for civil liberties and immigrants' rights.

Scapegoating and Racial Profiling

While trying to flee Lower Manhattan shortly after the attacks on the World Trade Center, a Sikh man found himself running not only from flames, but also from a trio of men yelling invectives about his turban. Two days later, a small group of men and boys gathered inside a mosque in Brooklyn Heights while outside a man drove past slowly and yelled, "Murderers" (Sengupta 2001b: EV1). Across the nation, word had spread that women in *hijab* (the identifying veil, in Arabic) should remain indoors. Fear of scapegoating swept through many Arabs and Muslims—as well as those who are neither but appear to be to the untutored American eye. Some mosques closed their doors out of such fear. The windows of the Islamic Center of Irving (Texas) were shattered by gunshots. In San Francisco, a bag of what appeared to be blood was left on the doorsteps of one mosque. In Alexandria, Virginia, a vandal threw two bricks through the windows of an Islamic bookstore; attached to the bricks were handwritten notes assailing Muslims. And in Richmond Hill, Queens, men beat a Sikh man with a baseball bat and shot at two others with a paint-ball gun (Sengupta 2001b, 2001c, 2001d).

Regrettably, acts of scapegoating and racial profiling also have been committed by law enforcement officers, the National Guard, and transportation security personnel. Sher J. B. Singh, an Indian Sikh and U.S. citizen, was removed from an Amtrak train in Providence, Rhode Island, handcuffed, and held for seven hours because, according to Singh, he wore a turban. Singh said the police and federal agents who questioned him knew nothing about the religion, the world's fifth largest. After the police searched the train, the agents told Singh they could not leave without taking someone into detention and told him that he would be released the next day (Glaberson 2001: EV2). After some officers taunted him because of his turban, Singh said they asked him general questions about Sikhism and never appeared to think he had any connection to terrorism. Some of those who have been questioned say the law enforcement officials have acknowledged that they were under pressure to hold people even if there was little reason to suspect them (Glaberson 2001).

At the Minneapolis airport, Dr. Jasjit S. Ahluwalia, an American Sikh and chairman of the department of preventative medicine at the University of Kansas School of Medicine, was stopped by a member of the National Guard who ordered him to remove his turban. Ahluwalia, who had already passed through a metal detector and scanned by a hand-held wand, was stunned by the request: "It is such an inappropriate question. It's like saying, 'Can I look under your bra?'" Numerous Sikhs have reported that since the September 11 attacks they have been targeted by airport police and security workers. More than two dozen Sikhs have filed complaints with antidiscrimination groups, asserting that they were forced to remove their turbans in public areas, a violation of their religious obligation to always keep their hair covered in public. Muslim women similarly have been ordered by airport security to remove their headscarves, also a violation of their faith. Kareem Shora, a legal advisor for the American Arab committee remarked, "This isn't even profiling. This is just outright discrimination and bigotry" (Goodstein 2001: B6).

Ziad Asali, president of the American-Arab Anti-Discrimination Committee (ADC), issued the following statement days following the attacks on the World Trade Center and the Pentagon:

> Unfortunately, as grief gives way to understandable anger, a pattern of collective blame and scapegoating against Arab Americans and Muslims seems to be emerging even before the culpability of any single individual has been established. Even if persons with connections to the Arab world or the Islamic faith prove to have had a hand in this outrage, there can be no reason or excuse for collective blame against any ethnic or religious community. Already we have received numerous disturbing reports of violent attacks, threats and harassment against Arab Americans and Muslims in many parts of the country and the pattern seems to be growing. As a result Arab Americans, in addition to feeling the intense depths of pain and anger at this attack we share with all our fellow citizens, are feeling deep anxiety about becoming the targets of anger from other Americans. We appeal to all Americans to bear in mind that crimes are the responsibility of the individuals who committed them, not ethnic or religious groups. (ADC 2001: EV1–2)

Immigration lawyers across the United States are instructing their clients to carry their documents with them at all times in the event that they are caught up in the government's sweep for terrorists. Compounding their anxiety, immigrants have been warned that immigration laws that were once rarely enforced have begun to take effect. Some immigration attorneys have said that, while the INS already enjoys broad powers to question, detain, and use secret evidence in prosecuting immigrants, they are concerned that the INS is now looking at the letter of the law and using it as a pretext to pick people up for questioning. Although it is technically a federal misdemeanor for immigrants not to carry their papers, the violation rarely called for a detention before September 11. David Leopold, an immigration attorney, acknowledged growing concern among his clients: "The key word is fear. Right now, for the first time, immigrants really feel their vulnerability. It's a scary time for them" (Kirchgaessner 2001: EV1).

As the DOJ vastly widened the scope of an investigation that, by December 2001, had yielded no direct link to the September 11 terrorist attacks, civil libertarians and other critics accused the government of engaging in wanton racial profiling that may scare away people who might be able to help (Butterfield 2001). In response to the DOJ's plan to interrogate 5,000 men who it believes might have information about the terrorist attacks, James Zogby, executive director of the Arab American Institute, said, "The kind of broad net-casting that was done right after September 11 may have been excusable, but at this point there has to be a better way of conducting this investigation" (Farragher and Cullen 2001: EV1). The DOJ has targeted for questioning men, ages 18 to 33, who have been in the United States legally on nonimmigrant visas since January 1, 2000, from countries from which known operatives of Osama bin Laden have entered the United States. Hussein Ibish, spokesperson for the ADC in Washington, was critical of the investigation: "This notion that all people of this category are red flags for scrutiny just stigmatizes young Arab men. It suggests that we're starting to rely increasingly on a crude type of stereotyping in our police work. And it encourages the public to find people of this description suspicious" (Farragher and Cullen 2001: EV2). Attorney General Ashcroft defended his tactics, insisting that the unconventional warfare triggered by the terrorist attacks calls for unconventional law enforcement methods.

Terrorism experts flatly disagreed. Professor Edith Flynn of Northeastern University described the tactic as "a fishing expedition" that suggested how little hard evidence the authorities have to proceed with in their attempts to prevent another terrorist attack. Flynn also questioned if it will work, "unless you have well-schooled questioners who could detect untruthfulness. Because of the inherent cultural differences, I really wonder how effective it will be" (Farragher and Cullen 2001: EV3). Although immigration rights' groups favor a thorough investigation, they are concerned that the DOJ's net is so broad it will inevitably ensnare men who are afraid to refuse to speak to federal officials out of fear of legal consequences. "It is inherently intimidating for an individual, especially one who has just arrived in this country, to be questioned by the FBI," said Lucas Guttentag of the ACLU. "It is not at all clear what the consequences of not talking to them would be, and whether the next knock on the door would come from the immigration service"(Farragher and Cullen 2001: EV3).

Mass Detention

In response to the September 11 attacks, the Bush administration abruptly announced a major expansion of its power to detain immigrants suspected of crimes, including plans that would allow the DOJ to detain indefinitely legal and illegal immigrants. (Previously, the department faced a 24-hour deadline on whether to release detained immigrants or charge them with a crime, or with violating the terms of their visa.) Given the Kafkaesque nature of indefinite detention, civil liberties advocates swiftly condemned the plan. David Martin, a law professor at the University of Virginia and a former general counsel of the INS, said, "There's definitely a civil liberties concern" in the new regulations. "I don't want to be alarmist about this. If we're talking about adding an additional 12 hours or 24 hours to detention, I don't think that's a problem. But if we are holding people for weeks and weeks, then I think there will be close scrutiny" (Shenon and Toner 2001: EV2). Just months before the September 11 attacks, the U.S. Supreme Court ruled against the government's use of indefinite detention of illegal immigrants, even when their homeland refuses to accept their return (*Zadvydas* v. *Underdown*). After much wrangling over the civil liberties issues contained in the new antiterrorism legislation, the Patriot Act was passed by Congress. Although the statute expanded the powers of the DOJ and the INS, it limited the length of detention to seven days before the government must charge the detainee with a crime. Once charged under the new law, however, detainees found to be engaged in terrorist activities can be held for six months (Rovella 2001).

The DOJ forged ahead with its broad powers, including the government's new rule to listen in on conversations between inmates and their lawyers—in effect suspending the Sixth Amendment right to effective counsel. Rachel King of the ACLU said the rule set a "terrifying precedent." It is "very scary," she said, adding, "It's nothing short of a police state" ("US to Listen In" 2001: EV1). Robert Hirshon, president of the American Bar Association, concurred, saying his group was "deeply troubled" by the rule because it ran "squarely afoul" of the U.S. Constitution and impinged on the right to counsel (2001: EV1). Even members of Congress were distressed by the new rule. Senator Patrick Leahy (D–Vermont), chairman of the Senate Judiciary Committee, stated in a letter to Ashcroft that the new policy raised grave concerns: "I am deeply troubled at what appears to be an executive effort to exercise new powers without judicial scrutiny or statutory authorization" (2001: EV2). Those new rules further empower an agency that already enjoys considerable authority:

> Under immigration law, the Justice Department is both accuser and judge, with its Immigration and Naturalization Service serving as police and prosecutor and its Executive Office for Immigration Review running special courts that decide whether resident aliens should be detained or deported. INS agents need no warrant to arrest noncitizens, and immigration courts don't provide lawyers for indigent suspects. (Bravin, Fields, Adams, and Wartzman 2001: EV1)

Professor David Martin elaborated on the government's use of power: "There may not be evidence right now to hold someone on a criminal charge." But with immigration charges, it often is "very easy to demonstrate a violation" of immigration law, allowing officials to deport or detain suspects (Bravin et al. 2001: EV1).

In less than two months following the September 11 attacks, the government had rounded up and detained more than 1,200 immigrants of Middle Eastern descent. Many concerned citizens took notice, most notably those who previously suffered similar forms of detention. Janice Mirikitani, San Francisco's poet laureate, said that when she read that the government is seeking the power to detain immigrants considered suspect and saw polls showing that Americans support racial profiling she felt a horrible sense of déjà vu. "Oh, no. Not again. For me, and other Japanese-Americans, what we immediately felt was great concern about what could happen to Afghan-Americans or Arab-Americans. It made us want to speak out and say, 'Never again'" (Nieves 2001: EV1). Mirikitani, age 59, was an infant when she was imprisoned by the federal government. Her entire family—both sets of grandparents, eight aunts, her parents, all American citizens—were rounded up after the Japanese attack on Pearl Harbor, herded into freight trains, and dumped in remote camps ringed with barbed wire, where they spent three and a half years during World War II. Fear and war hysteria led to the imprisonment of 120,000 Japanese Americans, nearly all from the West Coast (as well as nearly 11,000 Germans and German Americans and 2,000 Italians), who were considered possible allies of the nation's enemies, even though many of those imprisoned had sons and husbands serving in combat for the United States (Nieves 2001: EV1).

Abuse and Mistreatment

Weeks after September 11, evidence surfaced of abuse and mistreatment of those detained, prompting tremendous concern among human rights advocates:

> In Mississippi, a 20-year-old student from Pakistan reported that he was stripped and beaten in his cell by other inmates while jail guards failed to intervene and denied him proper medical care.
>
> In New York, prosecutors are investigating an Egyptian detainee's courtroom allegations of abuse by a guard, and the Israeli Consulate is concerned about five Israeli men who say they were blindfolded, handcuffed in their cells and forced to take lie detector tests.
>
> In three Midwestern states, U.S. immigration officials cut off all visits and phone calls for detainees for a full week after the attacks, a directive that officials now say was mishandled.
>
> And in Texas, a man from Saudi Arabia initially was denied an attorney and was deprived of a mattress, a blanket, a drinking cup and a clock to tell him when to recite his Muslim prayers, his lawyer said. (Serrano 2001b: EV1)

Such mistreatment amounts to scapegoating since it appears unlikely that any of those detainees played a role in the attacks on the World Trade Center or the Pentagon; none of them were held as a material witnesses and two were released after being interrogated. Indeed, the government's dragnet has failed to link most of those detained to the terrorism investigation. Most of those who were swept up were charged with immigration violations, most notably overstaying their visas. Attorney General Ashcroft insisted that there had been no wholesale abuse of detainees, even as four more cases surfaced in which young men allegedly were kept from their attorneys and confined in jails without proper food or protection. The new cases, in Florida and Pennsylvania, include a Pakistani man who lost 20 pounds while being detained alongside suspected murderers and other violent offenders, and an Iraqi teenager whose family said he came to America to escape one repressive regime and now fears he may have found another (Serrano 2001a, 2001b).

One of the more tragic incidents amid the sweep for terrorists was the death of Muhammad Rafiq Butt, who was found dead in Hudson County Correctional Center in New Jersey. Butt, a native of Pakistan and one of hundreds who had been picked up on the basis of tips from an anxious public, had been arrested for being in the country illegally. An autopsy revealed that Butt, 55, whose one-year stay in the United States seems to have been hapless from the very start, had coronary disease and died of a heart attack. His death forced the INS to do something it had not done during the 33 days it had him in custody—publicly explain the circumstances behind his arrest, detention, and death:

> It was revealed that he had been picked up after a tip to the Federal Bureau of Investigation from the pastor of a church near his home in South Ozone Park, Queens. His sole crime was overstaying his visitor visa. It took the F.B.I. a day to determine that it had no interest in him for its investigation into terrorism. He chose to appear at his deportation hearing without a lawyer, even though he spoke virtually no English and had little education. From jail, he made no calls to his relatives, nor to the Pakistani Consulate in New York. (Sengupta 2001b: EV1–2)

Torture of detainees is another controversial issue that has arisen since September 11. An experienced FBI agent involved in the investigation, in discussing the use of torture, is quoted as saying, "It could get to that spot where we could go to pressure" ("War on Terrorism" 2001: 25). Similarly, Robert Litt, a former DOJ official, argued that while torture ought not be "authorized," perhaps it could be used in an "emergency," as long as the person who tortures then presents himself to "take the consequences" (Williams 2001: 11). Those views appear to have some public support. A recent CNN poll revealed that 45 percent would not object to torturing someone if it would provide information about terrorism (Williams 2001). Journalists and human rights groups quickly responded. "We trust that the Bush administration is not seriously considering torture. . . . [Still] Ashcroft has been careless with the Constitution when it comes to the treatment of people arrested in the wake of

September 11, raising fears he will be similarly careless when it comes to using the broad new investigative powers recently granted him by Congress" ("Disappearing in America" 2001: A22; see Millett 1994). Amnesty International (2001) also condemned the use of torture and remains concerned over the well-being of detainees, especially in light of numerous reports that many of those arrested in the wake of the attacks were denied prompt access to lawyers or relatives. Moreover, questions about the mistreatment of detainees have yet to be answered fully because the government refuses to divulge such information to the public. Understandably, a policy of mass detention shrouded in secrecy and confusion has greatly distressed human rights and civil liberties groups.

Government Secrecy

Contributing to the Kafkaesque nature of mass detention, the government has maintained a policy of secrecy. Months following the investigation on the attacks of the World Trade Center and the Pentagon, Attorney General Aschroft repeatedly denied the public access to basic information about many of those in detention, including their names and current location. Such secrecy has been denounced by human rights and civil liberties advocates as well as by news organizations and even some political leaders who have complained that the attorney general has failed to explain adequately the need for those drastic measures. Kate Martin, director of the Center for National Security Studies, said, "The rounding up of hundreds of people secretly, secretly arresting them and putting them in jail where their families don't know where they are and not telling the public is unprecedented and extraordinary in this country" (Donohue 2001a: EV1). Martin added, "This is frighteningly close to the practice of 'disappearing' people in Latin America" where secret detentions were carried out by totalitarian regimes (Williams 2001: 11):

> In a high-security wing of Manhattan's Metropolitan Correctional Center, an unknown number of men with Middle Eastern names are being held in solitary confinement on the ninth floor, locked in 8- by 10-foot cells with little more than cots, thin blankets and, if they request it, copies of the Koran. Every two hours, guards roust them to conduct a head count.
>
> They have no contact with each other or their families and limited access to their lawyers. Their names appear on no federal jail log available to the public. No records can be found in any court docket in New York showing why they are detained, who represents them or the status of their cases. (Romano and Fallis 2001: EV1)

Steven Shapiro of the ACLU asked, "How many are being held? On what basis? What kind of judicial review is available? All of those seem to be important questions to answer"(Romano and Fallis 2001: EV1).

A 23-year-old Saudi student was held for 17 days, missing three weeks of school and being evicted from his San Diego apartment. He described his secret detention as a humiliating and terrifying experience (Romano and Fallis 2001). An attorney for three other men held in San Diego likened their detention to the sweeps for communists and sympathizers during the Red Scare of the 1920s; he complained that he was not even told where his clients were being held and was not permitted to contact them (Fox 2001: EV2). Harvey Grossman of the ACLU added, "There's been nothing as massive as this since the day after Pearl Harbor, when they rounded up 700 Japanese immigrants and held them incommunicado and without charges for a protracted period" ("Concerns Rise" 2001: EV2). Erwin Chemerinsky, a professor at the University of Southern California who specializes in constitutional law, could think of no other time in American history when the government had used so much judicial secrecy in a criminal investigation (Fox 2001).

Reports that detainees have been subjected to solitary confinement without being criminally charged as well as being denied access to telephones and attorneys have raised questions about whether detainees are being deprived of due process. Moreover, those deprivations clearly contradict assurances by the DOJ that everyone arrested since September 11 has access to counsel. By November 2001, key members of Congress began to challenge the sweeps of aliens in search of terrorists. Seven Democrats, most notably a coauthor of Ashcroft's antiterror legislation, Senate Judiciary Committee Chairman Patrick Leahy (VT), and the only senator to vote against it, Russ Feingold (WI), requested from the attorney general detailed information on the more than 1,000 people detained since the terrorist attacks. The lawmakers asked specifically for the identity of all those detained, the charges against them, the basis for holding those cleared of connection to terrorism, and a list of all government requests to seal legal proceedings, along with the rationale for doing so. The lawmakers stated that while the officials "should aggressively investigate and prevent further attacks," they stressed the DOJ's "responsibility to release sufficient information . . . to allow Congress and the American people to decide whether the department has acted appropriately and consistent with the Constitution" (Cohen 2001: EV1). Unlike people charged criminally, INS detainees are not entitled to government-appointed counsel; thus many are not represented. Some civil rights advocates complain that law enforcement officials are charging people with INS violations, holding them in solitary confinement, and then interrogating them before they can consult attorneys who might advise them not to talk (Cohen 2001). To abolish the DOJ's secrecy on detentions, a coalition of 21 groups, including Amnesty International, the American Friends Service Committee, the Arab American Institute, and the *Nation* magazine, filed a request under the Freedom of Information Act to release information about the detainees.

Interestingly, the DOJ then announced that it would no longer issue a running tally of the number of people detained around the nation as law enforcement officials investigate the September 11 hijackings and try to prevent further terrorist attacks. Instead, the DOJ would provide two, smaller pieces of information about its campaign of detentions: how many people are being held on charges of violating immigration laws and how many are in federal custody. The figures will reflect only the number of people held on INS or federal charges at any given time, not the cumulative total of who have been arrested and, in an unknown number of cases, released. According to the DOJ, the policy was changed because the previous method had placed too heavy a burden on state and local police departments to notify federal officials of arrests, thus making the tally prone to errors. That announcement prompted harsher criticism from civil liberties groups. "If it turns out what they've been giving out is confusing information, they ought to straighten that out, rather than withholding it," said Kate Martin, director of the Center for National Security Studies. Laura W. Murphy, of the ACLU, further argued, "We should not as a society tolerate a law enforcement apparatus that operates in virtual secrecy" (Goldstein and Eggen 2001: EV2; "Record Number Held" 2001).

The government's tactic of secrecy also continues to haunt even those detained—and released—before the September 11 attacks. As discussed in Chapter 4, the case of Mazen Al-Najjar, a Muslim cleric and former University of South Florida professor, figures prominently in the government's use of secret evidence. Although Al-Najjar had been released in December 2000 after being held for more than three and a half years on secret evidence, his case has taken on new and greater significance since September 11. In November 2001, Al-Najjar was rearrested outside his home and placed in INS detention as the government proceeded to deport him for overstaying a student visa from the early 1980s. In a swift decision, the U.S. Court of Appeals for the Eleventh Circuit upheld Al-Najjar's deportation. The DOJ argued that Al-Najjar has ties to terrorist groups and that his legal recourse for fighting deportation has simply run out. But attorneys for Al-Najjar contend that he is being used to test the government's powers to detain foreigners, particularly men of Middle Eastern descent, a power they say the government is misusing. David Cole, Al-Najjar's lead lawyer and a professor at the Georgetown University Law Center, reminds us of the importance of the case, especially in light of the government's campaign to use secret evidence against those detained since September 11: "This was one of the last secret evidence cases. The government has lost case after case in which it has sought to detain or deport aliens on the basis of secret evidence" (Canedy 2001: EV2). Martin Schwartz, one of Al-Najjar's other lawyers, added, "We don't believe that it is proper for I.N.S. to detain Mazen al-Najjar because the government has already failed to prove that he was either a threat to national security or a danger to the community" (Canedy 2001: EV2; Dow 2001).

The government prefers not to disclose to the public information on immigration and terrorism, but it is astonishing that such information rarely is shared among various government agencies. In the wake of the September 11 attacks, lawmakers from both parties are pushing for immigration legislation that would require the CIA, the FBI, the State Department, and other agencies to share information on suspected terrorists with the officials responsible for admitting foreigners into the United States. Intelligence-sharing has become a concern among members of Congress. Senator John Edwards (D–North Carolina) put it bluntly: "It's critically important that the people who issue visas have the information about who the bad guys are. The problem is the intelligence community, specifically the C.I.A., has not prior to September 11 been making that information available" (Clymer 2001: EV2).

While lawmakers from both parties remain focused on improving communication among key government agencies, their harshest criticism was aimed at the INS itself, especially in response to a tremendously embarrassing incident. Six months to the day after September 11th, the INS sent out a routine notice informing a flight school that Mohammed Atta and Marwan al-Shehhi, the hijackers who crashed into the World Trade Center, had been approved for student visas to study there. The INS said that it approved the visas for the two men in the summer of 2001, before either had been identified as suspected terrorists, and that it had failed to halt the normal process of having a sub-contractor notify the school. The error was far too painful to ignore, particularly since Congress had been criticizing the INS for sloppy management and inept record keeping. Representative John Conyers Jr. of Michigan blasted the INS: "I am astonished that while the INS is fixated on detaining and rounding up countless Arab-Americans without any justification, it has failed to take basic steps to ensure that visas are not issued to known terrorists" (Johnston 2002: A16). Days later, four top INS officials were replaced (Schmitt 2002a). Still, Congress moved forward with its most ambitious effort to overhaul the nation's immigration system. In April 2002, the House voted overwhelmingly (405 to 9) to abolish the INS and separate its functions between two new bureaus, one for immigration services and the other for enforcement (Schmitt 2002b). Lawmakers concede, however, that the bill is not a panacea. "It will take a long time for us to put our immigration affairs back in order. But this is an essential first step," replied Wisconsin Congressman F. James Sensenbrenner, Jr. (Schmitt 2002b: A26).

Final Thoughts on the Future of Immigrants' Rights

Understandably, the tragic events of September 11 have had a tremendous impact on American society, and as political leaders strive to balance national security with civil liberties, immigrants' rights will likely remain in flux. Regrettably, however, the DOJ's initial response to the threat of terrorism has pushed the envelope of civil liberties, especially in light of racial profiling and mass detentions compounded by a thick wall of secrecy. As the debate over immigration continues to be reshaped, it is important to briefly acknowledge two other problems exacerbated by the government's current campaign against terrorism: the adverse effects on refugees and continued profiteering by the corrections industry that uses INS detainees as raw materials.

The arrival of more than 20,000 refugees from around the world, cleared to enter to the United States so that they can escape persecution in their homelands, has been delayed indefinitely in the aftermath of the September 11 terrorist attacks.[1] A temporary moratorium on refugee admissions has resulted from both concerns about security and the fact that a White House consumed by its fight against terrorism has not issued its annual refugee quota. As a result, the nation's door remains closed to refugees, including women fleeing the Taliban, Iraqis fleeing the regime of Saddam Hussein, and children escaping civil war in Sierra Leone. Refugee resettlement groups say many of these people have been longtime residents of disease-prone refugee camps. Indeed, those refugees are indirect casualties of the terrorist attacks on America. While it is understandable that the government is increasingly vigilant of those coming to the United States, refugee experts insist that it is highly unlikely that a terrorist would pose as refugee in order to gain admittance. Refugees already undergo the most stringent background checks of any people seeking admission to the United States (Sengupta 2001c).

The government's campaign for homeland security also has fueled the corrections industry, especially given the more than one thousand foreigners who have been rounded up since the September 11 attacks.[2] In anticipation of internment camps and new prisons, stocks of private companies that build and operate prisons for governments recently increased as high as 300 percent. James MacDonald, prisons security analyst at First Analysts Securities, notes, "Unfortunately, these are becoming good investments" (Tharp 2001: EV1). As of November 2001, six publicly traded prison companies expect good financial news from the BOP, which has announced plans to expand its correctional capacity for INS detainees. The BOP recently opened the bidding process for two prisons to hold criminal aliens in Georgia and by early 2002, the government will have sought bids for three more prisons in the Southwest deserts that can hold more than 1,500 detainees. Among those companies poised to cash in on the new crop of detainees is Wackenhut Corporation. In Australia, Wackenhut has been housing detainees in former military bases converted to immigrant camps in which conditions are known to be abysmal (Gaylord 2001). CCA also is expected to be in the race for prison revenue. CCA was on the brink of bankruptcy in the summer of 2001, but a new management team and the sudden new business in the aftermath of the September 11 terrorist attacks changed its prospects. Financial analysts noted that many security companies received huge and immediate profits from supplying guards and new security.

Immigrant advocates continue to criticize the detention of people accused of noncriminal immigration violations in jails built to house criminals. The latest trend in detention further threatens to infuse the immigration system with a dangerous element of profiteering. "This is a really bizarre thing where our growth industry is our prison system. It is something that we have to be very concerned about," said James Haggerty, of the CLINIC (Donohue 2001b: EV2). In November 2001, economists announced that the United States had officially entered a recession; still, the corrections industry is likely to prosper during tough financial times. MacDonald agreed: "Crime always goes up in a bad economy. When there are good times and jobs are plentiful, people who get out of prison can usually find work and don't have to go back to their old ways. When the economy fails, so do the former inmates" (Tharp 2001: EV2).

As discussed throughout this book, 1996 was a benchmark year for repressive legislation that continues to erode immigrants' rights. With those lessons in clear view, immigrants' rights and civil liberties organizations must repeatedly caution the public and political leaders not to overreact to the tragic events of September 11. Fear of terrorism and anxiety over national security—albeit justified—must be contained so that they do not undermine the fair and just treatment of immigrants, refugees, and asylum seekers.

Notes

Chapter 1

Epigraphs: Parenti: *Lockdown America: Police and Prisons in the Age of Crisis* (1999: 154); Bontia: quoted in Hedges (2000a: B1); Sesay: quoted in Casimir (2001: EV1).

Chapter 2

Epigraphs: Buchanan 1996 (also see 1991, 2002); Guiliani: quoted in Firestone (1995: A1; also see Dugger 1997).

1. The following scholarly works illuminate the significance of moral panic and social constructionism: Best 1987, 1989, 1990; Chermak 1997; Chiricos 1996; Cohen and Young 1981; Ferrell 1996; Fishman 1978; Hall, Critcher, Jefferson, Clarke, and Roberts 1978; Hickman 1982; Hollywood 1997; Humphries 1999; Jenkins 1994a, 1994b; McCorkle and Miethe 1998; McRobbie and Thornton1995; Potter and Kappeler 1998; Reinarman and Levine 1997; Welch 2000a; Welch and Bryan 2000; Welch, Fenwick, and Roberts 1997, 1998; Welch, Price, and Yankey 2002a, 2002b.

2. Much like the debate over immigration, the debate over population has long been a polarizing one. Some opponents of population tend to abandon reasonable well-founded arguments and gravitate to extreme, catastrophic scenarios. In 1968, Paul Ehrlich's bestseller, *The Population Bomb*, offered a doomsday scenario in which world population would soar past the capacity of the planet to sustain it, leading to environmental disaster and mass starvation. Representing a similar perspective on immigration, in 1990, Lawrence Auster published a book with the catastrophic title *The Path to National Suicide: An Essay on Immigration and Multiculturalism*, a work that has been widely cited by anti-immigration proponents.

3. In criminalizing immigrants, Brimelow has a long memory, reminding his readers that Robert F. Kennedy was assassinated by an immigrant, Sirhan Sirhan, "born in Jerusalem, who entered the United States from Jordan under a special program for Palestinian refugees in 1956" (1995: 78).

4. Historically, there have campaigns to pathologize immigrants, thus influencing the course of legislation. In 1903, Congress prohibited idiots, epileptics, insane

207

persons, persons who had been insane within five years previously, and persons afflicted with a loathsome or dangerous disease. Moreover, that legislation also banned persons viewed as lazy, immoral, and politically radical, such as beggars, polygamists, and anarchists (Kraut 1994; Reimers 1998).

5. As another example of informal social control, in 1996 a group calling itself "U.S. Citizens Patrol" roamed the San Diego airport to intimidate and deter undocumented immigrants from entering the facility. Members of the group, wearing T-shirts labeled "U.S. Citizens Patrol" designed to appear as if they were government agents, approached airline ticketing employees and instructed them to check all identification as required by the Federal Aviation Administration. Eventually, a federal judge, at the urging of Latino residents, issued a temporary restraining order, thus confining their activities to outside the airport terminal (Yzaguirre 1996; see Parenti 1999).

Chapter 3

Epigraphs: Auster: *The Path to National Suicide: An Essay on Immigration and Multiculturalism* (1990: 53); Reimers, *Unwelcome Strangers: American Identity and the Turn against Immigration* (1998: 147).

1. Among the minor changes in the law affecting legal immigration was a new monetary limit on sponsoring immigrations. To bring one's relatives to the United States, one had to earn an income of 125 percent of the poverty rate, an increase from the former figure of the poverty level itself. Critics of the new income threshold argued that the policy discriminated against people from impoverished nations, in particular Central Americans (see Jonas and Dod Thomas 1999).

2. The operational and management functions of the INS are administered through INS headquarters in Washington, D.C., which oversees approximately 29,000 employees through three regional offices and the headquarters-based Office of International Affairs. These offices are responsible for directing the activities of 33 districts and 21 Border Patrol sectors throughout the United States and three district offices and 39 area offices outside U.S. territory. INS field offices provide direct service to applicants for benefits under the Immigration and Nationality Act and implement INS policies to carry out statutory enforcement responsibilities in their respective geographical areas. Overseas offices, in addition, serve as important information channels between INS and U.S. Foreign Service officers and foreign government officials abroad (INS 2000a).

3. Since 1996, when federal law drastically lowered the threshold for deportation in the wake of the Oklahoma City bombing, the number of immigrants removed from the United States has skyrocketed. From 1994 to 2000, the number of aliens held by the U.S. government for deportation proceedings rose from 74,479 to 167,342 (MacQuarrie 2000).

4. Efforts by the United States to secure its border with Mexico have funneled illegal crossings to more dangerous routes. In fact, between 1997 and 2000, more than 600 people have died crossing the United States–Mexico border (Stammer 2000; also see Chin 1999).

5. Since 1998, at least 294 INS employees—including inspectors, agents, and high-ranking officials—have been arrested and charged with crimes ranging from immigrant smuggling to sexual assault, bribery, extortion, and drug trafficking. Approximately 25 percent of the cases ended in guilty pleas or convictions; others resulted in terminations or other disciplinary actions (Walth et al. 2000).

Chapter 4

Epigraphs: Weissinger: *Law Enforcement and the INS: A Participant Observation Study of Control Agents* (1996: 48); Cooper, quoted in Sullivan and Walth (2000: EV2); Marx: "Ironies of Social Control . . ." (1981: 242).

1. Although the evacuation was reportedly organized around concerns for national security, critics insist that racism played a defining role in the detention of Americans of Japanese descent. Novelist John Steinbeck corresponded directly with President Roosevelt, reminding him that Japanese Americans were loyal citizens who condemned the attack on Pearl Harbor (Lewis 1995). Oddly, the relocation program was confined to the contiguous states, not reaching Hawaii where the concentration of those of Japanese ancestry was much higher. Lieutenant General John DeWitt, who oversaw the internment operation, publicly expressed sentiments construed as racist: "A Jap is a Jap. . . . it makes no difference whether he's an American or not." In his military reports, DeWitt characterized people of Japanese descent as "subversive" members of an "enemy race" whose "racial strains are undiluted" (Raskin 1991: 117). The U.S. Supreme Court supported DeWitt's evacuation plan under the umbrella of war powers. In *Korematsu* v. *United States* (1944), a case involving a Japanese American who defied the resettlement orders, the High Court ruled that Korematsu's constitutional rights were not violated. Conversely, critics argue the Court erroneously validated racial discrimination (Raskin 1991; Wiener 1995).

2. In 2001, 300,000 Bracero workers (and their heirs) filed a class-action suit against the governments of Mexico and the United States, claiming that they have never received money that was deducted from their paychecks. The money was to be transmitted from American banks to Mexican banks and given to the Braceros when they returned to Mexico. The retired workers are seeking hundreds of millions of dollars in reparations (Belluck 2001).

3. SSI benefits were later restored, but only for those immigrants who entered the country before August 22, 1996, the day the law went into effect.

4. Over the past few decades, other proposals featuring court-stripping provisions have been ruled unconstitutional because they were determined to be backdoor amendments to the Constitution. In such controversial areas as school integration, women's rights to reproductive autonomy, and separation of church and state (i.e., school prayer), Congress unsuccessfully tried to eliminate basic rights by prohibiting the courts' ability to enforce those rights. Eventually, "the public realized that taking away the court's power to enforce rights is tantamount to taking away the rights themselves" (Guttentag quoted in ACLU 1999a: 4).

5. The Anti-Terrorism and Effective Death Penalty Act of 1996 also features court-stripping provisions in which federal habeas corpus petitions were restricted

even in those cases in which a state court was not only wrong, but also unreasonably wrong. The effects of the Anti-Terrorism and Effective Death Penalty Act are especially significant in death penalty cases because federal habeas corpus petitions have been available where a prisoner raised, for the first time, claims of ineffective counsel or other procedural issues. However, under the new statute, such claims no longer merit a federal hearing, "because it would not be unreasonable for a state court to have failed to take into account an issue that was never raised" (Lewin 2000: EV1).

6. Mandatory detention, along with the new roster of deportable crimes, went into effect on October 9, 1998. Since then, many permanent residents who have been in the United States for many years and have U.S. citizen family members have been detained in INS facilities and county jails. Returning from a travel abroad, longtime residents have been taken into custody and transferred to the nearest INS detention center or county correctional facility without the possibility for release. The INS also runs background checks on those applying for U.S. citizenship. If the applicant has committed even a minor crime in the past, the INS revokes his or her resident alien ("green") card and immediately begins deportation proceedings (see Amnesty International 2000a: 3).

Chapter 5

Epigraphs: Tulsky: "Asylum Seekers Face Tougher Laws . . ." (2000a); Meissner: quoted in Tulsky (2000a); Weaver: "Stop Treating Refugees like Criminals." (2000).

1. The stern rule of the Taliban forbids the viewing of television and other forms of recreation; in fact, recently people in Afghanistan have been jailed for playing cards. Under the Taliban, thieves have had a hand cut off and homosexuals have been buried alive beneath a stone wall. In 2001, two prostitutes were hanged in Kandahar (Afghanistan) as more than 5,000 people watched (Bearak 2001).

2. Most European nations (and Canada) do not make detention automatic or mandatory, and most require judicial review of all detention cases (Walth 2000).

3. Detention of asylum seekers is inherently undesirable. All decisions to detain asylum seekers must be made on a case-by-case basis. Detention is justified only when it is strictly necessary to verify an asylum seeker's identity to a reasonable and practicable extent under the circumstances; determine whether an asylum seeker is asserting elements upon which a claim for asylum could be based; or protect national security, enforce criminal law, or protect public safety in the same circumstances and with the same legal protections afforded U.S. citizens. Detention also may be justified when an asylum seeker has a history of repeated or unjustified failures to comply with reporting requirements imposed by the INS or the immigration court, or has failed to leave the country following the exhaustion of all appeal procedures (Human Rights Watch 1998a: 7).

4. Lack of legal counsel needed to process their claims remains a persistent problem for refugees and asylum seekers who typically stay in detention for longer periods of time because their cases become backlogged in the bureaucracy of the INS (see Tulsky 2000b).

5. The INS has been criticized for its uneven enforcement of expedited removal and detention policies among its districts. Whereas some districts operate with considerable leniency, others have gained a reputation for their harsh enforcement of the 1996 immigration law (Lawyers Committee for Human Rights 1999a). After earning the nickname "De-Portland" in the media, the INS District Director in Portland, Oregon, David Beebe, resigned amid criticism from community leaders and Oregon's congressional delegation for mistreatment of international travelers at the Portland airport. The Portland INS chief detention officer, W. Scott Cihlar, said, "the fallout has prompted the local office to be more flexible. . . . We're trying to do the kinder, gentler thing" (Walth 2000: EV9).

6. In 1999, the controversial detention of Kosovar refugees gained national publicity as human rights groups sharply criticized the U.S. government for housing traumatized refugees in criminal facilities where physical abuse had been documented (Amnesty International 1999b; Lawyers Committee for Human Rights 1999b).

Chapter 6

Epigraphs: Roth: "Human Rights Watch Condemns . . ." (Human Rights Watch, 1998c: 1); Lipiner: quoted in Casimir (2001: EV2); Polidor: quoted in Benjamin (2001: EV3).

1. In 1999, five Mariel Cubans detained at the Saint Martin Parish jail in Louisiana seized control of the facility and took several hostages, including the warden. The detainees rioted to protest their long-term detention, some of whom had been confined for as long as seven years. Demanding safe passage from the United States, the standoff concluded after six days when hostages were released unharmed ("Hostage Standoff Ends" 1999). In an unusual move, the Cuban government accepted a petition that allowed the five Mariel hostage takers to return to the homeland; upon their arrival, they were transferred to a Cuban prison (Lacy and Firestone 1999; Martel 1999; Shenon 1999). Wayne Smith, the top-ranking American diplomat in Havana under Presidents Carter and Reagan, continues to voice his opposition to the embargo against Cuba. Reacting to the hostage-taking in the Saint Martin parish jail, Smith added, "You really have to sympathize with them [Cuban detainees]. What are they supposed to do, just sit there" (Lacy and Firestone 1999: A30). For discussions on riots and disturbances at facilities housing INS detainees, see Hamm (1995) and Welch (1997a, 1997b).

2. For its 1998 report, Human Rights Watch conducted research over an 18-month period, including visits to 14 jails in seven states and interviews with more than 200 INS detainees (1998a). Human Rights Watch also has received hundreds of letters and scores of telephone calls from detainees describing poor conditions and mistreatment in jails around the country. The seven states visited are Florida, Illinois, Louisiana, Maryland, Pennsylvania, Texas, and Virginia.

3. Although the INS claims that they do not keep records on the nationality of detainees, immigration and human rights lawyers who visit detention centers report that the vast majority of detainees are people of color (Marks 1995).

4. The UNHCR Guidelines on Detention of Asylum Seekers make clear that conditions of detention should be humane and prescribed by law and make special reference to the applicability of the norms and principles found in the U.N. Standard Minimum Rules and the U.N. Body of Principles. In particular, Guideline 6 states that the following conditions for asylum seekers should be provided: (i) the segregation within facilities of men and women, and children from adults and asylum seekers from convicted criminals; (ii) the possibility regularly to contact and receive visits from friends, relatives and legal counsel; (iii) the possibility to receive appropriate medical treatment and to conduct some form of physical exercise; and (iv) the possibility to continue further education or vocational training.

5. Another controversy stemming from INS detention practices is the use of forced sedation to control unruly detainees, especially during efforts to deport them (see Booth 1993; Lawyers Committee for Human Rights 1998b; Nhu and Hallye 2001; Viglucci 1994; Welch 1996a). Similarly, human rights groups are concerned over hunger strikes involving INS detainees protesting their harsh conditions of confinement ("Another Hunger Strike" 1998; Dow 1999; Sachs 1999b; Siegal 2000; Solomon 1999).

Chapter 7

Epigraphs: Leggs: quoted in Human Rights Watch (1997: 39); relative of Avila: quoted in Montero (2001: EV1); Human Rights Watch: *Slipping Through the Cracks . . .* (1997: 5).

1. According to the UNHCR, "An unaccompanied child is a person who is under the age of eighteen years, unless under the law applicable to the child, majority is attained earlier, and who is separated from both parents and is not being cared for by an adult who by law or custom has the responsibility to do so" (1996: 2).

2. UNHCR estimates that children make up more than half the world's refugee and internally displaced population, accounting for a population of 20 million children. Out of that population, an estimated 250,000 of these refugee children are separated from their parents (Lawyers Committee for Human Rights 2000b: EV2).

3. An estimated 20 percent of the children are released to relatives, while 60 percent voluntarily leave the United States before seeing a judge, said Wendy Young of the Women's Commission for Refugee Women and Children. "We worry about what happens to the other 20 percent," she said, charging that some kids are held indefinitely (Montero 2001: EV2).

4. In *Perez-Funez* v. *INS* (1985) a federal trial court in California found that the INS had violated the due process rights of unaccompanied minors by forcing them to accept voluntary departure from the United States (thus waiving their right to a hearing before an immigration judge) without their effective knowledge or consent. The *Perez-Funez* court concluded, "the situation faced by unaccompanied minors is inherently coercive" (F. Supp. 656, 662). The *Perez-Funez* court issued a nationally applicable injunction requiring the INS to ensure that unaccompanied minors have adequate opportunity to consult with an adult before signing a voluntary departure form. In *Orantes-Hernandez* v. *Meese* (1988), a federal trial court ruled that since undocumented immigrants have both statutory and constitutional rights to a

representative of their choosing, any INS regulations or practices that obstruct the right to counsel are invalid. The *Orantes-Hernandez* court added that INS detention officials must not only refrain from interfering with communication between detainees and their attorneys, but also are obligated to provide detainees with legal assistance (also see *Orantes-Hernandez* v. *Thornburgh* 1990).

5. The Los Angeles District of the INS usually has approximately 20 to 30 unaccompanied children in detention; until 1996, those children were placed in one of three county juvenile detention facilities: Eastlake, Los Padrinos, or Sylmar. Beginning in 1996, the INS began transferring most minors to the new contract "shelter care" facility in Arizona. Still, the INS continues to detain many minors in Los Angeles County facilities for short periods of time, and minors deemed by the INS to be a security risk will continue to be held in Los Angeles County (Human Rights Watch 1997: 19).

6. Human Rights Watch was permitted to visit the Arizona facility only on the condition that it not reveal its precise location.

7. It is estimated that one-half to three-fourths of the children detained in Arizona are Chinese, who typically stay there for months at a time (Human Rights Watch 1997).

8. In 2000, Southwest Key announced plans to move their facility (from Coolidge) to the Phoenix area to be closer to the INS courts and many of its programs. The new facility will have 65 beds, up from 48 at the former site (Beard 2000).

9. At the BCYC, the secure detention wing holds juveniles who have been charged or adjudicated delinquent. The "old" shelter care facility is used primarily for children in the custody of local child welfare authorities. In 1998, negotiations between BCYC and the INS led to the opening of a second 35-bed shelter care facility used primarily for children in INS custody.

10. It should be noted that at BCYC, children detainees are allowed telephone calls twice a week. Still, there complaints that many children go for weeks without being able to make phone calls (Human Rights Watch 1998d).

11. When Human Rights Watch interviewed other INS officials, it discovered comparable levels of ignorance regarding policies and procedures. John Salter, the Los Angeles INS district counsel, seemed equally uninformed: "There may be an INS policy. . . . I don't know." When we asked how the Los Angeles district INS ensured that minors passing through the B-18 staging area made telephone calls as required by *Perez-Funez*, Mr. Salter was vague: "Maybe Detention and Deportation documents that. . . . I don't know" (Human Rights Watch 1997: 40).

12. Furthermore, Melville admitted that she had not notified any local immigration attorneys of the change in policy resulting in the transfer of their clients to Arizona. Similarly, Leonard Kovensky, the Los Angeles acting assistant district director, told Human Rights Watch, "We inform attorneys of client transfers when we have the luxury to do so" (1997: 41).

13. District Counsel John Salter also defended procedural violations on the grounds that officials needed to "save time," and when asked whether he thought non-Spanish speaking children ought to receive translations of legal materials and rights advisories, he simply shrugged: "It's not in the regulations" (Human Rights Watch 1997: 41).

14. To keep asylum-seeking families together while undergoing the hearing process, the INS opened its first detention center for undocumented immigrant families in 2001. Located in central Pennsylvania, the dormitory-style Family Shelter Care Center makes use of a former nursing home. The average stay is expected to be three to six weeks at a cost to the government of about $200 per day, much cheaper than using hotel rooms pejoratively known as Motel Kafkas. "The overall goal here is the safe, secure and humane treatment of detainees," said Anthony Tangeman, an INS deputy commissioner in Washington. Still, a critic of the shelter noted that the facility is "just a very fancy jail with a pretty name. Anything that puts people in detention and keeps them locked up when they haven't committed a crime is a step in the wrong direction," said Kathleen Lucas, founder of the Coalition for Immigrants' Rights at the Community Level (May 2001: EV2).

15. The United Kingdom places unaccompanied children in the care of local authority social service departments, and in Canada they are placed in the care of a government child welfare agency, either the Children's Aid Society or the Ministry of Social Services. In Denmark, unaccompanied minors are cared for by nongovernmental organizations. Similarly, in the Netherlands such children are cared for by a nongovernmental organization called De Opbouw, which assumes guardianship of the children; the Dutch government pays for the cost of the children's care (Human Rights Watch 1997: 42).

16. Public interest attorneys report that even children with relatives in the United States often experience difficulties rejoining their families after being detained by the INS, because the INS requires family members to provide information about their immigration status before initiating the release process. The INS has been unwilling to assure them that it will not use this information to later apprehend and prosecute family members living illegally in the United States. Consequently, many families are afraid to approach the INS to obtain the release of their detained children; thus many children remain in INS detention in highly restrictive settings at significant government expense, despite the availability of relatives willing and able to provide for their care (Human Rights Watch 1997).

Chapter 8

Epigraphs: Lilly and Deflem: "Profit and Penalty . . ." (1996: 14); Mauer: "Letter to the Editor" (1998: 2); Pranis: "Letter to the Editor" (1998: 3).

1. Operating under the same umbrella of social control, other spheres of the criminal justice machinery have adopted a similar approach to public policy, most notably drug control. According to the Office of National Drug Control Policy (1996), 70 percent of the agency's budget was devoted to enforcement strategies while 30 percent was allocated to treatment and social services (see Welch, Bryan, and Wolff 1999; Welch, Wolff, and Bryan 1998).

2. The phenomenon of net-widening, fueling the prison industry, is well documented empirically. In their research, Irwin and Austin (1994) found that 80 percent of those in prison are not serious or violent criminals: Sixty-five percent of inmates were convicted of property, drug, and public-disorder crimes, while another 15 percent were returned for violating the conditions of their parole, for example, curfew violations, failure to participate in a program, or evidence of substance abuse.

More recently, Irwin, Schiraldi, and Ziedenberg (2000) estimated that the number of nonviolent prisoners in the United States exceeds one million.

3. According to Lilly and Knepper (1993), the corrections–commercial complex conforms to the subgovernmental model in four key aspects: (1) "Each of the participants in the corrections sub-government shares a close working relationship supported by the flow of information, influence, and money" (p. 157); (2) "There is a distinct overlap between the interests of for-profit companies and professional organizations and the interests of the federal agencies maintained by the flow of influence and personnel" (p. 158); (3) "The corrections-commercial complex operates without public scrutiny and exercises enormous influence over corrections policy" (p. 160); (4) "The corrections-commercial complex shows signs of becoming a fixture within national policy area of punishing lawbreakers as the participants define their activities in the public interest" (p. 161).

4. Incidentally, the world's leading private corrections company is the Corrections Corporation of America (CCA), based in Nashville, Tennessee. CCA holds more than 52 percent of the market share and owns approximately 43,000 beds in nearly 60 prisons in the United States, the United Kingdom, and Australia. Like other private corrections firms, CCA houses various types of prisoners, including federal, state, and local inmates along with INS detainees. By 1998, CCA's performance was in the top 20 percent of the stock market returns over the past 10 years (Bates 1998a; Welch 1999b; Yeoman 2000).

Chapter 9

Epigraphs: Filner: quoted in Malone and Trejo (2001: EV3); Wenski: quoted in Benjamin (2001: EV8); Brownback: quoted in Vekshin (2001: EV1).

1. The constitutional revolution in criminal procedure began with the 1961 case *Mapp* v. *Ohio* in which the Warren Court established the basic parameters of illegal search and seizure. Conservatives harshly criticized the Warren Court for its ruling in *Mapp*, arguing that it undermined the effectiveness of police. Five years later, the Warren Court delivered its decision in *Miranda* v. *Arizona* (1966), thereby requiring police to inform criminal suspects of their constitutional rights (also see *U.S.* v. *Wade* 1967).

2. In *Harris* v. *New York* (1971), *Kirby* v. *Illinois* (1972), and *Michigan* v. *Tucker* (1974), the Burger Court tempered due process by placing restrictions on the *Miranda* rule (also see *Berkemer* v. *McCarty*, *New York* v. *Quarles*, and *Nix* v. *Williams*, all in 1984). Soon other advances in due process established under the Warren Court also were eroded, shifting the balance of power to police and prosecutors and away from citizens. The Supreme Court in a series of cases gradually modified and weakened the exclusionary rule, thus permitting the admissibility of certain forms of evidence obtained illegally (see *Illinois* v. *Gates* 1983; *Massachusetts* v. *Sheppard* 1984; *U.S.* v. *Leon* 1984).

3. Indeed, President Reagan's crime control agenda benefited tremendously from the Court's commitment to strengthening the criminal justice system by delivering a key opinion that upheld the Bail Reform Act of 1984 (*U.S.* v. *Salerno* 1987) and another that rejected a claim that the Georgia death penalty process was unconstitutional because black defendants who murder white victims statistically are more

likely to receive a death sentence (*McCleskey* v. *Kemp* 1987). To aid the work of police, the Rehnquist Court further undermined the exclusionary rule (*Griffin* v. *Wisconsin* 1987; *Illinois* v. *Krull* 1987; *New York* v. *Burger* 1987). Advocates of due process were critical of those rulings as well as of the Court's controversial decision in *Colorado* v. *Connelly* (1987), concluding that a confession is not inadmissible as involuntary merely because it is prompted by mental illness.

4. Before 1996, noncitizens convicted of other serious crimes, including drug violations, were deportable. Still, they retained the right to apply for a "discretionary waiver of deportation" unless they had served at least five years in prison. In about half of the cases (a few thousand per year), that relief was granted, usually to immigrants whose family members were U.S. citizens or who could demonstrate evidence of rehabilitation or other compelling personal circumstances. Moreover, an immigrant could appeal to a federal court if the waiver was denied (Greenhouse 2001a; Schmitt 2001).

5. In related court decisions, in 2001, a divided U.S. Supreme Court upheld as constitutional a federal law that makes U.S. citizenship more difficult to obtain for children born abroad out of wedlock to American fathers than to American mothers. By a 5–4 vote, the court ruled the tougher requirements imposed on American fathers do not violate the constitutional guarantee of equal protection and do not amount to unconstitutional sex discrimination (Vicini 2001). Also in 2001, a federal appeals court ruled that pregnant women who are in the United States illegally have no right to prenatal care under Medicaid, a move that strengthens the cutback of benefits for undocumented immigrants (Wakin 2001).

6. Status adjustments will help those from nations with the heaviest rates of immigration into the United States, including Mexico, India, China, and the Philippines. However, critics argue that relatively few Central Americans are likely to be helped because many of their relatives also are here illegally and thus cannot serve as U.S. sponsors. In particular, immigrant advocates say that the new provisions discriminate against Guatemalans, Haitians, Hondurans, and Salvadorans who are denied the same benefits as Cubans and Nicaraguans. The dispute over Central American refugees began in the 1980s, when several waves of immigrants came to the United States fleeing political strife. Most, but not all, have been trapped in limbo over their immigrant status ever since. The exceptions are those arriving from Nicaragua before 1995, who along with Cuban refugees were given special amnesty under a 1997 law; some had fought for guerrillas supported by the Reagan administration. Other Central Americans, however, were never granted such amnesty. Most fled right-wing military regimes backed by the U.S. in wars with Marxist rebels. The 1997 law permitted some Salvadorans and Guatemalans to fight deportation under more lenient rules than before but stopped well short of the amnesty afforded Nicaraguans. Hondurans and Haitians were left out of that package altogether (Anderson and McDonnell 2000; Eggen 2001; Kahn 1996).

Epilogue

Epigraphs: Camarota: quoted in Hegstrom (2001: EV2); Human Rights Watch: "Human Rights Watch Response to Attacks . . ." (2000).

1. The refugees in this passage refer to those who are assisted in coming to the United States through the U.S. Refugee Resettlement Program and not to detained asylum seekers who enter the United States on their own.

2. Due to the September 11 attacks, the DOJ announced that it would move forward with its plans to reorganize the INS, dividing the agency into two separate bureaus, one dealing with service—such as citizenship or residency applications—and another with enforcement of immigration laws. According to Attorney General Ashcroft, the division will make the agency more effective in detecting foreign terrorists while expanding its detention and deportation operations (Viglucci and Chardy 2001).

References

EV refers to an electronic version of the publication. All websites were verified to be accurate as of July 2002.

"Access Denied: Children in INS Custody Have No Right to a Lawyer; Those Who Get One Risk Retaliation." 2001. *National Law Journal*, April: 1–2.

Acer, E., and G. Guerrero. 2001. "Asylum Parole Procedures Need More Reform." *Detention Watch Network News*, Spring: 16.

Acuna, R. 1996. *Anything But Mexican: Chicanos in Contemporary Los Angeles*. New York: Verso.

Adams, K. 1996. "The Bull Market in Corrections." *The Prison Journal*, 76(4): 461–467.

Adamson, C. 1984. "Toward a Marxian Theory of Penology: Captive Criminal Populations as Economic Threats and Resources." *Social Problems*, 31(4): 435–458.

Adler, J. 1994. "The Dynamite, Wreckage, and Scum in Our Cities: The Social Construction of Deviance in Industrial America." *Justice Quarterly*, 11(1): 7–32.

Alien Minors Shelter Care Program. U.S. Department of Justice, Community Relations Service. 1987. *Program Guidelines and Requirements*. Washington, D.C.: U.S. Government Printing Office.

"Alleged Mistreatment of Asylum Seekers in York County Prison." 2000. National Public Radio. *All Things Considered*. December 8.

Alvarez, L. 2000. "Congress Approves a Big Increase in Visas for Specialized Workers." *New York Times*, October 4: A1, A24.

American-Arab Discrimination Committee (ADC). 2001. "Statement by ADC President Ziad Asali." Press Release, Washington, D.C., September 14: EV1–3.

American Civil Liberties Union (ACLU). 1993. *Justice Detained: Conditions at the Varick Street Immigration Detention Center, A Report by the ACLU Immigrants' Rights Project*. New York: ACLU.

———. 1997. *The Rights of Immigrants*. www.aclu.org.

———. 1998a. *Trouble at the Border*. www.acul.org

———. 1998b. *In Search of Asylum*. www.aclu.org.

———. 1999a. "New Immigrant Law Threatens People and Principles: An Interview with Lucas Guttentag, Director of the ACLU Immigrants' Rights Project." (Reposted from, and with the permission of, *TexLaw*). www.aclu.org.

————. 1999b. *Expedited Removal*. www.aclu.org.

————. 2000a. *ACLU Joins Fix '96 Campaign for Justice for Immigrants*. www.aclu.org.

————. 2000b. *Stop the Use of Secret Evidence*. www.aclu.org.

————. 2000c. "ACLU Urges Congress to End Use of Secret Evidence." Press Release, May 23. Washington, D.C.: ACLU Media Relations Office.

————. 2000d. "Miami Federal Court to Consider Government's Use of 'Secret Evidence' in Detention of Academic." Press Release, April 17. Washington, D.C.: ACLU Media Relations Office.

————. 2000e. *The Aftermath of the 1996 Immigration Laws: Real Life Tragedies*. www.aclu.org.

————. 2000f. *Indefinite Detention*. www.aclu.org.

————. 2000g. "Federal Appeals Court Says INS Must Free Indefinitely Detained Immigrants." Press Release, April 10. Washington, D.C.: ACLU Media Relations Office.

Amnesty International.1997. *Children in INS Detention*. www.amnestyusa.org.

————. 1998a. *Human Rights Concerns in the Border Region with Mexico*. www. amnestyusa.org.

————. 1998b. *Treated as Criminal: Asylum Seekers in the USA*. www.amnestyusa.org.

————. 1999a. *Asylum-Seekers Detained in the USA: A Disproportionate and Harsh Measure*. www.amnestyusa.org.

————. 1999b. "Amnesty International USA Calls for End of Detention of Kosovar Refugees in Prisons: Cites History of INS & Pennsylvania Jails Poor Handling of Asylum Seekers." Press Release, May 14. Washington, D.C.: Amnesty International.

————. 2000a. *Rally to Demand an End to the Attacks on Immigrants and Protest Unfair Provisions of the 1996 Immigration Law*. www.amnestyusa.org.

————. 2000b. *Questions and Answers about Amnesty International and Refugees*. www.amnestyusa.org.

————. 2000c. *Protect Refugees! Pass the Refugee Protection Act*. www.amnestyusa.org.

————. 2001. "US Government May Be Considering Use of Torture for Detainees." Press Release, October 26. Washington, D.C.: Amnesty International.

Amon, E. 2000. A Battle against Secret Evidence. *The National Law Journal*, December 27: EV1–4.

————. 2000b. INS Will Upgrade Its Detainees Treatment: It Promises Lawyers Access, End to Routine Strip Searches. *The National Law Journal*, November 27: EV1–3.

Anderson, G. M. 2001. "Immigration Detention Is Just Another Term for Imprisonment." *America Magazine*, February 19: EV1–6.

Anderson, N., and P. J. McDonnell. 2000. "Immigration Reform Effort Comes up Short." *Los Angeles Times*, December 15: EV1–3.

Anderson, S., and J. Cavanagh. 1999. "Ten Myths About Globalization." *The Nation*, December 6: 26–27.

Andreas, P. 1998. *The U.S. Immigration Control Offensive: Constructing an Image of Order on the Southwest Border*. Cambridge, MA: Harvard University Press.

————. 2000. *Policing the U.S.-Mexico Divide*. New York: Cornell University Press.

"Another Hunger Strike Starts at Detention Center." 1998. *New York Times*, October 20: B8.

Archibold, R. 2000. "Between Cheek-Pinching and Pasta, Lazio Makes Appeals to Immigrants." *New York Times*, October 23: B5.

Arp, W., M. Dantico, and M. Zatz. 1990. "The Immigration and Control Act of 1986: Differential Impacts on Women?" *Social Justice*, 17, 2: 23–39.

"Ashcroft Visits INS a Target for Reorganization." 2001. CNN, April 17: EV1–2.

Asseo, L. 2001a. "Justices Mull Immigrant Deportation." *Associated Press*, April 24: EV1–2.

———. 2001b. "Court to Review Deportation Rules." *Associated Press*, January 12: EV1–2.

Auerbach, F. L. 1955. *Immigration Laws of the United States*. Indianapolis, IN: Bobbs-Merrill.

Auster, L. 1990. *The Path to National Suicide: An Essay on Immigration and Multiculturalism*. Monterey, VA: American Immigration Control Foundation.

Bacon, D. 1999a. "INS Declares War on Labor: Ethnic Cleansing Hits Immigrant Workers, in Midwest Meatpacking." *Nation*, October 25: 18–23.

———. 1999b. "INS Enforcers." *Nation*, January 4: 8, 24.

Baker, A. 2000. "Suspect in Racial Attack Tells of Life of Rage." *New York Times*, October 24: B6.

Barnett, R., and J. Cavanaugh. 1994. *Global Dreams: Imperial Corporations and the New World Order*. New York: Touchstone.

Bates, E. 1998. "Private Prisons." *Nation*, January 5: 11–18.

Bean, F. 1990. *Undocumented Migration to the United States: IRCA and the Experience of the 1980s*. Washington, D.C.: The Urban Institute.

Bearak, B. 2001. "This Job Is Truly Scary: The Taliban Are Watching." *New York Times*, June 1: A4.

Beard, B. 2000. "Mesa Beds Planned for Immigrant Children." *Arizona Republic*, December 12: EV1–2.

Beck, R. 1996. *The Case against Immigration: The Moral, Economic, Social and Environmental Reasons for Reducing Immigration Back to Traditional Levels*. New York: Norton.

Becker, H. 1963. *Outsiders: Studies in the Sociology of Deviance*. New York: Free Press.

Becker, J. 2000. "The Other Immigrant Children." *Miami Herald*, January 7: EV1–2.

Belluck, P. 2001. "Mexican Laborers in U.S. during War Sue for Back Pay." *New York Times*, April 29: A1, A36.

Benjamin, J. A. 2000a. "INS Eases Removal Guidelines." *Fort Lauderdale Sun Sentinel*, November 24: EV1–3.

———. 2000b. "More Gays, Harassed and Abused at Home, Are Seeking Asylum in U.S." *Fort Lauderdale Sun Sentinel*, December 10: EV1–4.

———. 2001. "96 Reform Law Lets INS Cast a Wide Net." *Fort Lauderdale Sun Sentinel*, April 22: EV1–9.

Bennett, D. 1989. *The Party of Fear: From Nativist Movements to the New Right in American History*. Chapel Hill: University of North Carolina Press.

Bennett, M. 1963. *American Immigration Policies: A History*. Washington, D.C.: Public Affairs Press.

Benson, L. B. 1997. "Back to the Future: Congress Attacks the Right to Judicial Review of Immigration Hearings." *Connecticut Law Review*, 29(4):1411–1500.

Bernstein, R. 1995. "The Immigration Wave: A Plea to Hold It Back." *New York Times*, April 19: C17.

Best, J. 1987. "Rhetoric in Claims-Making." *Social Problems*, 24(2):101–121.

———. 1989. *Images in Issues: Typifying Contemporary Social Problems*. New York: Aldine de Gruyter.

———. 1990. *Threatened Children: Rhetoric and Concern about Child Victims*. Chicago: University of Chicago Press.

———. 1999. *Random Violence: How We Talk about New Crimes and New Victims*. Chicago: University of Chicago Press.

Bjorhus, J. 1997. "Joint Effort by Police, INS Concern Immigrant Rights Groups." *Portland Oregonian*, November 2: 1.

"Blaming Immigrants." 2000. *New York Times*, October 14: A18.

Booth, W. 1993. "U.S. Accused of Sedating Deportees: Tranquilizers Given to Those Who Resist." *Washington Post*, October 7: A1, A20.

Borjas, G. 1990. *Friends or Strangers: The Impact of Immigration on the U.S. Economy*. New York: Free Press.

Bravin, J., G. Fields, C. Adams, and R. Wartzman. 2001. "Justice Department Quickly Moves to Use New Broad Authority in Detaining Aliens." *Wall Street Journal*, September 26: EV1–3.

Brewster, M. 2000. A Review of *Crack Mothers: Pregnancy, Drugs, and the Media* by Drew Humphries. *Social Pathology*, 6(2): 145–148.

Briggs, V. 1992. *Mass Immigration and the National Interest*. Armonck, NY: M.E. Sharpe.

Brimelow, P. 1992. "Time to Rethink Immigration." *National Review*, June 22: 30–46.

———. 1995. *Alien Nation: Common Sense about America's Immigration Disaster*. New York: Random House.

Brownstein, H. 1996. *The Rise and Fall of a Violent Crime Wave: Crack Cocaine and the Social Construction of a Crime Problem*. New York: Harrow and Heston.

Buchanan, P. J. 1991. "America Has a Right to Preserve Identity." *Conservative Chronicle*, August 28: 2.

———. 1996. Speech delivered at the Heritage Foundation, January 29. Washington, D.C.: Federal Document Clearing House, Inc.

———. 1999. *A Republic, Not an Empire: Reclaiming America's Destiny*. Lanham, MD: Regnery.

———. 2002. *The Death of the West: How Dying Populations and Immigrant Invasions Imperil Our Country and Civilization*. New York: Thomas Dunne Books/St. Martin's Press.

Bucio, V. 2001. "Where the Streets Are Mean and Brutal on Street Children Asylum-Seekers." *Houston Chronicle*, January 22: EV1–3.

Buckley, S., and S. Levine. 2000. "A Young Man's Homecoming to a Brazil He Does Not Know." *Washington Post*, November 29: EV1–5.

Bureau of Justice Statistics. 2001. *Prisoners in 2000*. Washington, D.C.: U.S. Department of Justice.

Burke, H. 2001. "INS Setting New Rules for Detainees." *Herald News* (NJ), January 3: EV1–4.

Burton-Rose, D. 1998. *The Celling of America: An Inside Look at the U.S. Prison Industry*. Monroe, ME: Common Courage.

"Bush Names Immigration Head." 2001. *Associated Press*, April 27: EV1–2."Bush Signs New Anti Terrorism Law." 2001. *Reuters*, October 26: EV1.

Bustamante, J. A. 1972. "The Wetback as Deviant: An Application of Labeling Theory." *American Journal of Sociology*, 77(4): 706–718.

Butterfield, F. 2001. "Police Are Split on Questioning of Mideastern Men: Some Chiefs Liken Plan to Racial Profiling." *New York Times*, November 22: A1, B6.

Calavita, K. 1992. *Inside the State: The Bracero Program, Immigration, and the I.N.S.* New York: Routledge.

———. 1996. "The New Politics of Immigration: 'Balanced-Budget Conservatism' and the Symbolism of Proposition 187." *Social Problems*, 43(3): 285–305.

Canedy, D. 2001. "Professor to Be Deported after Secret Evidence Case." *Associated Press*, November 27: EV1–2.

Carter, M. 2001. "Appeals Court Limits '97 Immigration Law." *Seattle Times*, January 24: EV1–2.

Casimir, L. 2001."Asylum Seekers Are Treated Like Criminals in the US." *New York Daily News*, February 16: EV1–4.

Catholic Legal Immigration Network (CLINIC). 2001. Project for the Indefinitely Detained (formerly the Coalition to Support Cuban Detainees). www.cscd.org.

Chambers, S. 2000. "A Lifeline for INS Detainees." *Newark Star-Ledger*, December 25: EV1–3.

Chardy, A. 2000a. "Krome Women to Be Moved." *Miami Herald*, December 12: EV1–3.

———. 2000b. "Jailed INS Detainees Cut Off, Advocates Say." *Miami Herald*, December 26: EV1–3.

Cheng, M. M. 2000."New INS Guidelines Soften '96 Laws." *New York Newsday*, November 26: EV 1–3.

Chermak, S. 1997. "The Presentation of Drugs in the News Media: News Sources Involved in Social Problem Construction." *Justice Quarterly*, 14(4): 687–718.

Chevigny, B. G. 2000. "Prison Activists Come of Age." *Nation*, July 24/31: 27–30.

Chin, K. L. 1999. *Smuggled Chinese: Clandestine Immigration to the United States*. Philadelphia: Temple University Press.

Chiricos, T. 1996. "Moral Panic as Ideology: Drugs, Violence, Race and Punishment in America." Pp. 19–48 in *Justice with Prejudice: Race and Criminal Justice in America*, M. Lynch and E. B. Patterson (Eds.). New York: Harrow and Heston.

Christensen, K., R. Read, J. Sullivan, and B. Walth. 2000. "Unchecked Power of the INS Shatters American Dream." *Oregonian*, December 9: EV1–8.

Christensen, K., J. Sullivan, and B. Walth. 2000. "Immigration Law Splinters Families." *Oregonian*, December 12: EV1–9.

Christianson, S. 1991. "Our Black Prisons." Pp. 62–75 in *The Dilemmas of Corrections* (2nd ed.), K. Hass and G. Alpert (Eds.). Prospect Heights, IL: Waveland.

Christie, N. 1994. *Crime Control as Industry*. Oslo: Universite-flag.

Chua, L. 1995. "The Closing of the American Mind: Peter Brimelow's Foreign Intervention." *Village Voice Literary Supplement*, April: 17.

Clear, T. R. 1994. *Harm in American Penology: Offenders, Victims, and Their Communities*. Albany: State University of New York Press.

Clendenning, A. 2000a. "Louisiana Tops in Jailing Long-Term INS Detainees." *Sunday Advocate* (Baton Rouge, LA), December 3: EV1–2.

———. 2000b. "U.S. Supreme Court to Take Up Detainee Issue." *The Associated Press*, December 3: EV1–3.

Clymer, A. 2001. "Lawmakers Want C.I.A. to Share Data on Foreigners." *New York Times*, November 2: EV1–2.

Cockburn, A. 2000. "The Radicalization of James Woolsey." *New York Times Magazine*, July 23: 26–29.

Cohen, L. P. 2001. "Denied Access to Attorneys Some INS Detainees Are Jailed without Charges." *Wall Street Journal*, November 1: EV1–3.

Cohen, S. 1972. *Folk Devils and Moral Panics.* London: Macgibbon and Kee.

Cohen, S., and J.Young. 1981. *The Manufacture of News: Deviance, Social Problems, and the Mass Media.* London: Constable.

Cole, D. 1997. "Blind Decisions Come to Court: What Happens when a Defendant Is Denied Access to the Evidence against Him." *Nation*, June 16: 21–22.

———. 1999. "Terrorist Scare: The Government Uses Secret Evidence to Find Aliens Guilty by Association." *Nation*, April 19: 26–28.

———. 2000. "Official Secrets Law." *Nation*, November 20: 8.

———. 2001. "A Legal Breakthrough for Immigrants." *New York Times*, July 1: WK13.

Commission on Immigration Reform (CIR). 1994. *U.S. Immigration Policy: Restoring Credibility.* Washington, D.C.: Government Printing Office.

"Concerns Rise of Civil Rights Being Ignored." 2001. *Chicago Tribune*, October 17: EV1–3.

Congressional Record. 1996. March 16: H2372–74. Washington, D.C.: Government Printing Office.

Cook, D. 1993. "Racism, Citizenship and Exclusion." Pp. 136–157 in *Racism and Criminology*, D. Cook and B. Hudson (Eds.). London: Sage.

Cooper, B. 1997. "Procedures for Expedited Removal and Asylum Screening under the Illegal Immigration Reform and Immigrant Responsibility Act of 1996." *Connecticut Law Review*, 29(4) 1501–1524.

Corbett, S. 2001. "From Hell to Fargo: The Lost Boys of Sudan Land in America." *New York Times Magazine*, April 1: 48–55, 75, 80, 84, 85.

Cose, E. 1992. *Prejudice, Politics, and the Populating of America.* New York: Morrow.

Council on American-Islamic Relations. 1995. *A Special Report on Anti-Muslim Stereotyping, Harassment, and Hate Crimes: Following the Bombing of Oklahoma City's Murrah Federal Building.* Washington, D.C.: CAIR.

Covington, J. 1995. "Racial Classification in Criminology: The Reproduction of Racialized Crime." *Sociological Forum*, 10(4): 547–568.

Cox, A. 1968.*The Warren Court: Constitutional Decision as an Instrument of Reform.* Cambridge, MA: Harvard University Press.

"Critical Resistance to the Prison-Industrial Complex." *Social Justice*, 2000. Special Issue. 27: 3.

Dalton, H. 1993. *Will America Drown? Immigration and the Third World Population Explosion.* Washington, D.C.: Scott-Townsend.

Daniels, R.1993. *Prisoners without Trial: Japanese-Americans in World War II.* New York: Hill and Wang.

Darling, J. 2000. "Adopted in U.S. as Toddler, Salvadoran Is Exiled to a Home He Never Knew." *New York Times*, November 27: EV1–3.

Davies, F. 2001. "Bush Choice for INS Raises Concerns." *Miami Herald*, May 1: EV1–2.

Davis, N., and C. Stasz. 1990. *Social Control of Deviance: A Critical Perspective*. New York: McGraw-Hill.

Delgado, H. 1992. *New Immigrants, Old Unions: Organizing Undocumented Workers in Los Angeles*. Philadelphia, PA: Temple University Press.

DePalma, A. 1992. "Winds Free 40 Aliens, Stirring Second Storm." *New York Times*, September 21: A10.

———. 2000. "'A Tyrannical Solution': Farmers Caught in Conflict over Illegal Migrant Workers." *New York Times*, October 3: C1–C2.

DeSipio, L., and R. O. de la Garza. 1998. *Making Americans: Remaking America: Immigration and Immigrant Policy*. Boulder, CO: Westview.

Dewan, S. K. 2001. "Immigrants Lining up to Marry as a Legal Deadline Approaches." *New York Times*, April 26: EV1–2.

Diamond, S. 1996. "Right-Wing Politics and the Anti-Immigration Cause." *Social Justice*, 23(3): 154–168.

Diaz, J. 2001. "More Gay Immigrants Seeking Refuge in U.S." *Miami Herald*, February 4: EV1–4.

Dillin, J. 2001. "Immigration Proposals Get Mixed Reviews." *Christian Science Monitor*, March 20: EV1–3.

"Disappearing in America." 2001. *New York Times*. November 10: A22.

Divine, R. 1957. *American Immigration Policy, 1924–1952*. New Haven, CT: Yale University Press.

Donohue, B. 2001a. "Rights Groups Prodding Feds for Information on Detainees." *Star-Ledger* (NJ), October 30: EV1–2.

———. 2001b. "Immigrants Fill a Drop in County Jail Populations." *Star-Ledger* (NJ), November 2: EV1–3.

Donziger, S. 1996a. *The Real War on Crime: The Report of the National Criminal Justice Commission*. New York: HarperPerennial.

———. 1996b. "The Prison-Industrial Complex: What's Really Driving the Rush to Lock 'Em Up." *Washington Post*, March 17: 24.

Dow, M. 1998. "Our Daily Ordeal Is Going Unnoticed: Cries for Help from Krome." *Haïti Progrès*, August 12–18: EV1–10.

———. 1999. "Hunger Strike of Asylum Seekers Detained in Queens." *Detention Watch Network News*, September: 9–10.

———. 2001a. "'Enforcement' Means You're Brutal." *Index on Censorship*, January 21: EV1–2.

———. 2001b. "We Know What INS Is Hiding." *Miami Herald*, November 11: EV1–3.

Dow, M., and J. Greene. 2001. "Protest against a Prison in Kendall—for the Right Reasons." *Miami Herald*, February 5: EV1–2.

Dowty, A. 1987. *Closed Borders: The Contemporary Assault on Freedom of Movement*. New Haven, CT: Yale University Press.

Drinan, R. F. 2001. *The Mobilization of Shame: A World View of Human Rights*. New Haven, CT: Yale University Press.

Dugger, C. 1997. "Giuliani Uses Conference to Rally Immigrant Cause." *New York Times*, June 10: B3.

Eggen, D. 2000. "Meissner Ends Embattled Tenure as Head of INS." *Washington Post*, November 20: EV1–3.

———. 2001. "Immigrants Left Out in the Cold." *Washington Post*, January 2: EV1–5.

Egelko, B. 2000. "INS Settles Two Suits Alleging Mistreatment." *San Francisco Chronicle*, November 21: EV1–3.

Ehrlich, P. R. 1968. *The Population Bomb*. New York: Ballantine.

Elvin, J. 1994/1995. "'Corrections-Industrial Complex' Expands in U.S." *The National Prison Project Journal*, 10(1): 1–4.

Espenshade, T. J. 1997. *Keys to Successful Immigration: Implications of the New Jersey Experience*. Washington, D.C.: Urban Institute.

Ethridge, P., and J. Marquart. 1993. "Private Prisons in Texas: The New Penology for Profit." *Justice Quarterly*, 10(1): 29–48.

Fagen, A. 2001. "Bill Seeks Better Deal for Detained Immigrant Children." *Congressional Quarterly Daily Monitor*, May 29: EV1–4.

Farragher, T., and K. Cullen. 2001. "Plan to Question 5000 Raises Issue of Profiling." *Boston Globe*, November 11: EV1–4.

Farrington, K. 1992. "The Modern Prison as Total Institution? Public Perception Versus Objective Reality." *Crime and Delinquency*, 38(1): 6–26.

Feeley, M., and J. Simon. 1992. "The New Penology: Notes on the Emerging Strategy of Corrections and Its Implications." *Criminology*, 30(4): 449–474.

Ferrell, J. 1996. *Crimes of Style: Urban Graffiti and the Politics of Criminality*. Boston: Northeastern University Press.

Fine, G. A., and L. Christoforides. 1991. "Dirty Birds, Filthy Immigrants, and the English Sparrow War: Metaphorical Linkage in Constructing Social Problems." *Symbolic Interaction*, 14: 375–393.

Firestone, D. 1995. "Giuliani Criticizes a U.S. Crackdown on Illegal Aliens." *New York Times*, August 23: A1, B2.

———. 1999. "Local Jails Deal with Federal Dilemma on Deportation." *New York Times*, December 17: A22.

Fishman, M. 1978. "Crime Waves as Ideology." *Social Problems*, 25: 531–543.

"Fixing the INS." 20001. *Oregonian*, December 15: EV1–3.

Flanigan, J. 1993. "Blaming Immigrants Won't Solve Economic Woes." *Los Angeles Times*, August 15: D1.

Florida Immigrant Advocacy Center, Inc. 1997. *Florida County Jails: INS's Secret Detention World*. Miami: Florida Immigrant Advocacy Center, Inc.

Fox, B. 2001. "Attacks Probed in Closed Courts." *Associated Press*, October 4: EV1–3.

Francis, D. R. 2001. "Immigration Focus Shifts from Economics to Security." *Christian Science Monitor*, October 22: EV 1–3.

Fraser, S. (Ed.) 1995. *The Bell Curve Wars: Race, Intelligence, and the Future of America*. New York: Basic Books.

"Freedom Flotilla: A Brave Skipper, a Grateful Family and Angry Florida Critics." 1980. *People*, May 26: 29.

Frey, W. H. 1995a. "Immigration and the Internal Migration 'Flight' from US Metropolitan Areas: Toward a New Demographic Balkanization." *Urban Studies*, 32 (4/5): 733–757.

———. 1995b. "Immigration and Internal Migration 'Flight': A California Case Study." *Population and Environment: A Journal of Interdisciplinary Studies*" 14 (March): 353–375.

———. 1996. "Immigrant and Native Migrant Magnets." *American Demographics*, November, 39.

Fried, J. P. 2000. "Close Prison Watch for Cleric in Bombing." *New York Times*, October 22: 37.

Gamboa, S. 2000. "Commission Begins Scrutiny of Immigration Laws Effects on Civil Rights." *Associated Press*, December 8: EV1–3.

Gans, H. 1995. *The War against the Poor: The Underclass and Antipoverty Policy*. New York: Basic Books.

Gaylord, B. 2001. "Australia Migrants, Many Children, Land at Troubled Camp." *New York Times*, December 2: A4.

Gearan, A. 2001. "High Court to Rule On Deportation." *Associated Press*, February 21: EV1–2.

General Accounting Office (GAO). 1990. *Immigration Reform: Employer Sanctions and the Question of Discrimination*. Washington, D.C.: Government Printing Office.

———. 1991. *Immigration Management: Strong Leadership and Management Reforms Needed to Address Problems*. Washington, D.C.: Government Printing Office.

———. 1995. *Illegal Immigration: INS Overstay Estimation Methods Need Improvement*. Washington, D.C.: U.S. Government Printing Office.

———. 1998. *Illegal Aliens: Changes in the Process of Denying Aliens Entry into the United States*. Washington, D.C.: U.S. Government Printing Office.

———. 2000. *Illegal Aliens: Opportunities Exist to Improve the Expedited Removal Process*. Washington, D.C.: U.S. Government Printing Office.

Gilens, M. 1999. *Why Americans Hate Welfare: Race, Media, and the Politics of Antipoverty Policy*. Chicago: University of Chicago Press.

Glaberson, W. 2001. "Detainees Accounts of Investigation Are at Odds with Official Reports." *New York Times*, September 29: EV1–3.

Glassner, B. 1999. *Culture of Fear: Why Americans Are Afraid of the Wrong Things*. New York: Basic Books.

Glazer, N. 1983. *Ethnic Dilemmas*. Cambridge, MA: Harvard University Press.

———. 1995. "Debate on Aliens Flares beyond the Melting Pot." *New York Times*, April 23: E3.

Glazer, N., and D. P. Moynihan. 1963. *Beyond the Melting Pot: The Negroes, Puerto Ricans, Jews, Italians, and Irish of New York City*. Cambridge, MA: MIT Press.

Goffman, E. 1961. *Asylums: Essays on the Social Situation of Mental Patients and Other Inmates*. Garden City, NY: Anchor.

Goldstein, A., and D. Eggen. 2001. "U.S. to Stop Issuing Detention Tallies." *Washington Post*, November 9: EV1–2.

Goode, E. 1990. "The American Drug Panic of the 1980s: Social Construction or Objective Threat?" *The International Journal of the Addictions*, 25(9): 1083–1098.

Goode, E., and N. Ben-Yehuda. 1994. *Moral Panics: The Social Construction of Deviance*. Cambridge, MA: Blackwell.

Goodstein, L. 2001. "American Sikhs Contend They Have Become a Focus of Profiling at Airports." *New York Times*, November 10: B6.

Gordon, C., and E. G. Gordon. 1979. *Immigration and Nationality Law*. New York: Bender & Company.

Gordon, D. 1991. *The Justice Juggernaut: Fighting Street Crime, Controlling Citizens*. New Brunswick, NJ: Rutgers University Press.

———. 1994. *The Return of the Dangerous Classes: Drug Prohibition and Policy Politics*. New York: Norton.

Gould, S. J. 1995. "Curveball." Pp. 11–22 in *The Bell Curve Wars: Race, Intelligence, and the Future of America*, S. Fraser (Ed.). New York: Basic Books.

Greenhouse, L. 2001a. "Supreme Court Will Decide on Deporting of Immigrants." *New York Times*, January 13: A10.

———. 2001b. "Justices Permit Immigrants to Challenge Deportations: 5–4 Ruling May Lead to Judicial Scrutiny of Other Actions by Executive Branch." *New York Times*, June 26: A1, A15.

———. 2000a. "U.S. to Expand Anti-Discrimination Rights for Illegal Immigrants Working in This Country." *New York Times*, October 28: A28.

———. 2000b. "Foreign Workers at Highest Level in Seven Decades: 12 Percent of Job Force, Increase in Immigrants Helps Companies Grow but Holds Down Pay of Unskilled." *New York Times*, September 4: A1, A12.

Grossman, P. 2000. "Two Jail Guards Charged in Sex Assaults." *Union Leader* (NH), December 20: EV1–3.

Guenter, S. 1990. *The American Flag, 1777–1924*. Rutherford, New Jersey: Farleigh Dickinson University Press.

Gusfield, J. 1963. *Symbolic Crusade: Status, Politics and the American Temperance Movement*. Urbana: University of Illinois Press.

Gutierrez, D. 1995. *Walls and Mirrors: Mexican Americans, Mexican Immigrants, and the Politics of American Ethnicity*. Berkeley: University of California P.

Hacker, A. 1992. *Two Nations: Black and White, Separate, Hostile, Unequal*. New York: Ballantine.

———. 1995. "Caste, Crime, and Precocity." Pp. 97–108, in *The Bell Curve Wars: Race, Intelligence, and the Future of America*, S. Fraser (Ed.). New York: Basic Books.

Hacker, T. 1996. "Jackson Raids Net More than 100 Illegal Workers." *Star Tribune* (Jackson Hole, WY), August 27: 1.

Hall, S., C. Critcher, T. Jefferson, J. Clarke, and B. Roberts. 1978. *Policing the Crisis: Mugging, the State and Law and Order*. New York: Holmes and Meiser.

Hallinan, J. T. 2001. *Going up the River: Travels in a Prison Nation*. New York: Random House.

Hamm, M. S. 1995. *The Abandoned Ones: The Imprisonment and Uprising of the Mariel Boat People*. Boston: Northeastern University Press.

Hansen, A. A. 1995. "Oral History and the Japanese American Evacuation." *Journal of American History*, 82: 625–639.

Harris, N. 1996. *The New Untouchables: Immigration and the New World Worker*. New York: Penguin.

Hawkins, R., and G. Tiedeman. 1975. *The Creation of Deviance*. Columbus, OH: C. Merrill.

Hedges, C. 2000a. "Condemned Again for Old Crimes: Deportation Law Descends Sternly, and Often by Surprise." *New York Times*, October 30: B1, B3.

———. 2000b. "Immigrant, Detained for 3 1/2 Years, Emerges from Labyrinth." *New York Times*, November 6: EV1–5.

———. 2001a. "Policy to Protect Jailed Immigrants Is Adopted by U.S." *New York Times*, January 2: EV1–4.

———. 2001b. "Suit Details the Beatings of Detainees in Louisiana." *New York Times*, January 2: EV1–3.

Heer, D. M. 1998. *Immigration in America's Future: Social Science Findings and the Policy Debate*. Boulder, CO: Westview.

Hegstrom, E. 2000. "Immigrants Taught to Sue for Unpaid Wages." *Houston Chronicle*, November 30: EV1–2.

———. 2001. "Immigration Rights Now Take Back Seat." *Houston Chronicle*, October 9: EV1–4.

Heller, M. 1994. "Too Many Immigrants?" *Hispanic Magazine*, April: 27.

Helton, A. 1989. "Detention of Refugees and Asylum Seekers." Pp. 4–22 in *Refugee Issues in International Relations*, G. Loescher (Ed.). Oxford: Oxford University Press.

Hentoff, N. 2001. "Terrorizing the Bill of Rights." *Village Voice*, November 20: 32.

Hernandez, R. 1995. "No Rational Argument for Ending Immigration." *Jersey Journal*, June 23: 8.

Herrnstein, R., and C. Murray. 1994. *The Bell Curve: Intelligence and Class Structure in American Life*. New York: Free Press.

Hickman, M. 1982. "Crime in the Streets—a Moral Panic: Understanding 'Get Tough' Policies in the Criminal Justice System." *Southern Journal of Criminal Justice*, 8: 7–22.

Higham, J. 1988. *Strangers in the Land: Patterns of American Nativism, 1860–1925*. New Brunswick, NJ: Rutgers University Press.

Hing, B. O. 1997. *To Be an American: Cultural Pluralism and the Rhetoric of Assimilation*. New York: New York University Press.

Hirschi, T. 1969. *Causes of Delinquency*. Berkeley: University of California P.

Hollywood, B. 1997. "Dancing in the Dark: Ecstasy, the Dance Culture, and Moral Panic in Post Ceasefire Northern Ireland." *Critical Criminology*, 8(1): 62–77.

Holmes, S. A. 1995. "The Strange Politics of Immigration." *New York Times*, December 31: E3.

———. 1996. "Candidates Criticized for Sound-Bite Approach to Problem of Illegal Aliens." *New York Times*, March 7: B10.

"Hostage Standoff Ends at Louisiana Jail." 1999. *New York Times*. December 19: 33.

Hubbard, C. 1996. "Feds Target Hispanic Workers." *Jackson Hole Guide*, August 28: 1.

Huber, J., and B. Schneider. 1992. *The Social Contexts of AIDS*. Thousand Oaks, CA: Sage.

Huddle, D. 1993. *The Net National Costs of Immigration in 1993*. Washington, D.C.: Carrying Capacity Network.

Hudson, A., and D. Boyer. 2001. "Lawmakers Closer on Taps Detention of Immigrants." *Washington Times*, September 27: EV1–3.

Human Rights Watch. 1993. *Brutality Unchecked: Human Rights Abuses along the U.S. Border with Mexico*. New York: Human Rights Watch.

———. 1997. *Slipping through the Cracks: Unaccompanied Children Detained by the U.S. Immigration and Naturalization Service*. New York: Human Rights Watch.

———. 1998a. *Locked Away: Immigration Detainees in Jails in the U.S.* New York: Human Rights Watch.

———. 1998b. *Crossing the Line: Human Rights Abuses along the U.S. Border with Mexico Persist amid Climate of Impunity*. New York: Human Rights Watch.

———. 1998c. "Human Rights Watch Condemns Detention Practices of INS: Urges End to Use of Local Jails to Hold Immigrants." Press Release, September 9. New York: Human Rights Watch.

———. 1998d. *Detained and Deprived of Rights: Children in the Custody of the U.S. Immigration and Naturalization Service*. New York: Human Rights Watch.

———. 2001. "Human Rights Watch Response to Attacks on the U.S. Civilian Life Must Be Respected." Press Release, September 12. www.hrw.org.

Humphries, D. 1999. *Crack Mothers: Pregnancy, Drugs, and the Media*. Columbus, OH: Ohio State University Press.

Hutchison, E. P. 1981. *Legislative History of American Immigration Policy, 1798–1965*. Philadelphia, PA: University of Pennsylvania Press.

"Illegal Immigrant Health Policy Told." 1993. *Los Angeles Times*, September 20: A12.

"The Immigrants: How They're Helping the U.S. Economy." 1993. *Business Week*, July 13: 12.

"Immigration Hurts City, New Yorkers Say in Poll." 1993. *New York Times*, October 18: B4.

Immigration and Naturalization Service (INS). 1995. *Interim Report, Executive Summary: The Elizabeth, New Jersey Contract Detention Facility Operated by ESMOR Inc.* Washington, D.C.: INS.

———. 1999. "Strengthening the Nation's Immigration System." *Fact Sheet*. Washington, D.C.: U.S. Government Printing Office.

———. 2000a. "This Is INS." http://www.ins.usdoj.gov/graphics/aboutins/thisisins/overview.htm.

———. 2000b. "INS to Adopt New Detention Standards to Be Implemented at All Facilities Housing INS Detainees." Press Release, November 13.

———. 2001. "This Is INS." http://www.ins.usdoj.gov/graphics/aboutins/thisisins/overview.htm.

———. 2002. "This Is INS." http://www.ins.usdoj.gov/graphics/aboutins/thisisins/overview.htm.

Indefinite Detention Project of the Catholic Legal Immigration Network Inc. 1999. *Mission Statement*. www.cscd.org.

———. 2000. *Quarterly Report for the Indefinite Detention Project: October-December*. www.cscd.org.

———. 2001. Final Annual Report for the Indefinite Detention Project. www.cscd.org.

"INS Standards Need Teeth." 2001. *St. Petersburg Times*, January 8: EV1–2.

Irwin, J. 1985. *The Jail: Managing the Underclass in American Society*. Berkeley: University of California Press.

Irwin, J., and J. Austin. 1994. *It's about Time: America's Imprisonment Binge*. Belmont, CA: Wadsworth.

Irwin, J., V. Schiraldi, and J. Ziedenberg. 2000. "America's One Million Nonviolent Prisoners." *Social Justice*, 27(2): 135–147.

Jaffe, J. 1972. *Crusade against Radicalism: New York during the Red Scare*. Port Washington, NY: Kennikat.

James, S. 2002. "Private Prison Operators Upbeat on Results." *Reuters*, May 2: EV1–2.

Janofsky, M. 2001. "Undocumented Immigrants Rush for Legal Status." *New York Times*, May 1: EV1–3.

Jansen, B. 2000. "Deal Sought on Illegal Farm Labor." *Associated Press*, December 4.

Jelinek, P. 2000. "Gender Considered in New Asylum Rule; INS News Release." *The Associated Press*, December 7: EV1–2.

Jenkins, P. 1994a. "'The Ice Age': The Social Construction of a Drug Panic." *Justice Quarterly*, 11(1): 7–31.

———. 1994b. *Using Murder: The Social Construction of Serial Homicide*. New York: Aldine de Gruyter.

Johnston, D. 2002. "6 Months Late, I.N.S. Notifies Flight School of Hijackers' Visas." *New York Times*, March 13: A16.

Jonas, S., and S. Dod Thomas. 1999. *Immigration: A Civil Rights Issue for the Americas*. Wilmington, DE: SR Books.

Jones, B. J., B. Gallagher, and J. McFalls. 1989. "Toward a Unified Model for Social Problems Theory." *Journal for the Theory of Social Behavior*, 19: 337–356.

Jones, M. 1960. *American Immigration*. Chicago: University of Chicago Press.

Judis, John. 1997. "Huddled Elites." *New Republic*, December 23: 23–26.

Kafka, F. 1937. *The Trial*. New York: Alfred A. Knopf.

Kahn, R. 1996. *Other People's Blood: U.S. Immigration Policies in the Reagan Decade*. Boulder, CO: Westview.

Kastenmeier, R. W. 1988. "Mariel Cubans Deserve Due Process Too." *Washington Post*, March 24: 12A.

Katz, J. 1988. *Seductions of Crime: Moral and Sensual Attractions in Doing Evil*. New York: Basic Books.

Kelley, T. 2000. "Suspect Admits Attacking Immigrants, the Police Say." *New York Times*, October 12: B5.

Kerwin, D. 1997. "Detention: Our Sad National Symbol." Pp. 137–147 in *In Defense of the Alien*, L. Tomasi (Ed.). New York: Center for Migration Studies.

———. 2000. *The Needless Detention of Immigrants in the United States*. Washington, D.C.: Catholic Legal Immigration Network.

Kirchgaessner, S. 2001. "Some Immigration Lawyers Wary of INS Powers." *Financial Times*, September 30: EV1–3.

Knobel, D. 1996. *"America for the Americans": The Nativist Movement in the United States*. New York: Twayne.

Kraut, A. 1994. *Silent Travelers: Germs, Genes, and the "Immigrant Menace."* New York: Basic Books.

Labovitz, P. 1995. "Immigration—Just the Facts." *New York Times,* March 25: A15.

Lacy, M., and D. Firestone. 1999. "In Rare Deal, U.S. and Cuba Halt Standoff." *New York Times,* December 20: A30.

Lamm, R., and G. Imhoff. 1985. *The Immigration Time Bomb: The Fragmenting of America.* New York: Ruman Talley Books.

"Law Students Needed to Represent Asylum Seekers." 2001. *ABA Student Lawyer,* 29(5): 74.

Lawyers Committee for Human Rights. 1998a. *Slamming the 'Golden Door': A Year of Expedited Review.* www.lchr.org.

———. 1998b. *Lawyers Committee Testimony on INS Detention.* Testimony Delivered by Eleanor Acer: Before the U.S. Senate Committee on the Judiciary, Immigration Subcommittee. September 16. www.lchr.org.

———. 1999a. *Refugees behind Bars: The Imprisonment of Asylum Seekers in the Wake of the 1996 Immigration Act.* www.lchr.org.

———. 1999b. "Responding to the Kosovo Refugee Crisis." Statement of the Lawyers Committee for Human Rights submitted to the Senate Committee on the Judiciary, Immigration Subcommittee. April 14. www.lchr.org.

———. 2000a. Testimony delivered by Daniel Shanfield, Staff Attorney, Lawyers Committee for Human Rights: Before the United States House of Representatives Committee on the Judiciary Subcommittee on International Operations and Human Rights. April 13. www.lchr.org.

———. 2000b. *Help Restore Fairness to the Treatment of Refugees! Urge Congress to Enact the Refugee Protection Act (S 1940).* www.lchr.org.

LeDuff, C. 2000a. "Immigrants Were Beaten After a Promise of Work." *New York Times,* September 20: B1.

———. 2000b. "For Migrants, Hard Work in Hostile Suburbs." *New York Times,* September 24: A1, A42.

Lemann, N. 1995. "Too Many Foreigners: Immigration at Current Levels, the Author Believes, Threatens the Republic." *New York Times Book Review,* April 16: 3.

Lemert, E. 1972. *Human Deviance, Social Problems, and Social Control.* Englewood Cliffs, NJ: Prentice-Hall.

LeMoyne, J. 1990. "Florida Center Holding Aliens Is under Inquiry: Additional Complaints Made of Abuse." *New York Times,* May 16: A16.

Lester, W. 2001. "Attacks Change Immigration Debate." *Associated Press,* October 12: EV1–3.

Levin, M. 1971. *Political Hysteria in America: The Democratic Capacity for Repression.* New York: Basic Books.

Lewin, T. 2000. "Curbs in Immigrants' and Inmates' Rights, Too." *New York Times,* December 26: EV1–3.

Lewis, A. 1999. "Accent the Positive." *New York Times,* October 10: A23.

———. 2000. "Correcting a Mistake." *New York Times,* September 23: A17.

Lewis, C. 1995. "John Steinbeck's Alternative to Internment Camps: A Policy for the President, December 15, 1941." *Journal of the West,* 34: 55–61.

Lilly, J. R., and M. Deflem. 1996. "Profit and Penality: An Analysis of the Corrections–Commercial Complex." *Crime & Delinquency,* 42(1): 3–20.

Lilly, J. R., and P. Knepper. 1993. "The Corrections–Commercial Complex." *Crime & Delinquency*, 39(2):150–166.

Lutton, W., and J. Tanton. 1994. *The Immigration Invasion*. Petoskey, MI: Social Contract.

MacQuarrie, B. 2000. "Immigrant Felons Stir Worry in Dorchester." *Boston Globe*, December 11: EV1–3.

Malone, D., and F. Trejo. 2001. "Asylum Changes Sought: Congress Hears from Detained Immigrants." *Dallas Morning News*, May 3: EV1–4.

Manis, J. 1974. "The Concept of Social Problems: Vox Populi and Sociological Analysis." *Social Problems*, 21(Winter): 305–315.

———. 1976. *Analyzing Social Problems*. New York: Praeger.

Mann, C. R., and M. Zatz. 1998. *Images of Color, Images of Crime*. Los Angeles: Roxbury.

Manning, P. 1980. *The Narc's Game: Organizational and Informational Limits on Drug Law Enforcement*. Cambridge, MA: MIT Press.

Margasak, L. 2001. "Court Rules against Open-Ended Jail." *Associated Press*, June 28: EV1.

Marks, S. 1995. Lawyers Committee for Human Rights. Personal Communication, March 1.

Marks, S., and J. Levy. 1994. *Detention of Refugees: Problems in Implementation of the Asylum Pre-Screening Officer Program*. Briefing Paper, September. New York: Lawyers Committee for Human Rights.

Marshall, I. H. 1997. *Minorities, Migrants, and Crime*. Thousand Oaks, CA: Sage.

Martel, B. 1999. "Inmates Surrender after Standoff, Will Be Sent Back to Cuba." *USA Today*, December 20: 5A.

Martinez, D. 2001. "New INS Guidelines Soften Edge of '96 Laws." *Miami Herald*, January 2: EV1–3.

Marx, G. T. 1981. "Ironies of Social Control: Authorities as Contributors to Deviance through Escalation, Nonenforcement, and Covert Facilitation." *Social Problems*, 28: 221–246.

Mata, A. 1998. "Stereotyping by Politicians: Immigrant Bashing and Nativist Political Movements." Pp. 145–155, in *Images of Color, Images of Crime*, R. Mann and M. Zatz (Eds). Los Angeles: Roxbury.

Mauer, M. 1998. "Letter to the Editor." *Nation*, March 16: 2.

———. 1990. *Young Black Men and the Criminal Justice System: A Growing National Problem*. Washington, D.C.: The Sentencing Project.

Mauer, M., and T. Huling. 1995. *Young Black Americans and the Criminal Justice System*. Washington, D.C.: The Sentencing Project.

May, T. D. 2001. "Center for Immigrant Families Opens." *Associated Press*, March 15: EV1–2.

McCorkle, R., and T. Miethe. 1998. "The Political and Organizational Responses to Gangs: An Examination of a 'Moral Panic' in Nevada." *Justice Quarterly*, 15(1): 41–64.

McDonnell, P. J. 2000. "Change Planned in Asylum Rules on Domestic Abuse." *Los Angeles Times*, December 7: EV1–2.

———. 2001. "Ruling Allows Asylum for Foreign Victims of Abuse." *Los Angeles Times*, March 22: EV1–3.

McFadden, R. D. 2000. "Suffolk Residents Protest Illegal Immigrants and Day Laborers." *New York Times*, October 15: 42.

McRobbie, A., and S. Thornton. 1995. "Rethinking Moral Panics for Multi-Mediated Social Worlds." *British Journal of Sociology*, 46(4): 559–574.

Medina, M. I. 1997. "Judicial Review—A Nice Thing? Article III, Separation of Powers and the Illegal Immigration Reform and Immigrant Responsibility Act of 1996." *Connecticut Law Review*, 29(4): 1525–1564.

Miller, J. 1996. *Search and Destroy: African American Males in the Criminal Justice System*. New York: Cambridge University Press.

Millett, K. 1994. *The Politics of Imprisonment: An Essay on the Literature of Political Imprisonment*. New York: W.W. Norton.

Millman, J. 1997. *The Other Americans: How Immigrants Renew Our Country, Our Economy, and Our Values*. New York: Penguin.

Mills, C. W. 1956. *The Power Elite*. New York: Oxford University Press.

Montero, D. 2001. "Three Hellish Months in a Juvenile Jail." *New York Post*, January 29: EV1–3.

Montgomery, L. 2000. "Immigrants in Small-Town Jails Generate an Infusion of Cash for Counties." *Washington Post*, November 25: EV1–3.

Moore, T. 2000. "Sudan's 'Lost Boys' Find a Home in U.S." *Associated Press*, November 9: EV1–2.

Morley, H. R. 2001. "Bergen Jail May Soon House Deportees: Sheriff Hammering Out Deal with INS." *Bergen Record* (NJ), March 5: A1, A4.

Morris, M. 1985. *The Beleaguered Bureaucracy*. Washington, D.C.: The Brookings Institute.

"Motel Kafka." 1993. *New York Newsday*, October 24: 2–3.

Murphy, P. 1972. *The Constitution in Crisis Times, 1918–1969*. New York: Harper & Row.

Musalo, K., L. Gibson, S. Knight, and J. E. Taylor. 2000. *The Expedited Removal Study: Evaluation of the General Accounting Office's Second Report on Expedited Removal*. San Francisco: University of California, Hastings College of Law, Center for Human Rights and International Justice.

National Immigration Forum (NIF). 1997. *Finding Common Ground: A Primer for Environment and Population Advocates Concerned about Immigration*. Washington, D.C.: NIF.

Naureckas, J. 1995. "The Jihad that Wasn't." *Extra*, July: 6–10: 20.

Neff, J. 1981. "1500 Aliens Arrested Every Day in 12 Mile Border Stretch." *Staten Island Advance*, June 17: 1.

"New York's Prison Building Fever." 1997. *New York Times*, July 24: A20.

Nhu, T. T., and H. Jordan. 2001. "Suit Seeks to Block INS from Sedating Deportee." *San Jose Mercury News*, May 4: EV1–3.

Nieves, E. 2001. "Recalling Internment and Saying 'Never Again.'" *New York Times*, September 28: EV1–2.

Nisbett, R. 1995. "Race, IQ, and Scientism." Pp. 36–57, in *The Bell Curve Wars: Race, Intelligence, and the Future of America*, S. Fraser (Ed.). New York: Basic Books.

Nishimoto, R. 1995. *Inside an American Concentration Camp: Japanese-American Resistance at Poston*. Tuscon: University of Arizona Press.

Nuzum, M. 1998. "The Commercialization of Justice: Public Good or Private Greed?" *The Critical Criminologist*, Summer: 1, 5–8.

Office of National Drug Control Policy. 1996. *National Drug Control Strategy*. Washington, D.C.: Government Printing Office.

Ojito, M. 1997a. "Old Crime Returns to Haunt an Immigrant: Facing Deportation, Dominican May Become a Test Case for New Law." *New York Times*, October 15: B1–B2.

———. 1997b. "U.S. Frees Immigrant Jailed for 1974 Misdemeanor." *New York Times*, October 25: B1, B3.

Orlando Sentinel. 1993. "Anti-Immigration Gains Support." July 27: 1.

Osborn, K. 2001. "DUI Gets Aliens a Free Trip Home." *Fox News*, January 24.

Ostrow, R. J. 1990. "Bush Signs Law Boosting Immigration Quotas by 40%." *Los Angeles Times*, November 30: 39.

Packer, H. L. 1964. "Two Models of the Criminal Process." *University of Pennsylvania Law Review*, 113(November): 1–68.

———. 1968. *The Limits of the Criminal Sanction*. Stanford, CA: Stanford University Press.

"Palestinian Jailed on Secret Evidence Released." 2000. *Associated Press*, December 15.

Parenti, C. 1996. "Making Prisons Pay: Business Finds the Cheapest Labor of All." *Nation*, January 29: 11–14.

———. 1999. *Lockdown America: Police and Prisons in the Age of Crisis*. New York: Verso.

Pastor, M. 1992. *Latinos and the Los Angeles Uprising: The Economic Context*. Claremont, CA: Tomas Rivera Center.

Peet, J., and D. Schwab. 1995. "Critics Praise INS for 'Candid' Report." *The Star Ledger*, October 22: 8.

Perea, J. 1997. *Immigrants Out! The New Nativism and the Anti-Immigrant Impulse in the United States*. New York: New York University Press.

Pianin, E., and T. B. Edsall. 2001. "Terrorism Bills Revive Civil Liberties Debate." *Washington Post*, September 14: EV1–3.

Piven, F. F., and R. Cloward. 1971. *Regulating the Poor: The Functions of Public Welfare*. New York: Vintage.

Plant, R. 1986. *The Pink Triangle: The Nazi War Against Homosexuals*. New York: Henry Holt and Company.

Platt, A. 1994. "Rethinking and Unthinking 'Social Control.'" Pp. 72–79 in *Inequality, Crime, & Social Control*, George S. Bridges and Martha A. Myers (Eds.). Boulder, CO: Westview.

Portes, A., and R. Rumbaut. 1996. *Immigrant America: A Portrait* (2nd ed.). Berkeley: University of California Press.

Potter, G., and V. Kappeler. 1998. *Constructing Crime*. Prospect Heights, IL: Waveland.

Povich, E. S. 2001. "Ashcroft Seeks Broad Laws." *New York Newsday*, September 20: EV1–3.

Pranis, K. 1998. "Letter to the Editor." *Nation*, March 16: 2–3.

"The Prison Boom." 1995. *Nation*, February 20: 223–224.

"Prison Guards Charged with Beating Inmate." 2000. *Associated Press*, December 6.

"Public Opinion and Demographic Report." 1994. *American Enterprise*, January–February: 97.

Purdy, M., and C. W. Dugger. 1996. "Legacy of Immigrants' Uprising: New Jail Operator, Little Change." *New York Times*, July 7: A1, A18.

Quiroga, A. 1995 "Copycat Fever: California's Proposition 187 Epidemic Spreads to Other States." *Hispanic Magazine*, 18–24.

Raskin, J. 1991. "Remember Koretmatsu: A Precedent for Arab-Americans?" *Nation*, February 4: 117–118.

Rather, J. 2000. "Long Island Official Wants to Sue I.N.S. to Spur Action." *New York Times*, August 25: B5.

Read, R. 2000a. "Overwhelmed, Demoralized INS Develops Culture of Abuse, Racism." *Oregonian*, December 14: EV1–9.

———. 2000b. "Rejected Foreigners Have No Voice in Changing the System." *Oregonian*, December 15: EV1–3.

"Record Number Held in Prison; State Rise Slows." 2001. *New York Times*, March 26: A12.

Rector, R. 1996. "The U.S.-Retirement Home for Immigrants." *The Social Contract*, Summer: 279.

Reimers, D. M. 1992. *Still the Golden Door: The Third World Comes to America* (2nd ed.). New York: Columbia University Press.

———. 1998. *Unwelcome Strangers: American Identity and the Turn against Immigration*. New York: Columbia University Press.

Reinarman, C., and H. Levine. 1997. *Crack in America: Demon Drugs and Social Justice*. Berkeley: University of California Press.

Reiss, A. 1951. "Delinquency as the Failure of Personal and Social Control." *American Sociological Review*, 16: 196–207.

Reitz, J. G. 1998. *Warmth of the Welcome: The Social Causes of Economic Success for Immigrants in Different Nations and Cities*. Boulder, CO: Westview.

Rizza, N. J. 1996. "INS Detention: Impact on Asylum Seekers." Refugee Reports, A News Service of the US Committee for Refugees, XVII(8): EV1–4.

Robbins, M. 2001. "DWI Order May Help Immigrants." *San Antonio Express-News*, March 6: EV1–3.

Robertson, I. 1981. *Sociology* (2nd ed.). New York: Worth.

Robertson, J. E. 2000. "Psychological Injury and the Prison Litigation Reform Act: A 'Not Exactly' Equal Protection Analysis." *Harvard Journal on Legislation*, 37(1): 105–158.

———. 2001. "Prison Reform, A Faustian Bargain: Commentary on Prospective Relief before and after *French* v. *Miller.*" *Criminal Law Bulletin*, March-April: 194–208.

Rodriguez, C. 2000. "Law Puts Immigrants in Jeopardy of Deportation for Minor Crimes." *Boston Globe*, December 28: EV1–2.

———. 2001. "AFLCIO embraces essential workers." *Boston Globe*, May 2: EV1–3.

Rohde, D. 1999. "Judge Rules Egyptian Linked to Terrorism Should Be Freed." *New York Times*, July 31: B1, B4.

Rohter, L. 1992. "'Processing' for Haitians Is Time in a Rural Prison." *New York Times*, June 21: E18.

Romano, L., and D. S. Fallis. 2001. "Questions Swirl around Men Held in Terror Probe." *Washington Post*, October 15: EV1–5.

Rosenblatt, R. 2001. "Immigrants Gain Support Survey Shows." *Los Angeles Times*, May 14: EV1–2.

Ross, K. 2000. "Residents Bombard Wackenhut over Prison Site." *Miami Herald*, November 2: EV1–3.

———. 2001. "Sexual Abuse Fears Reach beyond Krome." *Miami Herald*, January 7: EV1–2.

Rovella, D. E. 2001. "Clock Ticks on Terrorism-Related Detentions." *National Law Journal*, October 31: EV1–3.

Ruiz, V. L. 1998. *From out of the Shadows*. New York: Oxford University Press.

Russell, K. 1998. *The Color of Crime: Racial Hoaxes, White Fear, Black Protectionism, Police Aggression and Other Macroaggressions*. New York: New York University Press.

Sachs, S. 1999. "Men Awaiting Asylum Rulings Begin Protest Seeking Release." *New York Times*, July 30: B7.

———. 2001. "File Suggests Profiling of Latinos Led to Immigration Raids." *New York Times*, May 1: B1, B6.

Sack, K. 2001. "Judge Finds Labor Law Broken at Meat-Packing Plant." *New York Times*, January 4: A18.

Sale, C. 1994. INS Memorandum from Office of the Deputy Commissioner to District Directors, Subject: Parole Authorization, September 14. Washington, D.C.: INS.

Samora, J. 1971. *Los Majodos: The Wetback Story*. Notre Dame, IN: University of Notre Dame Press.

Sanchez, G. 1993. *Becoming Mexican American*. New York: Oxford University Press.

Sanchez, L. 2001. "Legal Help for Juvenile Immigrants Urged." *San Diego Union*, February 17: EV1–2.

Scaperlanda, M. 1997. "Who Is My Neighbor? An Essay on Immigrants, Welfare Reform, and the Constitution." *Connecticut Law Review*, 29 (4): 1587–1626.

Schiller, D. 2001. "INS Posts Detention Standards." *San Antonio Express-News*, January 3: EV1–2.

Schmitt, E. 2000. "G.O.P. Fight with Clinton on Immigrants Splits Party: Defeat of Bill Could Hurt Bush Campaign." *New York Times*, October 22: 16.

———. 2001. "Court to Take Up Deportation Rules." *New York Times*, April 22: 16.

———. 2002a. "4 Top Officials on Immigration Are Replaced." *New York Times*, March 16: A1, A9.

———. 2002b. "Vote in House Strongly Backs an End to I.N.S." *New York Times*, March 16: A1, A16.

Schneider, A., and H. Ingram. 1993. "Social Construction of Target Populations: Implications for Politics and Policy." *American Political Science Review*, June: 334–347.

Schneider, J. W., and J. I. Kitsuse. 1985. "Social Problems Theory." *Annual Review of Sociology*, 11: 209–229.

Schneider, L. 1975. "Ironic Perspective and Sociological Thought." Pp. 323–339, in L. Coser (Ed.), *The Idea of Social Structure*. New York: Harcourt Brace Jovanovich.

Schuck, P. H. 1998. *Citizens, Strangers, and In-Betweens: Essays on Immigration and Citizenship*. Boulder, CO: Westview.

Sengupta, S. 2001a. "Pataki Courts Immigrants, but His Ally Is Seen as Their Foe." *New York Times*, May 11: B4.

———. 2001b. "Arabs and Muslims Steer through an Unsettling Scrutiny." *New York Times*, September 13: EV1–3.

———. 2001c. "Ill Fated Path to America Jail and Death." *New York Times*, November 5: EV1–4.

———. 2001d. "Refugees at America's Door Find It Closed after Attacks." *New York Times*, October 29: EV1–3.

Serrano, R. 2001a. "Detainees Face Assaults and Other Violations Lawyers Say." *Los Angeles Times*, October 15: EV1–3.

———. 2001b. "Ashcroft Denies Wide Detainee Abuse." *Los Angeles Times*, October 17: EV1–4.

Shaheen, J. 1984. *The TV Arab*. Bowling Green, Ohio: Bowling Green University Press.

Shapiro, B. 2001. "All in the Name of Security: The Administration Is Using September 11 to Curtail Our Civil Liberties." *Nation*, October 22: 20–22.

Shaw, G. 2001. "High Court to Hear Cases Involving Permanent Residents." *New York Newsday*, March 25: EV1–2.

Shenon, P. 1999. "Cubans Freed from U.S. Jail Return Home to New Prison." *New York Times*, December 22: A12.

Shenon, P., and R. Toner. 2001. "U.S. Widens Policy on Detaining Suspects." *New York Times*, September 19: EV1–4.

Sheridan, M. B. 2001. "Tougher Enforcement by INS Urged." *Washington Post*, September 18: EV1–3.

"Sheriff's Beating Case Ends in Hung Jury." 1998. *Dallas Morning News*, July 11: 1.

Siegal, N. 2000. "After 2 Years in Deportation Fight, a Hunger Strike." *New York Times*, B5.

Silver, I. 1974. *The Crime-Control Establishment*. Englewood Cliffs, NJ: Prentice-Hall.

Simon, J. 1995. *Immigration: The Demographic and Economic Facts*. Washington, D.C.: National Immigration Forum.

Simon, R., and S. Alexander. 1993. *Ambivalent Welcome: Print Media, Public Opinion, and Immigration*. Westport, CT: Praeger.

Skolnick, J. 1994. *Justice without Trial: Law Enforcement in Democratic Society*. New York: Macmillan.

"Smashing Secrecy." 1999. *Nation*, November 15: 5.

Smith, P. 1995. *Democracy on Trial: The Japanese American Evacuation and Relocation in World War II*. New York: Simon and Schuster.

Smothers, R. 1998. "3 Prison Guards Guilty of Abuse of Immigrants." *New York Times*, March 7: A1, B4.

———. 1999. "Judge Bars Use of Secret Data to Hold Immigrant." *New York Times*, October 21: B1, B10.

Snowden, L. L. 1995. "Due Process, Deterrence, and Violence: Issues Surrounding Refugee Detention in Western Europe and the United States." Paper Presented at the Law and Society Annual Meeting, Toronto (June).

Solomon, A. 1995. "The Worst Prison System in America." *Village Voice*,, August 8: 25–30.

———. 1999. "Wackenhut Detention Ordeal." *Village Voice*, September 7: 29–30.

Sontag, S. 1989. *AIDS and Its Metaphors*. New York: Farrar Straus Giroux.

———. 1993. "Report Cites Mistreatment of Immigrants: A.C.L.U. Says Aliens Are Detained Too Long." *New York Times*, August 12: B1, B8.

Spector, M., and J. Kitsuse. 1977. *Constructing Social Problems*. Menlo Park, CA: Cummings.

Spitzer, S. 1975. "Toward a Marxian Theory of Deviance." *Social Problems*, 22 (June): 638–651.

Spoto, M. 1998. "Corrections Firm Sued for Firing Whistle-Blower." *Star Ledger* (NJ), May 3: 43.

Stammer, L. B. 2000. "Catholic Bishops Call for Immigration Reform." *Los Angeles Times*, November 17: EV1–2.

"Standing up for Immigrants." 1995. *New York Times*, August 27: E14.

Stefancic, J., and R. Delgado. 1996. *No Mercy: How Conservative Think Tanks and Foundations Changed America's Social Agenda*. Philadelphia: Temple University Press.

Stein, D. 1994. "Population, Migration, and America: Is Immigration a Threat to National Security?" *Speech to the National War College Class of 1995*. August 24.

Stewart, J. 1985. "Breaking up Government's Monopoly on Prison Cells." *New York Times*, March 3: E22.

"Study Finds Immigrants Doing Well in America." 1999. *New York Times*, July 3: A9.

Sullivan, J. 1995a. "6 Guards in New Jersey Charged with Beating Jailed Immigrants." *New York Times*, October 13: A1, B5.

———. 1995b. "More Illegal Immigrants Released Since Melee Shut New Jersey Jail." *New York Times*, October 16: A1, B4.

———. 2000a. "Prison Conditions Severe Even for Jails." *Oregonian*, December 9: EV1–10.

———. 2000b. "INS Locks Children Away Next to Criminals." *Oregonian*, December 12: EV1–4.

Sullivan, J., and M. Purdy. 1995. "In Corrections Business, Shrewdness Pays." *New York Times*, July 23: A1, A28.

Sullivan, J., and B. Walth. 2000, "Ex-Lawmaker Watches Reforms Exceed Intent." *Oregonian*, December 9: EV1–3.

Tagami, T. 2000a. "INS Arrests 14 Hispanics in Sting Operation at Courthouse." *Herald-Leader*, November 21: EV1–3.

———. 2000b. "Roadblock Reveals Problem for Courts." *Herald-Leader*, November 26: EV1–6.

Tanton, J., and W. Lutton. 1993. "Immigration and Criminality in the U.S.A." *Journal of Social, Political, and Economic Studies* (Summer) 8: 210–226.

———. 1994. *The Immigration Invasion*. Petoskey, MI: Social Contract.

Taylor, M. H. 1997. "Promoting Legal Representation for Detained Aliens." *Connecticut Law Review*, 29 (4): 1647–1711.

Tebo, M. G. 2000. "Locked up Tight." *ABA Journal*, November: EV1–9.

Teepen, T. 1996. "Locking in the Profits." *Atlanta Constitution*, December 10: 21.

"Tensas Sheriff Indicted in Jail Beating." 1998. *Advocate*, February 27: 1.

Tharp, P. 2001. "Prison Companies Get Hot." *New York Daily News*, October 4: EV1–2.

Thomas, P. 1994a. "Rural Regions Look to Prisons for Prosperity." *The Wall Street Journal*, July 11: B1, B8.

———. 1994b. "Making Crime Pay: Triangle of Interests Creates Infrastructure to Fight Lawlessness: Cities See Jobs, Politicians Sense a Popular Issue—And Business Cashes In." *The Wall Street Journal*, May 12: A1.

Thompson, G. 1999. "Prayers Answered, Flock Rallies: Immigrants Hail Pastor's Release from Drug Charges." *New York Times*, March 8: B1.

Thompson, M. 2001. "Senators Meet with Mexican Leaders to Discuss Changes in Border Policies." *San Jose Mercury News*, January 11: EV1–2.

Tonry, M. 1996. *Ethnicity, Crime, and Immigration*. Chicago: University of Chicago Press.

———. 1998. "Racial Disproportion in U.S. Prisons." Pp. 287–301 in *Incarcerating Criminals*, T. Flanagan, J. Marquart, and K. Adams (Eds.). New York: Oxford University Press.

Toy, V. 1999. "Rally Faults Immigration Law Used in Pastor's Drug Arrest." *New York Times*, February 12: B1, B10.

Tulsky, F. 2000a. "Asylum Seekers Face Tougher U.S. Laws, Attitudes." *San Jose Mercury News*, December 10: EV1–9.

———. 2000b. "Asylum Seekers Face Lack of Legal Help." *San Jose Mercury News*, December 30: EV1–2.

———. 2000c. "Detained Immigrants Who Allege Sex Abuse Are Transferred to Jail." *San Jose Mercury News*, December 13: EV1–2.

Uchitelle, L. 2000. "I.N.S. Is Looking the Other Way as Illegal Immigrants Fill Jobs: Enforcement Changes in Face of Labor Shortage." *New York Times*, March 9: A1, C16.

Ufford, L. 2000. "ACLU Pushes against 'Secret Evidence.'" *ACLU-Civil Liberties Reporter*, 34(3): 1, 4.

Ungar, S. J. 1995. *Fresh Blood: The New American Immigrants*. New York: Simon and Schuster.

United Nations Convention on the Rights of the Child. 1989. G.A. Res. 44/25, November 20. New York: United Nations.

United Nations High Commissioner for Refugees (UNHCR). 1995. *United Nations High Commissioner for Refugees' Guidelines on the Detention of Asylum Seekers*. Geneva: UNHCR.

———. 1996. *Note on Policies and Procedures in Dealing with Unaccompanied Children Seeking Asylum*. Geneva: UNHCR.

U.S. Congress, House.1981. *Department of State, Justice, and Commerce, the Judiciary, and Related Agencies Appropriations for 1981. Hearings before a Subcommittee of the Committee on Appropriations House of Representatives*, 96th Congress, 2nd Session, page 538. Washington, D.C.: U.S. Government Printing Office.

———. 1986. *Atlanta Federal Penitentiary*. Judiciary Committee. Subcommittee on Courts, Civil Liberties, and the Administration of Justice. Washington, D.C.: U.S. Government Printing Office.

———. 1990. *HHS Authority over Immigrants and Public Health*. Hearing before the Subcommittee on Health and the Environment of the Committee on Energy and Commerce, 101st Congress, 1st Session. Washington, D.C.: U.S. Government Printing Office.

———. 1993. *World Trade Center Bombing: Terror Hits Home*. Hearing before the Subcommittee on Crime and Criminal Justice for the Committee on the Judiciary, 103rd Congress, 1st Session. Washington, D.C.: U.S. Government Printing Office.

———. 1994a. *Criminal Aliens*. Hearing before the Subcommittee on International Law, Immigration, and Refugees of the Committee on the Judiciary, 103rd Congress, 1st Session. Washington, D.C.: U.S. Government Printing Office.

———. 1994b. *Border Violence*. Hearing before the Subcommittee on International Law, Immigration, and Refugees of the Committee on the Judiciary, 103rd Congress, 1st Session. Washington, D.C.: U.S. Government Printing Office.

U.S. Congress, Senate. 1994. *Criminal Aliens*. Hearing before the Subcommittee on International Law, Immigration, and Refugees of the Committee on the Judiciary, 103rd Congress, 2d Session. Washington, D.C.: U.S. Government Printing Office.

———. 1995. *Criminal Aliens in the United States*. S. Rept., 104–148. Committee on Governmental Affairs, 104th Congress, 1st Session. Washington, D.C.: U.S. Government Printing Office.

U.S. Department of Justice. 2000. "Proposed Rule Issued for Gender-Based Asylum Claims." Press Release, December 7: Washington, D.C.: U.S. Department of Justice.

"U.S. Religious Leaders Call for Asylum Reform." 2001. *Associated Press*, April 30: EV1–2.

"US to Listen in on Some Inmate-Lawyer Talks." 2001. *Reuters*, November 13: EV1–3.

Valdez, D. W. 2000. "Group alleges 80 civil rights abuses along border." *El Paso Times*, December 19: EV1–2.

Vekshin, A. 2001. "Senate Committee Urged to Reform Asylum Laws." *Bergen Record*, May 4: EV1–2.

Vicini, J. 2001. "U.S. High Court Rejects Challenge to Citizenship Law." *Reuters*, June 11: EV1–2.

Viglucci, A. 1994. "INS Deports Nigerian without Telling Lawyers." *Miami Herald*, January 12: 2B.

Viglucci, A., and A. Chardy. 2001. "Immigration Scrutiny a Dramatic Shift in Focus." *Miami Herald*, November 16: EV1–4.

Viorst, M. 2000. "Pollard & Haddam: Prisoners of Secret Evidence." *Nation*, February 28: 18–20.

Vlahos, K. B. 2001. "Lawmakers Propose Tighter Rules on Immigrants." *Fox News*, October 26: EV1–3.

"Wackenhut Corrections Opens Val Verde Correctional Facility." 2001. *PRNewswire*, January 19: EV1–2.

Wakin, D. J. 2001. "Court Restricts Prenatal Care for Immigrants: Those in U.S. Illegally Are Ruled Ineligible." *New York Times*, May 23: B1, B4.

Walth, B. 2000. "Asylum Seekers Greeted with Jail." *Oregonian*, December 13: EV1–9.

Walth, B., K. Christensen, and R. Read. 2000. "INS One of the Most Corrupt Federal Law-Enforcement Agencies." *Oregonian*, December 11: EV1–4.

"War on Terrorism." 2001. *Washington Post*, October 22: 25.

Weaver, S. 2000. "Stop Treating Refugees like Criminals." *Los Angeles Times*, April 27: EV1–3.

Weiser, B.1997. "In Lawsuit, I.N.S. Is Accused of Illegally Detaining Man." *New York Times*, September 16: B2.

Weissinger, G. 1996. *Law Enforcement and the INS: A Participant Observation Study of Control Agents*. Lanham, MD: University Press of America.

Welch, M. 1991. "Social Class, Special Populations and Other Unpopular Issues: Setting the Jail Agenda for the 90s." Pp. 17–23 in *Setting the Jail Research Agenda for the 1990s: Proceedings from a Special Meeting*, G. L. Mays (Ed.). Washington, D.C.: U.S. Department of Justice, National Institute of Corrections.

———. 1994. "Jail Overcrowding: Social Sanitation and the Warehousing of the Urban Underclass." Pp. 251–276 in *Critical Issues in Crime and Justice*, A. R. Roberts (Ed.). Thousand Oaks, CA: Sage.

———. 1996a. "The Immigration Crisis: Detention as an Emerging Mechanism of Social Control." *Social Justice: A Journal of Crime, Conflict & World Order*, 23(3): 169–184.

———. 1996b. *Corrections: A Critical Approach*. New York: McGraw-Hill.

———. 1996c. "Prisonization." Pp. 357–363 in *Encyclopedia of American Prisons*, M. McShane and F. Williams (Eds.). New York: Garland.

———. 1997a. "Questioning the Utility and Fairness of INS Detention: Criticisms of Poor Institutional Conditions and Protracted Periods of Confinement for Undocumented Immigrants." *Journal of Contemporary Criminal Justice*, 13(1): 41–54.

———. 1997b. A Feature Review of *The Abandoned Ones: The Imprisonment and Uprising of the Mariel Boat People* by Mark S. Hamm (Boston: Northeastern University Press), *Social Pathology*, 3(3): 202–206.

———. 1997c. "Regulating the Reproduction and Morality of Women: The Social Control of Body and Soul." *Women & Criminal Justice*, 9(1): 17–38.

———. 1998. "Problems Facing Immigration and Naturalization Service (INS) Centers: Policies, Procedures, and Allegations of Human Rights Violations." Pp. 192–221 in *Turnstile Justice: Issues in American Corrections*, T. Alleman and R. L. Gido (Eds.). Englewood Cliffs, NJ: Prentice-Hall.

———. 1999a. "The Immigration Crisis: Detention as an Emerging Mechanism of Social Control." Pp. 191–206 in *Immigration: A Civil Rights Issue for the America*, S. Jonas and S. D. Thomas (Eds.).Wilmington, DE: Scholarly Resources. (Reprinted from Welch, 1996a.)

————. 1999b. *Punishment in America: Social Control and the Ironies of Imprisonment.* Thousand Oaks, CA: Sage.

————. 2000a. *Flag Burning: Moral Panic and the Criminalization of Protest.* New York: de Gruyter.

————. 2000b. "The Correctional Response to Prisoners with HIV/AIDS: Morality, Metaphors, and Myths." *Social Pathology,* 6(2): 121–142.

————. 2000c. "The Role of the Immigration and Naturalization Service in the Prison Industrial Complex." *Social Justice: A Journal of Crime, Conflict & World Order,* 27(3): 73–88.

————. 2002a. "Detention in I.N.S. Jails: Bureaucracy, Brutality, and a Booming Business." Pp.180–196 in *Turnstile Justice: Issues in American Corrections* (2nd ed.), R. L. Gido and T. Alleman (Eds.). Englewood Cliffs, NJ: Prentice-Hall.

————. 2002b. "Assembly Line Justice." *Encyclopedia of Crime and Punishment,* D. Levinson (Ed.). Great Barrington, MA: Berkshire Reference Work/Sage.

Welch, M., and J. Bryan. 2000. "Moral Campaigns, Authoritarian Aesthetics, and Escalation: An Examination of Flag Desecration in the Post-*Eichman* Era." *Journal of Crime and Justice,* 23(1): 25–45.

Welch, M., N. Bryan, and R. Wolff. 1999. "Just War Theory and Drug Control Policy: Militarization, Morality, and the War on Drugs." *Contemporary Justice Review,* 2(1): 49–76.

Welch, M., M. Fenwick, and M. Roberts. 1997. "Primary Definitions of Crime and Moral Panic: A Content Analysis of Experts' Quotes in Feature Newspaper Articles on Crime." *Journal of Research in Crime and Delinquency,* 34(4): 474–494.

————. 1998. "State Managers, Intellectuals, and the Media: A Content Analysis of Ideology in Experts' Quotes in Featured Newspaper Articles on Crime." *Justice Quarterly,* 15(2): 219–241.

Welch, M., and D. Gunther. 1997a. "Jail Suicide under Legal Scrutiny: An Analysis of Litigation and its Implications to Policy." *Criminal Justice Policy Review,* 8(1): 75–97.

————. 1997b. "Jail Suicide and Crisis Intervention: Lessons from Litigation." *Crisis Intervention and Time-Limited Treatment,* 3(3): 229–244.

Welch, M., E. Price, and N. Yankey. 2002a. "Moral Panic over Youth Violence: *Wilding* and the Manufacture of Menace in the Media." *Youth & Society,* 34(1): 3–30.

————. 2002b. "Youth Violence and Race in the Media: The Emergence of *Wilding* as an Invention of the Press." *Race, Gender & Class,* In Press.

Welch, M., L. Weber, and W. Edwards. 2000. "'All the News That's Fit to Print': A Content Analysis of the Correctional Debate in the *New York Times.*" *The Prison Journal,* 80(3): 245–264.

Welch, M., R. Wolff, and N. Bryan. 1998. "Decontextualizing the War on Drugs: A Content Analysis of NIJ Publications and Their Neglect of Race and Class," *Justice Quarterly,* 15(4): 719–742.

"Why Our Borders Are out of Control." 1993. *Newsweek,* August 9: 25.

Wiener, J. 1995. "Japanese-Americans Remember: Hard Times at Heart Mountain." *Nation,* March 15: 694.

Wilkins, L. T. 1994. "Don't Alter Your Mind—It's the World That's Out of Joint." *Social Justice*, 21(3): 148–153.

Williams, P. J. 2001. "By Any Means Necessary." *Nation*, November 26: 11.

Wilson, W. J. 1987. *The Truly Disadvantaged: The Inner City, The Underclass, and Public Policy*. Chicago: University of Chicago Press.

———. 1996. *When Work Disappears: The World of the New Urban Poor*. New York: Knopf.

Women's Commission for Refugee Women and Children.1998a. *Forgotten Prisoners: A Follow-Up Report on Refugee Women Incarcerated in York County, Pennsylvania*. New York: Women's Commission for Refugee Women and Children.

———. 1998b. *Protecting the Rights of Children: The Need for U.S. Children's Asylum Guidelines*. New York: Women's Commission for Refugee Women and Children.

———. 2000. *Behind Locked Doors—Abuse of Refugee Women at the Krome Detention Center*. New York: Women's Commission for Refugee Women and Children.

Wood, G. 1997. *Survey of the Chandler Police Department-INS/Border Patrol Joint Operation*. Phoenix, AZ: Office of the Attorney General, Civil Rights Division.

Yeoman, B. 2000. "Steel Town Lockdown." *Mother Jones*, May/June: 38–47.

Yoo, D. 1996. "Captivating Memories: Museology, Concentration Camps, and Japanese American History." *American Quarterly*, 48: 680–699.

Yoshino, R. 1996. "Barbed Wire and Beyond: A Sojourn through Internment—A Personal Recollection." *Journal of the West*, 35: 34–43.

Young, W. 1998. *Testimony before the Senate Judiciary Subcommittee on Immigration*. September 16. Washington, D.C.: Women's Committee on Refugee Women and Children.

Yzaguirre, R. 1996. "Elections Mean Open Season on U.S. Hispanics." *Houston Chronicle*, June 21: 1.

Zatz, M. 1987. "Chicago Youth Gangs and Crime: The Creation of a Moral Panic." *Contemporary Crisis*, 11: 129–158.

Zucker, N. L., and N. Flink. 1987. *The Guarded Gate: The Reality of American Refugee Policy*. San Diego: Harcourt Brace Jovanovich.

Cases

Aguirre-Cervantes v. *INS*, 242 F.3d 1169 (9th Cir. 2001)

Al-Najjar v. *Reno*, 97 F.Supp. 2d 1329 (2000)

Alvarez-Mendez v. *Stock*, 941 F.2d 956 (9th Cir. 1991)

Barrera-Echavarria v. *Rison*, 35 F.3d 436 (9th Cir. 1994)

Berkemer v. *McCarty*, U.S. SupCt 35 CrL 3192 (1984)

Calcano-Martinez v. *INS*, 121 S. Ct. 849 (2001)

Castro-Cortez v. *INS*, 239 F.3d 1037 (9th Cir. 2000)

Colorado v. *Connelly*, 197 S. Ct. 851 (1987)

Cuban American Bar Association v. *Christopher*, 43 F.3d 1412 (11th Cir. 1995)

Flores v. *Reno*, 507 U.S. 292, 113 S. Ct. 1439 (1993)

Gisbert v. *U.S. Attorney General*, 988 F.2d 1437 (5th Cir. 1993)

Griffin v. *Wisconsin*, 55 U.S.L.W. 5156 (1987)

Harris v. *New York*, 401, U.S. 22 (1971)

Illinois v. *Gates*, 103 S. Ct. 2317 (1983)

Illinois v. *Krull*, 197 S. Ct. 1160 (1987)

INS v. *St. Cyr*, 121 S. Ct. 848 (2001)

Kirby v. *Illinois*, 406 U.S. 682 (1972)

Korematsu v. *U.S.*, 65 S. Ct. 193 (1944)

Ma v. *Ashcroft*, 257 F.3d 1095(2001)

Ma v. *Reno*, 208 F.3d 815 (9th Cir. 2000)

Mapp v. *Ohio*, 367 U.S. 463 (1961)

Marbury v. *Madison*, 5 U.S. 137 (1803)

Massachusetts v. *Sheppard*, U.S. SupCt 35 CrL 3296 (1984)

McCleskey v. *Kemp*, 197 S. Ct. 1756 (1987)

Michigan v. *Tucker*, 417 U.S. 433 (1974)

Miranda v. *Arizona*, 384 U.S. 436 (1966)

Najjar v. *Reno*, 97 F. Supp. 2d 1329 (S.D.Fl. 2000)

New York v. *Burger*, 55 U.S.L.W. 4890 (1987)

New York v. *Quarles*, U.S. SupCt 35 CrL 3135 (1984)

Nix v. *Williams*, U.S. SupCt 35 CrL 3119 (1984)

Orantes-Hernandez v. *Meese*, 685 F. Supp. 1488, 1510 (C.D. Cal. 1988)

Orantes-Hernandez v. *Thornburgh*, 919 F. 2d. 549 (9th Cir. 1990)

Perez-Funez v. *INS*, 619 F. Supp. (C.D. Cal. 1985)

Plyer v. *Doe*, 102 S. Ct. 2382 (1982)

U.S. v. *Chapa-Garza*, 243 F.3d 921 (5th Cir. 2001)

U.S. v. *Leon*, U.S. SupCt 35 CrL 3273 (1984)

U.S. v. *Salerno*, 107 S. Ct. 2095 (1987)

U.S. v. *Wade*, 388 U.S. 218 (1967)

Yamataya v. *Fisher*, 189 U.S. 86, 23 S. Ct. 611, 47 L. Ed. 721 (1903)

Zadvydas v. *Underdown*, 185 F.3d 279 (5th Cir. 1999), 121 S. Ct. 876 (2001)

Index

247